ALSO BY DONALD LOFLAND

Powerlearning

THOUGHT VI

THOUGHT
VIRUSES

DONALD LOFLAND, PH.D.

HARMONY BOOKS

NEW YORK

Published by Harmony Books, a division of Crown Publishers, Inc., 201 East 50th Street, New York, New York 10022. Member of the Crown Publishing Group.

Random House, Inc. New York, Toronto, London, Sydney, Auckland

http://www.randomhouse.com/

Harmony and colophon are trademarks of Crown Publishers, Inc.

Printed in the United States of America

Book design by Susan Hood

Library of Congress Cataloging-in-Publication Data

Lofland, Donald J.
Thought viruses / Donald Lofland — 1st ed.
p.   cm.
Includes index.
1. Neurolinguistic programming.   I. Title.
BF637.N46L64   1997
158.1—dc21   97-869
CIP

ISBN 0-517-70577-X

10 9 8 7 6 5 4 3 2 1

First Edition

THIS BOOK IS DEDICATED TO THE MEMORY OF DANA BUTTERFIELD,
WHOSE WAY OF THINKING AND MAKING MEANING
INSPIRED THIS WORK, AND TOUCHED THE LIVES
OF SO MANY PEOPLE
AROUND HER.

CONTENTS

ACKNOWLEDGMENTS

I'd like to express my gratitude to the many people who have made this work possible, especially the following:

- Frank Weimann, my agent, who has recognized and supported my visions;
- Adrienne Ingrum, who has been so instrumental in getting my visions into print;
- Robert Dilts, who conceived of the notion of thought viruses, and who introduced this country and me personally to N.L.P.;
- Lynn Larson, whose emotional support, faith in my ideas, and editing help got me through this last year.

PART ONE

THOUGHT VIRUSES

1

THE BREEDING GROUND: COHERENCE AND MAKING MEANING

THE MEANING OF THINGS LIES NOT
IN THE THINGS THEMSELVES,
BUT IN OUR ATTITUDE
TOWARDS THEM.

—ANTOINE DE SAINT-EXUPÉRY

July 20, 1969. It was morning and the sun was well above the horizon, but the sky was pitch black. The first American astronauts to reach the moon peered in anticipation toward Earth from this barren lunar landscape. Years of rigorous training had brought them to a peak of physical, mental, and emotional coherence, yet they were about to witness an experiment in a new form of coherence that would have monumental scientific repercussions.

Except for these two alien Earthlings, the moon was lifeless. Or was it? Amino acids, the building blocks of life, actually speckled the lunar surface in meteorites. What is living and what isn't?

Deep in remote areas of the rain forests on that watery blue sphere in the sky, microscopic bundles of protein and genetic material lurked, patiently waiting to spring to life. By themselves, they were as lifeless as the moon, but inside a host cell, when man ventured into these regions, they would once again possess the miracle of life—the ability to reproduce. In time, HIV, Ebola, and other viruses would scourge this planet.

Computer viruses were not yet recognized, yet such a computational glitch at this very moment in Mission Control might abort the experiment about to take place and possibly jeopardize the lives of the astronauts. Marie, one of the programmers, was also unaware of the possibility of computer viruses. She knew that her software contributions were totally successful, yet felt a strange letdown with that success. She looked across at her husband, Jason, clearly the man of her dreams, and wondered why she occasionally did things that might sabotage their relationship. She thought of her cousin dying of terminal cancer, and sneezed in an allergic response to microscopic quantities of July pollen.

The moon, at an average 239,000 miles from the Earth, can be an extraordinarily lonely place. It is, however, a position for perspective. Looking at our world from the "outside" can impart a strong sense of what's important in life and what isn't. When you think about your own life, and perhaps imagine being near the end of it, do you have a sense of what *your life* was really about? How would you need to live? What would you need to accomplish? What experiences would you like to have had? How would you need to *be* in order to look back at the end, smile, and think, "Now *that* was a successful life!" On the other hand, what stands in the way of setting a course for yourself in life, where you can look back at the end, and feel total pride in the way you've lived? Maybe you are on track already, but if you're not, what stands in your way? Is it

- procrastination?
- being caught up just trying to make a living and getting through the day?
- poor health?
- fear of failure or fear of success?
- not having the quality of intimate relationships you desire?
- not knowing how to effectively manage your finances?
- having allergies?
- periodic fatigue or depression?

Suppose that one day you found out that all *internal* obstacles that stood between you and your ability to achieve your desired destiny were caused by a group of strange, newly discovered biological viruses. And suppose that there was also a nutritious antiviral remedy, with no side effects, that you could get from your local physician. Wouldn't you be the first in line? Or suppose you discovered that all these internal obstacles were mysteriously caused by computer viruses in your home computer. If antiviral software was available, wouldn't you immediately purchase and install the program?

No doubt these scenarios seem unlikely to you. But suppose I told you that *all* internal obstacles that stand between you and where you want to be in life are the results of glitches in thinking that strikingly parallel biological and computer viruses—glitches we might call *thought viruses*. Perhaps that would sound more plausible. Suppose that a form of Thought Virus Therapy was now available. Within a short time you could

- finally break through self-defeating patterns, such as fear of failure/success, procrastination, and internal conflict
- learn highly effective alternatives to drugs for alleviating allergies and depression
- discover the missing link that would make mind/body healing three times more effective
- recognize the five major "land mines" that destroy most intimate relationships
- learn how thought viruses kill vastly more people than AIDS, Ebola, and all other deadly biological viruses combined
- move beyond thought viruses so you could use your brain with laserlike precision for achieving personal dreams and spiritual fulfillment

That is what this book is about: recognizing thought viruses as the common basis for self-defeating patterns, and applying easy-to-use antiviral remedies to improve health, relationships, career, social cohesiveness, and personal fulfillment.

Personal fulfillment had to be in the forefront of what the astronauts were experiencing, as they stood triumphantly on the moon, gazing toward Earth, and anticipating the experiment about to be performed. "There it is," observed the astronauts, as the flash of light from earth ricocheted off the corner reflectors the astronauts had lain in place. It then precisely retraced its path back to that point on Earth from which it originated. This light, clearly visible to the astronauts, can be seen from the moon at levels as low as 15 watts—the energy output of an average night light. What they could *not* see were the millions of watts from the lights of New York City at night. Why can a much dimmer 15-watt light be clearly visible, while whole cities on Earth fail to illumine the lunar sky?

COHERENCE

Coherence made the difference. Each speck of light from this strange new source vibrated in synchrony with every other speck of light. All of these added together constructively to produce a coherent beam. Ordinary light, on the other hand, consists of specks or photons that mostly work against each other destructively. So 15 watts of coherent light can "outshine" millions of watts of noncoherent light.

When a person is in good health, the body functions coherently. All systems work together in harmony to sustain life and produce a feeling of well-being. Part of the power of a computer is the coherent functioning of the circuitry, which produces complicated computations with lightninglike speed. When a biological virus invades the body, functioning becomes noncoherent. The body has to work against itself by destroying its own cells—those infected by the viruses. The results of a viral infection can be quite varied, ranging from a relatively benign cold sore to the lethargy of a fever, to the inner organs being liquefied, as in the case of Ebola. A computer virus invading the computer software or memory also causes noncoherence in the computer's functioning. The result can be as innocuous as the keyboard keys producing a clicking sound on the eighteenth day of each month to total destruction of data in the hard drive.

A recent article in *Newsweek* stated that the human brain is the most complex creation in the known universe. Some people estimate that in the human brain, with 10 billion cells, there are 10^{800} (one with 800 zeros behind it) possible paths of interaction among the cells. We were given the gift of nature's most superb engineering feat, but we were not given an instruction manual. It is also not always user-friendly.

Just how coherent is the average person's brain? How free are we from thought viruses? To get some sense of this, we might ask how many people in this country come from clear-thinking, emotionally healthy, or what we might call *functional* families. First of all, according to the well-known family psychologist Terrance Gorski, a functional family is one that demonstrates to a child, and provides him or her with, all the intellectual, emotional, and relationship skills necessary to function effectively as an adult.

Intellectual skills provide people with the ability to make sense of external and internal reality. This results in a minimum of perceptual deletions, distortions, and denial. Emotional skills, in turn, prepare people to (1) recognize their own feelings, (2) express those feelings to others, and (3) be able to listen to, and care about, others' feelings without getting defensive. Relationship skills allow people to relate successfully throughout the full spectrum of possible human relationships, including the most challenging—intimate love relationships.

How many of us observed our own caregivers fully living life this way and giving us all these tools as a child? Gorski estimates optimistically maybe 20 to 30 percent of us.

YOUR LEVEL OF COHERENCE

The following exercise may provide some insight as to your own level of coherent thinking.

Exercise 1
How Coherent Is Your Thinking?

Answer the following questions about yourself. Be honest.

1. Do you find that from time to time you don't act like yourself, or you experience an emotional state you are later displeased with?
2. Do you procrastinate?
3. When you are exposed to certain pollen, chemicals, foods, or animals, do you experience allergies?
4. When you were in school, did you have learning blocks in certain subjects?
5. Do you experience fear of failure or fear of success?
6. Do you have difficulty making decisions?
7. When single and dating, did you experience fear of rejection when approaching a new potential partner?
8. When in a relationship, do you sometimes do stupid things that help sabotage the relationship?
9. Do you indulge certain addictions, such as smoking, food, chocolate, caffeine, even though you know those addictions are not good for you?
10. Do you experience depression?

If you, like most of us, answer yes to some of these questions, at least on occasion, you can make great strides toward improving your health, having the quality of relationships you desire, reducing internal conflict, breaking through learning blocks, or perhaps alleviating allergies or depression by following the exercises and guidelines in this book.

What counts the most in life is not so much what happens to us or what doesn't, but rather how we *make meaning* out of what life presents us. The happiest, most well-adjusted people I know of share this magical trait—the ability to make meaning from life's experiences in a way that truly serves them—a way that is free from the devious twists of thought viruses. To better understand thought viruses and how they affect us, first let's consider the breeding ground for thought viruses—how we make meaning. We'll briefly explore:

1. coherent thinking
2. Neuro-Linguistic Programming, which provides an understanding of how we think, and is a basic tool in Thought Virus Therapy
3. the twin forces that normally motivate us
4. how we make meaning based on the emotional state we are experiencing
5. how what we feel physically, and our internal maps of reality, affect the way we make meaning
6. how beliefs, values, and learning affect the way we make meaning
7. how thought viruses gum up all of the above processes

COHERENT THINKING

Seven years ago Dana, a dear friend of mine, was diagnosed with advanced ovarian cancer. Only about 15 percent of people with this type of cancer survive. The only treatment available to her was aggressive chemotherapy and the occasional poking of tubes into her lungs and other organs to remove excess fluid that had accumulated. From time to time she would tell me horror stories about the additional suffering she endured from mishandled medical procedures, red tape of paperwork, lack of financial relief, and the fact that she was dying at only forty-two years old. What was truly remarkable to me, however, was that no matter how deep her pain and suffering, she could almost always manage to find something humorous in the situation, or at least tell about it in a humorous way.

She was a woman who totally embraced her own uniqueness in a most playful, charming, and childlike way. She told me of a time when she even sold her house so she could buy a tugboat to live on, because she thought that would be an adventure. Naturally, people were magnetized by her ability to be in the here and now, and to see the bright or humorous side of whatever was happening to her. I suspect she was more alive in her dying than most people are in the best of health. As you might imagine, visitors streamed into the hospital to bask in her presence and to learn her secret of living before she died.

Every religious and spiritual tradition tells us this is how we should live—seeing the bright side, seeing the good in whatever is taking place. Unfortunately, for the most part, they don't say *how* to live this way. How can a person like Dana keep going emotionally and spiritually and maintain her inner charm under the worst of conditions? How can a Thomas Edison fail thousands of times at building a lightbulb and keep on going, not even knowing it would eventually work? How can some people maintain the inner focus to learn a new foreign language in a month or two? These, I believe, are all examples of the power of truly coherent thinking.

Notice, from time to time, those special days when everything seems to go your way. You do just the right thing at the right time; the tennis game is exceptional; you come up with all the right answers in an important meeting. Sometimes it might seem that you couldn't have planned that day any better. Do days like this just randomly happen, or is there something more to it?

Exercise 2
Those Special Days

List all the qualities you can think of that make those special days unique. How do you feel physically? What emotions do you feel? How does the world look? Do you notice any special sounds? What beliefs are you aware of on those special days? Take a minute or two and write down as many characteristics as quickly as you can.

Here are some of the most frequently listed qualities in answer to the above exercise. Check them against your list.

- I feel relaxed.
- Everything falls into place.
- I feel spontaneous.
- I am happy and energetic.
- The day looks brighter.
- Things really click for me.
- Other people pick up on my mood.
- These days are too rare!

How do those qualities compare with your experience? Such days are a result, at least in part, of coherent thinking. On the other hand, noncoherent thinking allows us to get depressed over much smaller issues than Dana faced—the monthly bills, discord in our personal relationships, or having to clean out the cat's litter box. Living and being true to our inner uniqueness, as Dana did, is an important part of making meaning in life. It might even be a key for having those special days more often.

I decided to make uncovering the secret of how Dana made meaning one of my top personal growth goals. It wasn't until a year later, when I took a summer certification program in Neuro-Linguistic Programming (NLP), that I got my first clue.

NEURO-LINGUISTIC PROGRAMMING

Neuro-Linguistic Programming, or NLP, was developed in 1975 by John Grinder and Richard Bandler at the University of California, Santa Cruz, and popularized some years later by Tony Robbins in his best-selling book *Unlimited Power.* NLP provides simple yet powerful techniques for changing behavior, changing our emotional states, influencing others, and modeling excellence. Those methods are now being applied in education, personal relationship therapy, business, sports, and personal motivation for achieving dreams and goals.

Grinder and Bandler began their work by modeling and duplicating the "magical" results of a few top communicators, therapists, and healers: Milton Erickson, Virginia Satir, and Fritz Perls. While studying NLP, I began to see a vision of possibilities in the power of coherent thinking. In addition, Robert Dilts, one of my trainers, was one of the first people I heard use the term *thought viruses* to describe a strange set of glitches in human thinking that produce self-defeating behavior and distort mental coherence. In NLP, mental coherence also equates with the term *congruence*—not being at odds with ourselves and having our unconscious parts working together harmoniously.

NLP deals with how we process sensory experience, how we represent the information inside our heads, and how we make meaning out of what we experience in life.

The prefix *neuro-* refers to neurology or the nervous system.

Linguistic refers to language patterns, i.e., how language *influences* how we think, and what our choice of words *reveals* about our unconscious model of reality. Connected with language patterns are patterns of thought. There are essentially three ways of thinking:

- *visual* thinking, in which we make pictures inside our heads
- *auditory* thinking, in which we have internal dialogue or self-talk
- *kinesthetic* thinking, which concerns internal feelings or emotions

Visual, auditory, and kinesthetic (V/A/K) are the *modalities* of thought and perception.

Programming refers to a sequence of external and internal sensory experiences, V, A, or K, that we go through to arrive at an emotional state, such as being motivated, feeling frustrated, being focused, or feeling depressed. For instance, when I want to procrastinate, I might

- *see* that the garage needs to be cleaned out (visual external, or V^e)
- *hear* a stern internal voice telling me *I have* to do this (auditory internal or A^i)
- *hear* another internal voice, perhaps my rebellious side saying, "I don't want to do it." (auditory internal or A^i)
- *picture* all the tedious details necessary to accomplish the chore (visual internal V^i) and finally
- *feel* paralyzed with the internal conflict of having to do it versus not wanting to do it (kinesthetic internal K^i)

In summary, my program or strategy for procrastinating is as follows:

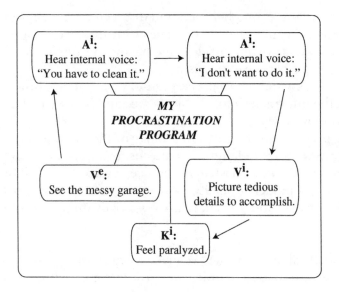

The reason my procrastination program works so well is that it is *incongruent*—that is, inner parts of me are in conflict with each other. Understanding this gave me my first clue to understanding Dana's secret of how she thought and lived.

CLUE NUMBER 1: BE CONGRUENT IN YOUR THINKING. WORK TO-WARD HAVING YOUR MENTAL AND EMOTIONAL PARTS ALIGNED WITH YOUR OWN INNER UNIQUENESS AND CHARM.

Of course, part of this involves making peace among conflicting inner parts and getting more in touch with what makes you unique as a human being, and what path in life is most true to your uniqueness.

Another key toward understanding the breeding ground for thought viruses is to explore the twin forces that lead to motivation.

WHAT MOTIVATES US IN LIFE?

Some proponents of NLP feel that only two forces drive all human behavior and motivation. These are the *fear* of feeling bad (experiencing painful emotional states) and the *desire* to feel good (experiencing pleasurable emotional states). What most of us want in life—happiness, love, comfort, power, success, and so on—are simply *states* that feel good.

Exercise 3
The Motivation Behind Your Goals

Divide a piece of paper into three vertical columns. In the first column, list five top goals you would like to achieve within one year. Next to each of those, in the second column, write what is important to you about achieving that goal. In the third column, write down the emotion or feeling you would experience by achieving each goal.

Is one of your goals to have more money? If so, why do you want more money? You might respond that you could buy certain things. I would ask further why you want to buy those things. Perhaps you would reply that it makes you feel powerful to be able to buy what you want. *Feeling powerful,* then, is the pleasurable state you are after, and having money is one means to achieve that state. If your goal is to be in a relationship, again, that is not likely the core goal. What is important to you about having the quality of relationship you desire? Maybe you love the feeling of being in love, maybe you feel more secure in a relationship, or maybe you feel more connected with a sense of companionship. Again, these pleasurable states are the real goals you desire. Having a new car might provide you with a state of freedom. Having a spiritual path might give more meaning to your life.

Exercise 4
Fearful Emotional States

Quickly write down five emotional states you would do almost anything to avoid. These might include such states as humiliation, depression, overwhelming feelings, anger, confusion, or fear.

Suppose a friend asks you to come and do something you've never done before, like salsa dancing, browsing through a computer trade show, or bungie jumping. As you evaluate each of these possibilities, what emotions does your brain connect with the activity? If you associate boredom, possible humiliation, or fear for your physical survival, and these are among the states you'd do almost anything to avoid, you're not too likely to go. On the other hand, if you associate possible adventure, exhilaration, or social connection, you're more likely to participate. Part of how we understand and make meaning out of what life presents us is by unconsciously judging whether it will lead to a pleasurable or a painful state.

HOW WE EVALUATE LIFE EXPERIENCES

If this is true, then what determines whether what we are experiencing in life is emotionally painful or pleasurable? Aside from clear-cut physical pain, it's not always obvious. One person might go to a dance lesson and make a lot of mistakes, yet feel exhilarated and have a great time, while another person finds the experience humiliating. Or one person may meet the romance of his or her dreams, fall in love, and feel delighted with life, while another, who is just as much in love, is petrified of being close.

From an NLP perspective, a painful or pleasurable evaluation of life experience is determined by (1) our physiologies, (2) our models or maps inside our heads of the way the outside appears to be (these we call our *internal representations*), and (3) how our models of reality match up with our expectations, values, and associations.

We naturally expect learning and making meaning to produce a reasonably accurate internal map of reality. What I have discovered, however, is that under the wrong circumstances, learning and making meaning can produce glitches in thinking that lead to incongruence—Robert Dilts's "thought viruses."

PHYSIOLOGY

How we feel physically—the *physiology*, has a profound effect on how we make meaning. Are we rested? Are we tired? Are we energetic? Often when we have special days and experience coherent thinking, it's after a good night's sleep, or a dynamic exercise session, or any activity from which we feel physically alive and vibrant.

Physiology is influenced positively by appropriate diet, exercise, getting enough rest, and being free of drugs. Other factors, however, such as posture, occasional slow, deep breathing, and how we use our facial muscles can have a pronounced impact on physiology. For example, in a study of people experiencing manic-depressive symptoms, one group of patients was asked to spend fifteen or twenty minutes a day smiling. After doing this for a short time, they experienced a marked improvement as compared with a control group. As it turns out, smiling stimulates production of the neuropeptides and neurotransmitters that the brain normally produces during a state of well being.

Taking on the physiology of an emotional state we desire, *as if* we were experiencing that state, is one of the quickest ways to produce the state.

Exercise 5
The "As If" Frame

Suppose that what you were about to learn in this book would transform your life and empower you beyond your wildest dreams. If you knew with certainty that this was about to happen, how would you be *sitting*? Now go ahead and sit that way. Notice how you would be *breathing* if you felt totally empowered and in control of your destiny. Breathe that way, and notice how you feel. What would your *facial expression* be in this state? Go ahead and put on this expression. Once you've done all this, again notice how you feel.

INTERNAL REPRESENTATIONS

Have you ever seen one of those TV nature specials where the camera is used to show us the world as cats see it? Cats have exceptional night vision. Then this is contrasted with the way snakes see the world; snakes can see infrared. For further contrast, a fly's eye is depicted; a fly, with compound eyes, sees multiple images of the world. Each animal sees the world in a strikingly different and unique way. If these animals could somehow communicate with each other and describe the world they were seeing, which animal would be seeing it "correctly"?

Some people might say *none* of them. They might think humans are the only animals that see the world correctly. Keep in mind, however, that birds have much more refined visual acuity than we do. Each animal, in fact, through vision and the rest of the senses, creates a unique internal model or internal map of the world.

Evidently, we do not directly perceive reality at all, but rather a *neurological model,* the Internal Representations created by our senses. Understand, however, that our internal maps do not precisely represent what is happening around or within us. A presupposition of NLP is that THE MAP IS NOT THE TERRITORY.

The menu is not the meal. The equation is not the physical reality. Each, however, provides a more or less accurate way to *represent* the reality. Consciously we focus on one or several things at a time, so most of the myriad impressions bombarding our senses each second are filtered out unconsciously. Our values, beliefs, and expectations can also cause distortions, deletions, and generalizations in how we perceive things.

DISTORTIONS. Have you ever dined at a restaurant with friends and had to agree on a tip? One friend says you received timely service, because your friend usually goes to a restaurant where service is much slower. Another friend thinks the waitress was very rude, because she interrupted conversations each time she came to the table. You thought she was warm and friendly, because she reminded you of your favorite aunt. You each experienced the same waitress, but your perceptions of her were *distorted* by past associations and expectations of how she should do her job.

DELETIONS. Just now, as you are reading this section, are you consciously aware of your breathing (or were you, *before* I brought it to your attention)? Are you aware of your heartbeat? How about feelings in your left elbow, or sounds of traffic outside? Actually, thousands of perceptions reach our brain each moment, but we only pay conscious attention to one or, at most, several of them at once. The positive side of this is that we can consciously focus on those few things that we have decided need our attention. The negative side is that the vast majority of sensory input we perceive, we are deleting from our conscious awareness.

GENERALIZATIONS. Suppose it's a hot summer day, so you and some friends go to the beach for a picnic. One friend has her attention distracted much of the time by a family whose members are arguing and insulting each other. She concludes that people at this beach aren't very friendly. Another friend focuses on a group of musicians playing African rhythms on their drums, and concludes that people at this beach are creative and play well together. Perhaps you notice the people fishing, the ones playing Frisbee, and others playing volleyball, so you conclude that people at this beach are sports-minded.

Part of learning and understanding how reality works involves formulating rules or generalizations. Generalizations are essential to making life more predictable, *and* they can be limiting or erroneous when formed too quickly or without enough data.

Distortions, deletions, and generalizations are like filters that limit and distort our internal maps. Aside from that, even undistorted perception is not likely the same for each of us. Do we all see the color blue in the same way, or hear the same sounds at a concert, or experience the same taste of a strawberry? I doubt it. More likely we each have completely unique Internal Representations of these and other experiences. Our internal perceptions are probably as individual as snowflakes. Unfortunately, most of us unconsciously assume everyone else has the same internal map of reality as we do. This leads to some real challenges when trying to relate with or manage other people.

Once we have created an internal model of what we are experiencing in life, the next step in making sense out of it occurs when we unconsciously evaluate it. We do this by comparing the internal model with beliefs, values, and associations we have *learned* in the past. Notice the key point here is *not* that we are comparing *actual reality* with what we expect it to be, but rather we are comparing our more or less distorted *internal model* with the way we think things ought to be.

"Dan, I was so humiliated being with you at that party," snapped Doris. "You were flirting with that brunette in the corner, and *everyone* knew it!"

Doris was upset *in part* because she had an expectation or an unspoken rule that when she is in a relationship, her partner shouldn't be flirting with another woman, especially in front of her. Fair enough, *if* Dan happens to have the same belief or rule. But there are two problems here. For one thing, Dan might have a different belief about flirting, even though he is in a relationship. If this is the case, they have different beliefs and values they will need to resolve.

The second problem is that Doris was comparing her rule or expectation against her *internal interpretation* of what Dan was doing. This may be completely different from his feelings and actions.

How did she know he was really flirting? How, without talking with anyone else in the room, did she know that "everyone" knew he was flirting?

Doris, like most of us, got upset because an unconscious rule or expectation was violated. But violated by what? In this case her rule was not violated by reality, but rather by a distorted internal interpretation. Dan knew the brunette, wanted to introduce her to Doris, but couldn't remember the brunette's name. Such a waste of emotional energy!

Such unconscious evaluations are what result in pleasurable, fearful, or painful states. Think about how a person could win the lottery and wind up after some time feeling depressed. Most likely, part of this person believes it is not okay to have this much money, and that belief conflicts with an Internal Representation of having too much money. How could a great teacher like Socrates, when sentenced to death and forced to drink hemlock, use the experience to teach his students what he was experiencing as the hemlock took effect? His way of thinking *associated* learning from new experiences—even dying—with pleasure. These unconscious evaluations leading to pleasure or fear of pain are based on what and how we have learned in the past.

BELIEFS, VALUES, AND LEARNING

Learning has a dark side. On the one hand, it allows us to make sense of life, first through *memory,* by *associating* related events and experiences; second, through *beliefs* or *expectations* based on our understanding of how and why things happen as they do; and third, through *parts*—patterns of thinking specifically set up to protect us in some way or disassociate us from some experience or memory that might otherwise be too painful. Virtually every aspect of life involves learning, and learning is essential for creating our internal map of reality to guide us through life.

On the other hand, learning can result in the formation of glitches in thinking. Associations, so basic to memory, can be erroneous. Beliefs, which normally allow understanding in life, can be inappropriately limiting or disempowering. Mental parts or patterns, set up to protect us, can be at odds with other parts and thus create internal conflict.

In summary, coherent thinking occurs

1. with supporting physiology
2. when we create our internal map of what we are experiencing, with a minimum of distortions, deletions, and generalizations
3. when the beliefs, values, and associations we use unconsciously to evaluate our experience are more or less accurate, productive, and effective in moving us toward pleasurable states and away from fearful or painful states

NONCOHERENT THINKING

What causes noncoherence or incongruence, mentally and emotionally? Why does motivation sometimes get reversed? How do we at times become fearful of positive states and drawn toward the negative? From my fourteen years of experience in working with clients and more than 15,000 seminar participants, I am convinced the problem involves the glitches in thinking to which I have alluded that do strikingly resemble biological and computer viruses. As discussed previously, these can come about from the dark side of learning: erroneous associations, limiting or disempowering beliefs, and conflicting inner parts. Significant emotional experiences form the fertile breeding ground for these viruses. Thought viruses include the following:

- fear of failure or fear of success
- self-sabotaging patterns
- math anxiety or other learning blocks
- inappropriate worry and guilt
- destructive expressions of anger
- compulsions and addictions
- internal conflict, which many physicians and psychologists feel is an important cause or trigger for chronic, degenerative disease
- destructive communication patterns in intimate relationships

Once we understand the types and structures of viruses (see chapter 2), the uniqueness of each of the four types of viruses (see chapters 3–6), Thought Virus Therapy (chapter 7), and how clearing up thought viruses can enhance health, career, love relationships, and personal growth (chapters 8–14), then we will have a vision of possibilities for the coherent, congruent thinking of people like Socrates and my friend Dana. Dana in fact admired great thinkers and historical figures who displayed such clarity of thought, people like Edison, Einstein, and the first astronauts to reach the moon.

Meanwhile, the astronauts peered toward the Earth in awe after experiencing the power of this strange new coherent light. If they had thought about *coherent thinking,* they might have wondered what mental power this type of coherence could release, and how the Earth might be transformed.

At that very moment, though, on Earth, an epidemic of non-coherence was well under way. Even though this epidemic would kill more people than all of the forthcoming biological viral epidemics put together, strangely it would not be recognized itself as a viral epidemic for another twenty-six years. Meanwhile, three of the greatest healers and therapists of the time—Milton Erickson, Fritz Perls, and Virginia Satir—were laying the groundwork for antiviral remedies.

2

VIRUSES

OUR GREATEST FOES,
AND WHOM WE MUST CHIEFLY COMBAT,
ARE WITHIN.

—MIGUEL DE CERVANTES

Wil, a client of mine, was once a university professor. He had spent the last eight years on a spiritual quest at a meditation retreat facility. He had decided not to return to the university, so he was completing a training program for a new profession. One day I called him to see how things were going, and he replied, "Not so good." Since completing the schooling, he had contracted a nasty toe infection. He had gone to see a physician several times over the last couple of months. The physician had given him antibiotics and attempted to drain the infection, but the infection persisted. Because of the infection, Wil could not wear shoes, so he hadn't been able to go out on job interviews.

I said, "Wil, I bet when you go out on a job interview, you really have to be on your toes, don't you?"

"Why, yes!" he replied.

I speculated, "You can't very well be on your toes if they are infected, can you?"

"No, I guess you can't."

"Do you think there's something going on here besides the bacterial infection?" I probed.

"I don't know. Maybe."

He then sidetracked the issue, and proceeded to tell me about a science fiction story he had just read. A couple of physicists had unlocked the secret of time travel. They had the choice of going back to any past time they wanted, so they chose to go to the Jurassic period and experience the dinosaurs. Making sure they were well armed and well equipped with scientific instruments, they proceeded back in time.

What they discovered was completely different from what anyone expected. A group of giant extraterrestrials were living on Earth at that time. They had found a way to reduce gravity on the Earth's surface to one sixth of its present value.

The giant aliens were actually breeding the dinosaurs to use for warfare on other planets. The physicists disagreed with such abuse of the Earth's resources and discovered a way to change gravity back to its normal pull, so the dinosaurs and the giant aliens were crushed.

The aliens, however, wound up "surviving" in the form of viruses. Their revenge was to infect every living thing on Earth, from bacteria, to plants, every animal, and eventually humans. The only way life on Earth could evolve was for each life form to develop an immune response to the invading viruses. When artificial intelligence appeared in the form of computers, viruses changed to an appropriate form to infect the computers. Again, the only way for computers to survive was through creation of antiviral programming immune systems.

Wil told me that the highest step in evolution on Earth was human thought, the by-product of our life form's specialty, the cerebral cortex. Unfortunately, the viruses had also transmuted to infect human thought. Some spiritual traditions had predicted a new evolutionary step in consciousness, an "Age of Enlightenment" in the near future, somewhere after the turn of the millennium. However, this would not occur until we recognized viruses in our thinking for what they were and evolved an appropriate immune response.

Understand, that after eight years of seclusion and deep meditation, Wil had a strong spiritual bent to his thinking. I don't know if he remembered the story correctly, but I enjoyed his interpretation.

Bringing him back to the issue of his toe, "Maybe you have a virus," I suggested. He assured me that the infection was bacterial and not viral, but agreed to a consultation to see what emotions, beliefs, or past conditioning might be playing into his ongoing infection. I actually suspected that a thought virus might have triggered the infection, or perhaps it was hindering his body from healing.

Have *you* had the feeling, at times, of being your own worst enemy—that you occasionally do things unconsciously that block your success? When I first heard Robert Dilts use the term *thought viruses* to describe such self-defeating thinking patterns, I thought it was a nice metaphor. Part of me wondered if there was anything more to it. Do these glitches have structure? Do they reproduce, and carry on a devious life of their own, the way biological and computer viruses do? What similarities do they share with biological and computer viruses? What differences? How do they infect and how are they spread?

To answer these questions, I began researching biological and computer viruses and to look more carefully at the *structure* of thought glitches as I consulted with my clients.

BIOLOGICAL VIRUSES

September 1915. World War I is in progress. New lethal weapons—mustard gas, the machine gun, and the tank—will be introduced in this "war to end all wars." Millions of lives will be lost. Yet the most deadly weapon of all is just being put together in southern China. The unsuspected delivery system is migrating ducks.

In the winter and spring of 1918–19, three years after the naturally occurring *viral mutation* in southern China, the world experienced a pandemic outbreak of influenza that killed more than 20 million people. This was nearly 1 percent of the world population and constituted more lives than were lost in all the battles of World War I put together. Even now, influenza typically originates in southern China and takes about three years to reach the United States. The way we produce flu vaccines is by studying the influenza that occurred among ducks, pigs, and people in southern China three years before.

A virus is a bundle of DNA or RNA genetic material enclosed by protein. It is sometimes referred to as "bad news wrapped in protein" or "rebel genetic material." Viruses apparently infect every life form on the planet, from ducks to mushrooms to bacteria to people. Some viruses infect only one species. For example, smallpox only infects humans. Others, such as influenza, can cross the boundaries from one species to another and infect ducks, pigs, and humans.

How lethal a virus is, and how easily it spreads, is measured by

the so-called *biosafety level.* Lethal as HIV is, it is not particularly effective in spreading, and rates only a Biosafety Level 2. At the top
of the scale, Biosafety Level 4 viruses—"hot viruses"—kill quickly,
spread easily, and have no cure. The tropical viruses Lassa fever,
Ebola, and Sabia fall into this category.

Viruses have occurred throughout recorded history. An ancient Egyptian inscription[1] dating back to 1500 B.C. shows a man
with a shriveled leg, probably caused by polio. In the thirteenth
and fourteenth centuries, bubonic plague killed one quarter of
Europe's population. Smallpox, brought to the New World for the
first time by Cortés and his small group of invaders, is believed to
have killed about one third of the Aztec population.

How lethal a virus is depends on the type of cell it infects, and
how quickly it multiplies. Outside of a host cell, a virus displays no
life functions. When it attaches itself to a cell, the whole virus may
enter the cell, or it may just insert its genetic material. Once inside
the cell, the virus directs the cell's machinery to duplicate the
virus. The virus may reproduce slowly, with an occasional virus
slipping out through the cell's membrane (a process called *bud-
ding*), or it may reproduce explosively and rupture the cell,
thereby destroying it.

Typically a virus will infect certain types of cells. Influenza and
the common cold attack respiratory cells; hepatitis affects the
liver; and HIV attacks our very defense against viruses, the T-killer
white blood cells.

Our natural defense against viral invasions is the immune system. White blood cells called T-helper cells scan human cells to
detect ones infected with a virus. Cells have a protein code deposited on the outside of the cell membrane to indicate what activity the cell is engaged in. A virus-infected cell normally has a
different protein code, which the T-helper cells can detect. Once
an infected cell is detected, the immune system sends an army of
T-killer cells to destroy our own infected cells and their viral con-
tents.

A few craftier viruses can hide out from the immune system.
The cold-sore virus (herpes simplex) hides out in nerve cells, except for an occasional outbreak. The HIV virus hides out in nodules impervious to the immune system and located on lymph
nodes during the relatively dormant years prior to the onset of
AIDS. Unfortunately, during this time, HIV is multiplying and
mutating. When the nodules finally burst, the immune system is

faced with huge numbers of different mutations of the original virus, and is simply overwhelmed.

Most of the exotic hot viruses or killer viruses come from remote regions of tropical rain forests. The possibility of a viral epidemic like HIV, which is projected to infect 40 million people by the end of the century,[2] was unthinkable a bit more than fifteen years ago. The problem is that with agriculture, tourism, and urbanization encroaching on the tropical rain forests, more people have the potential to be directly exposed to killer viruses. And as Richard Preston, the author of *The Hot Zone,* points out, the natural habitat for these killer viruses is only twenty-four hours' flying time from any major city in the world. A massive hot-virus epidemic, such as that portrayed in the movie *Outbreak,* is all too possible.

Ironically, however, the more quickly the virus reproduces, and the more deadly it is, the less likely it will survive for long. In remote regions, victims of Ebola or other hot viruses die so quickly it is easy to quarantine the victims and stop the spread. Fortunately, Ebola is not airborne, and is extremely unlikely to mutate into an airborne strain. If, however, there were an airborne hot virus lurking somewhere in the rain forest that somehow got transported to a major city, a catastrophe could be at hand. With our continued encroachment on tropical rain forests, AIDS is not likely to be the last viral scourge.

COMPUTER VIRUSES

Deep within a high-security area guarded by infrared motion sensors, steel bars, and appropriate locks, IBM maintains a collection of potentially the most dangerous software in the world.[3] The laboratory in Hawthorne, New York, has collected 500 out of the 6,000 or so known computer viruses. With new computer viruses appearing at a rate of more than one hundred per month, antivirus software companies are hard pressed to keep pace.

A computer virus is a small piece of programming code with instructions to reproduce—that is, to make copies of itself wherever possible. By replicating itself, the virus multiplies, spreading to new programs and other computers. Besides the instructions to reproduce, the virus carries a program for some type of mischief. For example, a virus called Ripper randomly swaps pairs of numbers, creating chaotic spreadsheets. The "Sunday Virus" shuts down computers only on Sundays, and orders workaholics to take the day off and have some fun. Other, more malicious viruses can make a computer's monitor screen go blank or cause its hard drive to crash. Some experts estimate the cost to industry of restoring data lost to computer viruses at $3 billion per year.

Computer viruses have been known for about a decade, but they only became popularly known with the Michelangelo virus scare of March 6, 1992. This virus threatened to hinder hard-drive access for computers all around the world. The scare turned out to be mostly a false alarm, with only a few infections. It did, however, inspire companies and individuals to install antivirus programs.

Unlike biological viruses, their computer counterparts are man-made, written by pranksters or disgruntled people with an ax to grind. Computer viruses are not airborne, so computers must be infected by intimate contact—primarily infected floppy disks. Computers can also be infected, however, through programs downloaded from the Internet or through a telephone modem.

After a computer contracts a virus, the virus can spread to other software within the computer and potentially to other computers. Viruses attach themselves to various programs, but in most cases someone must run the program to activate the virus in order for it to replicate and do its damage.

Antivirus programs detect viruses by looking for common instructions to self-replicate, and by comparing the sizes of files against the size they should be. This is effective because virus codes usually increase the file size. Viruses, however, are becoming more devious, using encryption and other means to disguise their work and hide their presence. IBM is developing an innovative computer virus "immune system" that would detect new viruses, create new digital antibodies, and send a "kill" signal for all computers on a shared network to destroy the intruders.

Stephen Hawking, the well-known theoretical physicist and best-selling author of A Brief History of Time, has speculated that computer viruses may be the closest we've come to creating a new life form. The ability to reproduce gives "life" to these programs. Fred Cohen, a computer scientist and consultant, has further speculated that computer viruses may have positive benefits as "live" information runners on the Internet.[4] They could distribute software, clean out old files, or gather information from multiple databases. Tom Ray, a University of Delaware ecologist, has developed a virus "game preserve" called Tierra. This is a computer ecosystem in which competing viruses are allowed to interact, mutate, and evolve.

THOUGHT VIRUSES

Diane, one of the participants at my NLP Practitioner Training, was highly allergic to cats. At one point we were covering a section on "NLP and Health." About one third of the participants were medical doctors, a few of them being specialists in allergies.

When we came to the section on allergies, the trainers suggested that allergies were caused by a virus. I always thought they were caused by cat dander, pollen, certain foods, environmental toxins, and so forth. To illustrate the point that a *thought virus* might be involved, the trainers had Diane come up to the front of the room to demonstrate a mental process that in many cases allows allergy symptoms to disappear.

Diane was so sensitive to cats that when she even mentally pictured a cat, her eyes would start watering and her nose would start running. The trainer then guided Diane through an allergy process that we'll present in chapter 9. After thirty minutes of this process, Diane reached a point where she could imagine and picture cats in vivid detail with no allergic symptoms. This was not the end, however. The final test was to see if she could be in the presence of a real cat without the allergic response.

Our training was on the University of California campus in Santa Cruz. There are normally many cats that wander through the coastal redwoods on campus, so we went to look for one to test Diane. Unfortunately, we couldn't find one. In fact, the word must have gotten out to the cats about Diane, because none of us saw a cat for the next few days. Diane's viewpoint on cats seemed much improved, however, so at least the mental and emotional side of the issue—the thought virus—had apparently been cleared up.

WHAT IS A THOUGHT VIRUS?

Dr. Tad James, a major NLP trainer, has provided a definition we can apply to thought viruses.[5] His definition also begins to suggest

viral structures. He suggests we all have *parts* of the unconscious
that, to a greater or lesser degree, are *functionally detached* from the
rest of the nervous system. Communication between a *part* (what
I call a thought virus) and the rest of the unconscious is more or
less limited. The virus, then, is a portion of the nervous system
that literally takes on a life of its own. It filters and distorts the ways
we make meaning in life, and leads to noncoherent, incongruent
thinking.

The degree of incongruence that the thought virus produces is
related to how strongly the boundary around the virus blocks
communication between the virus and the rest of the unconscious
mind. Part of Thought Virus Therapy, in fact, involves dissolving
or "blowing out" this boundary, and allowing the virus to integrate
back into the wholeness of the unconscious.

VIRUS TYPES

In my research I have identified four distinct types of thought
viruses: *trigger viruses, limiting viruses, Gemini viruses,* and *killer
viruses.* Each of the first three has a unique structure, and each
corresponds to errors in learning—the "dark side" of learning discussed in chapter 1. Killer viruses—literally that—are a combination of the other three.

TRIGGER VIRUSES. Associations, so basic to memory, can be erroneous and lead to a *trigger virus.* If you are in a love relationship,
have you ever noticed that your partner occasionally has a certain
mannerism or tone of voice that for no logical reason makes your
skin crawl? Or perhaps you are peacefully driving along the highway, then for no reason someone impatiently passes you at high
speed, and gives you an obscene gesture. You don't even know the
person, and his behavior really has nothing to do with you, yet
your blood boils. Or maybe whenever you pick up a math book
you break into a cold sweat.

These are all examples of trigger viruses. A certain external experience automatically triggers an old craving or a negative emotional state. Somewhere in the past, the unconscious erroneously
linked together the external trigger and the negative emotion.

LIMITING VIRUSES. Beliefs, which normally allow understanding in life, can be inappropriately limiting or disempowering and become *limiting viruses*.

- "I'd love to have my own business, but I just don't have the courage or patience to get one started."
- "I'll never be as smart as my older sister."
- "I'd love to have money, but that means I'd have to take advantage of others, and I could never do that."

These are a few examples of limiting viruses—limiting decisions or limiting beliefs that disempower us. The structure of a limiting virus, like other thought viruses, contains a positive intent. That is why it is so hard to consciously change beliefs. In fact, most of us are convinced that we can't change beliefs, even if they disempower us.

GEMINI VIRUSES. Mental parts or patterns set up to protect us, can oppose other internal parts and create internal conflict. The two conflicting parts are like the twins of the astrological sign Gemini, ultimately seeking equilibrium by balancing opposite values. Have you ever had an experience in which you didn't act like yourself, or perhaps you felt an emotional state you were later unpleased with? Maybe you've noticed sometimes that part of you wants to do one thing, like working on your income tax, while another part of you wants to get enough sleep so you can be fresh the next day. Each part has a positive intent and each one has its own set of beliefs and values. In fact, a well-developed part can become a minor personality.

Parts in conflict are thought viruses, in that they result in inner conflict and incongruent behavior. The viruses are twins because any inner mental part that is involved in inner conflict must have an opposite part to oppose. What's amazing is that conflicting twin parts almost always have the same positive intent for the experiencer.

KILLER VIRUSES. These result in addictions, compulsive self-destructive behaviors, and a tendency toward violence. These are usually combinations of trigger, limiting, and Gemini viruses that literally do kill—more than 1 million Americans per year. These viruses are the most complex in structure and the most deep-seated psychologically. Once the individual who has this virus is willing to change, and is convinced he *must* change, the methods of Thought Virus Therapy are among the quickest and most profound for alleviating these maladies.

THE STRUCTURES OF THOUGHT VIRUSES

In some cases, viruses can even have their own beliefs and values, which might be entirely different from those the person normally embraces. Unlike biological and computer viruses, however, no matter how self-destructive or limiting the thought virus is, it always has a positive intent for the individual. The positive intent is incongruent with the actual behavior the virus produces, so this creates incongruence, internal conflict, and noncoherence in the victim's thinking.

As an example, Lucy, a friend of mine, had a nice solid oak dining set. I noticed that whenever I was visiting her, and her family was eating, no one would eat at the table. Everyone ate separately, in different places. When I asked her about this, she said that she and her ex-husband had had many arguments and fights at the table during mealtime. She and her children now stayed away from the table, *to avoid feelings of disharmony.* This type of response is called a *spatial trigger* or a *spatial anchor.* As a trigger virus, the thought of sitting at the table created a feeling of disharmony. The positive intent of the virus was to avoid feelings of disharmony. However, the behavior, in which everyone ate separately in different parts of the apartment, created a feeling of disharmony. The intent and the behavior were incongruent.

A trigger virus occurs when a visual (V), auditory (A), or kinesthetic (K) trigger is unconsciously associated with a negative kinesthetic state (K$^-$), that is, a negative emotion, behavior, or compulsion. The connection between the trigger and the state is called a *synesthesia.* V/K is a visual-kinesthetic synesthesia, A/K an auditory-kinesthetic synesthesia, and K/K a kinesthetic-kinesthetic synesthesia.

A limiting virus occurs with the unconscious adoption of a lim-

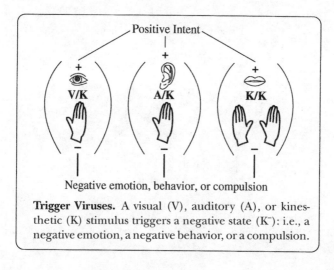

Trigger Viruses. A visual (V), auditory (A), or kines-thetic (K) stimulus triggers a negative state (K⁻): i.e., a negative emotion, a negative behavior, or a compulsion.

iting belief or a limiting decision. Quite often the positive intent has to do with safety or "protecting" the experiencer from embar-rassment or humiliation. The virus creates a hole or a blind spot, in that we *delete* perception or experience that might imply such positive meaning as "Maybe I really am attractive," or "Maybe I could become wealthy," or "Maybe I could learn that foreign lan-guage." The negative behavior occurs because we act as if the lim-iting belief were true.

Gemini viruses occur with the creation of an internal part with

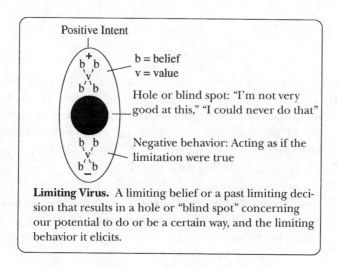

Limiting Virus. A limiting belief or a past limiting deci-sion that results in a hole or "blind spot" concerning our potential to do or be a certain way, and the limiting behavior it elicits.

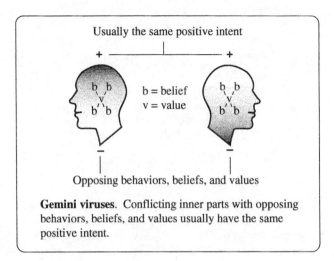

Usually the same positive intent

b = belief
v = value

Opposing behaviors, beliefs, and values

Gemini viruses. Conflicting inner parts with opposing behaviors, beliefs, and values usually have the same positive intent.

behaviors, beliefs, and values opposed to an opposite twin part. Quite often, when we elicit the highest purpose or positive intent for each twin, they are the same. Achieving inner calm and being at peace with oneself often amounts to integrating conflicting twin parts.

Again, trigger, limiting, and Gemini viruses are the fundamental or primary viruses. These can combine in a myriad of ways to form more complex viruses, including killer viruses.

HOW DO THOUGHT VIRUSES BREED AND INFECT?

Mistakes in learning provide the mechanics of thought-virus formation. The breeding ground seems to be significant emotional experiences. Many psychologists believe that we begin life with an experience of wholeness or oneness. Through significant emotional experiences (the painful ones) and the formation of thought viruses, that wholeness is shattered.

Dr. Tad James has also provided a model for how the wholeness is lost. This is illustrated in the chart on page 33. The vertical axis represents the *intensity* of the significant emotional experience. The bottom represents a state of wholeness. As you move up vertically, the intensity of the emotional experiences increase fragmentation of the wholeness. The intensity itself depends on

- how *strong* the emotional state was
- the *rate* at which change into the emotional state occurred
- *how many times* the state occurred

For example, a child may have experienced a *gradual* increase in parental violence many times as the parent gradually became drunk. Another child may have had just as intense an experience from a single incident in which the parent *suddenly and unpredictably* became violent.

In this model, a person with no negative significant emotional experiences would begin at the bottom from a state of wholeness. Within wholeness would be the usual array of notions, ideas, and feelings. Moving upward with increasing intensity of emotional experience, at some point there should be a threshold for creation of glitches in thinking—thought viruses. The greater the in-

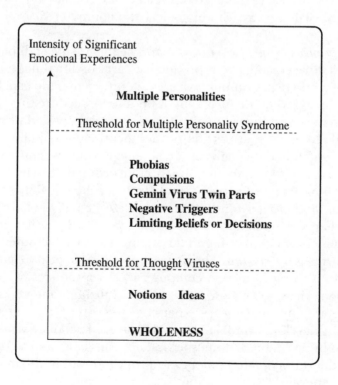

tensity of the emotional experiences, the stronger the boundaries between the thought virus and the rest of the nervous system. Communication between the part of the nervous system forming the thought virus and the rest of the nervous system is further impeded, and the virus becomes more independent and functionally detached.

The extreme of this occurs toward the top of the scale, with the formation of multiple personalities. Here communication among the parts is so blocked that the various personalities are unaware of each other. It is well known that multiple personalities often result from abusive childhoods in which the abuse was heavy and occurred frequently, and in which changes of state were quick and unpredictable.

COMMON CHARACTERISTICS OF THOUGHT VIRUSES

In my research, I've discovered seven common characteristics that thought viruses share with biological and computer viruses.

1. *The virus cannot live or remain active outside of a host.* Biological viruses show no ability to reproduce or carry on life functions outside of a host cell. Computer viruses are only active and capable of reproducing when the program or booting procedure they are attached to is running. Thought viruses are only activated when the neural circuitry (that portion of the unconscious containing the virus) is activated through certain language patterns, sensory stimulation, or thinking about a situation involving that virus or part.

If you have fear of success, you have to *see* the possibility of success, or *think about it,* for that fear to be activated. If you have a specific allergy, you need to *see* the cat or *experience* the pollen for the neural network containing the thought virus to be activated.

2. *Viruses can reproduce.* The only purpose a biological virus seems to have is to reproduce. A computer virus reproduces by design. Thought viruses can reproduce by generalizing context. For example, if I once had a scary experience with one particular snake, I might develop a phobia about all snakes. The killer viruses involved in drug abuse, domestic violence, smoking, and so on also have the unfortunate tendency to propagate within a family and from generation to generation.

3. *Viruses are self-centered.* The biological virus has no concern for the host cell; its only concern is to use the host cell as a means to reproduce. The computer virus has no concern for the program it is a part of, or for the computer itself; it simply reproduces and carries out the mischievous instructions in its code. Thought viruses ultimately *do* have the benefit of the experiencer as a highest purpose. Owing, however, to inhibited information flow across the virus boundary, the virus acts on its own twisted agenda. It is "unaware" of its own incongruence; the self-defeating behavior it produces is not in line with its highest intent. As an example, we often crave foods to which we are allergic. We eat the food to feel good, and wind up not feeling good.

4. *Viruses produce noncoherence in the infected system.* The invasion of biological viruses causes the body to have to work against itself—that is, to destroy its own cells infected with the virus. Computer viruses cause the computer to work against itself with opposing instructions from the programs versus the viruses. As discussed previously, thought viruses lead to internal conflict and self-defeating beliefs and behavior.

5. *The purpose of the virus may be incongruent with its activity.* If a biological virus is too successful at reproducing, it will destroy the host, be unable to reproduce, and ultimately perish itself. A computer virus that is successful to the extent of shutting down the computer then loses the ability to spread to other computers. And as I have pointed out, the highest purpose of the thought virus is *incongruent* with the behavior it produces.

6. *Some viruses can enter the system and hide from the system's awareness.* The herpes virus is one type that hides out in nerve cells, invisible to the system until it becomes active in an outbreak. The Stealth computer virus can be invisible to antivirus software by intercepting checkup messages and sending back a message that everything's okay. Many thought viruses are entirely outside of the conscious awareness of the experiencer. A woman vows that "I'll never be like my mother." Outside of her conscious awareness, she becomes just like her mother. A man gets angry with his lover over that certain tone of voice, unaware that the tone is just a trigger.

7. *Viruses can have positive uses.* Biological viruses are the basic tool of genetic engineering, which will likely become a major means of healing in the medical field. Computer viruses may one day become "live" information runners on the Internet. In chapter 7 we'll see that integrating the virus back into the wholeness of

the unconsciousness involves maintaining and using the positive intent of the virus. Furthermore, positive triggers can be used constructively as a means toward desirable states, such as motivation, adventure, and focus. They also can be used to *reprogram* unproductive behavioral patterns.

But if thought viruses are analogous to biological and computer viruses, aren't viruses associated with epidemics? If so, what epidemics would relate to thought viruses?

When you think about it, what is the most deadly epidemic of our time? Is it AIDS, Ebola, influenza, government spending? Each of these certainly takes a deadly toll, but the most pervasive and insidious epidemic of our time claims more than 1 million American lives per year and many more casualties. It is a social epidemic based on distorted thinking that results in drug abuse, preventable degenerative disease, depression, social violence, and lack of personal and family fulfillment in the midst of the greatest levels of affluence, technological comfort, and information availability in the history of this planet. Thought viruses are the unrecognized basis of the distorted thinking responsible for this epidemic.

Recognizing that there is a social epidemic and understanding that all of these problems share the common ground of distorted noncoherent thinking are the first steps in solving these problems. Life forms on this planet have evolved immune systems to protect against viruses, and computers have software to ward off computer viruses, but what immune response is there for thought viruses?

During a biological plague such as the bubonic plague in Europe in the Middle Ages, not everyone got the disease. A few people even started to get sick, but then managed to recover. This second group is particularly interesting, because they developed antibodies to ward off the disease. In principle, we can *model* these people's immune response, by isolating the antibody from their blood and reproducing it for others.

In the case of thought viruses, trying to get beyond them by simply changing our behavior or using willpower does not work, because the unconscious is committed to maintaining the positive intent of the virus. The antiviral remedies of counseling or traditional psychotherapy can work, but often require considerable time and expense. What else could there be that would be more practical? I found a clue by observing and thinking about my friend Dana.

CLUE NUMBER 2: *MODEL* PEOPLE (LIKE DANA) ARE THOSE WHO ARE RELATIVELY FREE FROM OR WHO HAVE RECOVERED FROM THOUGHT VIRUSES.

Aside from Dana, where would I find such people, and even if I could, how would I model them? With these questions in mind, answers began presenting themselves over the next couple of years after Dana's passing. One answer came in the form of an ancient mental technique from the Himalayas. Other answers began emerging from my training with NLP and in working with clients and seminar participants.

One of the most profound contributions of NLP in the direction of coherent thinking is precision modeling—modeling excellent sports figures, modeling creative thinkers, modeling therapists who move people beyond virus-infected thinking, and modeling the people themselves who have shaken such a faulty mentality. I have discovered and assembled a set of antiviral treatments that I call Thought Virus Therapy. Much of the concern of psychotherapy and spiritual practices is to reintegrate the psyche towards its original wholeness. Thought Virus Therapy provides practical steps to accomplish this.

I remember discussing this social epidemic with Diane during our NLP training, about three days after she had experienced the NLP process for allergies. She excitedly told me that she had finally encountered a cat. She said that she cautiously approached the cat and had no allergic symptoms. She picked the cat up, again with no symptoms. Finally, she rubbed her nose in the cat's fur and still had no symptoms. Her allergic symptoms were gone. Professionals who practice this process with clients report an 80 percent success rate for people with *specific* allergies.

A few years after this, I was telling my friend Wil about Diane and the cat as we tried to figure out what was going on with his infected toe. After about forty-five minutes of processing with him and questioning various parts of his unconscious, what came up was that part of him really did want to start his new career, but an-

other part felt that to do so would be an insult to his father. His father, who had died when Wil was quite young, had not been much
of a go-getter in terms of career.

Wil was clearly suffering from the inner conflict of a Gemini
virus. I worked another forty-five minutes to help him resolve father issues and to reintegrate the conflicting parts. I didn't hear
from him for a few days. Then he called and said that his toe had
started draining the afternoon after our consultation, and was finally healing. Within a week it was back to normal.

3

TRIGGER VIRUSES

The night sky in mid-August, as seen from the peaks of the Sierra Nevada in California, is exquisite. A few years ago I lay on my sleeping bag, gazing up at this spectacle. I had backpacked to about a 10,000-foot elevation—well above low-lying haze, smog, and city lights that dim the night sky for urban dwellers. In places the stars appear more dense than the pitch-black space between the stars. Mid-August also provides the spectacle of the Perseid meteor shower, as Earth's orbit intersects remnants of the tail of a comet. Such "falling stars" can trigger a brilliant streak stretching halfway across the sky, yet most of these meteors are only about the size of a grain of sand. They burn up harmlessly, well above the ground, as atmospheric friction vaporizes them.

In 1908, farmers in Tunguska, in Siberia, observed a meteorite that was not so harmless. Its explosion was large enough to flatten and char an area thirty-two miles in diameter. From the size of the explosion, scientists calculated that the meteorite must have been enormous, but no trace of meteoritic material was ever found. What triggered this enormous explosion? If it was a meteorite, why did it do the *reverse* of what you'd expect, and leave no trace of its existence? Like the Tunguska meteorite, events can produce effects opposite to what you might expect. The actual cause of the explosion remains a mystery to this day, although scientists have proposed some provocative theories to explain it.

While I was on my backpacking trip, I remember thinking about the Tunguska explosion, and reading Dr. Deepak Chopra's best-selling book *Quantum Healing* for the first time. In it he told of a patient who was addicted to heroin. Dr. Chopra treated this patient, and for about a year he was free of his former addiction and held down a steady job. Then, while the former patient was riding on a train in an old familiar setting, something suddenly and mysteriously *triggered* an uncontrollable urge to take heroin. He irrationally returned to his addiction.

Dr. Chopra's holistic approach to mind/body healing, called *quantum healing*, promotes physical, mental, emotional, and spiritual healing through traditional western medicine, Ayurvedic remedies, and meditation. Still, something is missing in the puzzle of mind/body healing.[1]

As I read Dr. Chopra's account, I wondered further why, when we have clear goals and visions for ourselves, even the *thought* of certain experiences keeps us from achieving them.

TRIGGERS

What is missing began to crystallize the first time I met Amy. Amy was an attractive, bright medical student—the daughter of a friend of mine. We were seated for dinner, when my friend brought in the salads for us. Amy inexplicably stood up, walked across the room, took her keys out of her purse, replaced them, and then returned to the dinner table. When my friend brought out the rest of the dinner, Amy repeated this little ritual. When dessert arrived, she did the same thing. My friend then asked Amy what she was doing with her keys. She responded tersely that it was important for her to be assured that her keys were in their proper place. "You can't go anywhere without your keys, can you?" Somehow food being served *triggered* a compulsion in Amy to know that her keys were secure.

Have you ever walked into a department store and smelled a perfume you haven't smelled in ten years? Suddenly you're taken back in time to the way you felt ten years ago. Perhaps you are driving down the highway when you hear a song on the radio you haven't heard since you were in high school. Suddenly there you are, back at a high school dance. Maybe you see Robin Williams in a new movie. He assumes a certain expression or posture, and even before he says something funny, you start laughing. These are all examples of *triggers,* which, in NLP, are also called *anchors.* The smell, the song, the look on the comedian's face are external triggers that are unconsciously connected with, or *anchored to,* a memory or a state.

Have you experienced any triggers today? Have any external or internal experiences automatically stimulated a state or a memory? The answer is probably many more than you might imagine. Did you

- wake up to an alarm clock this morning?
- feel someone touch you?
- respond to signals from your stomach regarding the need for food?
- hear a cat purr?
- feel a sense of urgency when your watch indicated the appropriate time to leave for work?
- experience certain feelings when you noticed that the sky was blue and the sun was shining brightly, or perhaps that it was cloudy or rainy?
- drive up to a stop light or stop sign?
- see someone smile?

These few examples show how pervasive triggers are. In fact, some psychologists feel that how we make meaning, and our resulting behavior, is controlled entirely by such stimulus-response triggers.

THE VALUE OF TRIGGERS

Triggers, as they occur in everyday life, serve us in three ways:

TRIGGERS ARE ESSENTIAL FOR MEMORY FORMATION AND RETRIEVAL. I wonder how many times you've had an experience like this: You are working on a project when suddenly you get distracted and look over at a newspaper. The article is about an increase in the price of gasoline, so you think about the Middle East. That reminds you of Africa, at which point you think of famine caused by the civil wars there. Now you start thinking about food and notice you are hungry. Suddenly it occurs to you that you were supposed to meet your friend at a restaurant five minutes ago, so off you go. The association of one idea with another is the basic mechanics of effective encoding and recall that is so essential to memory.

Trying to recall one unconnected memory among millions of

others would be like walking into a library and finding the books arranged randomly, with no numbering system. The more organized the numbering system, the easier it will be to find the book. Similarly, the more visual, auditory, and kinesthetic associations or triggers we use to encode new knowledge, the easier it will be to access the memory. Triggers allow us, then, to associate events, memories, and states for the purpose of easy access to memory.

TRIGGERS CAN PROVIDE SAFETY AND PROTECTION. My mother told me that I took to physics at an early age. When I was about fourteen months old, I was fascinated by watching people plug electrical devices into wall sockets and seeing the magical things that happened as a result. I apparently decided to experiment with this myself. I found a bobby pin with the two sides bent open wide enough so it looked like it would fit into the electrical outlet. Making sure my mother was looking the other way, I managed to plug in the bobby pin. She tells me that the electrical jolt knocked me halfway across the room, and of course blew a fuse. As you can imagine, I never repeated that experiment.

What happens the first time a child touches fire, plays with a bee, or gets shocked electrically is the formation of a trigger we never forget (at least unconsciously). Triggers are also prevalent throughout the rest of the animal kingdom—the first time a puppy plays with a skunk or a young bear cub goes after a porcupine.

TRIGGERS ALLOW US TO MAKE MEANING OUT OF A THREATENING SITUATION IMMEDIATELY AND WITHOUT HAVING TO THINK ABOUT IT. When a person is out camping and a grizzly bear suddenly appears, ready to charge, the unconscious *immediately* triggers the fight-or-flight response—no need or time to stop and analyze the situation. In life-threatening circumstances, the unconscious recognizes the need for immediate action—run away, or fight.

THE PROBLEM WITH TRIGGERS

As we saw in chapter 2, a trigger virus results from the erroneous association of an external stimulus with an emotional state. For this link to occur, the stimulus needs to happen at or just before the peak of the emotional state. Suppose a dear friend of yours was killed in an automobile crash. At the funeral, a well-meaning friend touches you on the shoulder and expresses sympathy. A few minutes later, another friend comes up to you and sympathetically touches you in exactly the same way. Finally, just at the peak of your grieving, a third friend touches you the same way. Now they become unconsciously linked—that particular touch and the state of grieving.

Ten years later you are at a fine restaurant, celebrating your birthday with some close friends. One of your friends gets up to make a phone call, returns, touches you on the shoulder, and—whammo!—you're depressed. Have you ever had an experience like this? You are moving through your day, feeling fine, when suddenly, for no obvious reason, you feel on edge or anxious or depressed. Quite possibly a trigger virus has been activated.

Just as triggers can serve us in three ways, trigger viruses can disempower us in three ways:

TRIGGERS CAN BE DEHUMANIZING. We experience *this* stimulus and automatically experience *that* response. There's only one choice. The impatient driver gives us an obscene gesture and *automatically* we are upset. Advertisers use sex or portray some peak adventurous experience to sell beer, and on some level we take interest. Your lover or a family member speaks in that obnoxious tone of voice, and you automatically lose your patience.

Some psychologists believe that for us to feel fully human, any perceptual experience should allow us a variety of possible responses, at least two or three. To have only one is to become machinelike.

TRIGGERS TAKE AWAY CONTROL OF OUR EMOTIONAL WELL-BEING. Positive and negative triggers or associations are unconsciously being formed and activated all the time. Erroneous ones may disempower us by taking away our control over the states we experience. Notice the states that might be unconsciously triggered in a typical day.

- It is raining for the twelfth day in a row, so you start the day feeling depressed.
- Your spouse or lover rubs your shoulders and you feel relaxed.

- You listen to the morning news and feel angry.
- You see the garage in need of organizing and start to feel tired.
- You hear your favorite music on the radio and feel rejuvenated.
- You encounter a homeless person seeking a handout and feel uncomfortable.
- You make a mistake while working on an important project and feel annoyed with yourself.
- You look at a picture of family members and feel a sense of pride.

The problem here is that most of us experience emotions that randomly go up and down during a typical day in triggered response to what is happening around us. We are like emotional basketballs, randomly bouncing this way and that. Deepak Chopra calls this mode of functioning *object referral* behavior. Emotional well-being depends on external circumstances.

Most of us are not even consciously aware of what is triggering our emotional responses. We have lost control of the states we might prefer to be experiencing. Tony Robbins says that the single most important key to his phenomenal success has been the ability to manage his states. For most of the rest of us, states just happen.

TRIGGERS IN THE FORM OF *TRIGGER VIRUSES* LEAD TO INCONGRUENCE. A trigger becomes a *trigger virus* when it has no useful connection with the context in which it occurs, *or* it causes mental and emotional incongruence. Amy's repeated compulsion to verify the safety of her keys had no obvious connection with being served dinner, and her behavior embarrassed her. The person who picks up a math book and has a fight-or-flight survival response is acting out of context. The feeling of annoyance that gets triggered when you just *look* at your boss or that colleague you dislike may not enhance your job performance.

If a trigger automatically results in behavior, a compulsion, or an emotional state that interferes with your job, your relationships, your health, or your sense of well-being, then it is a *trigger virus.* Remember that a thought virus, by definition, is a portion of the unconscious that is more or less functionally detached from the rest of the nervous system, and serves its own self-interest or positive intent. The unconscious positive intent may be memory, safety, or survival. The resulting behavior or states may include anger, overwhelming feelings, depression, frustration, anxiety, fatigue, worry, or guilt. If you are experiencing any of these on a regular basis, trigger viruses may be the cause. If you sometimes indulge behaviors or compulsions you are later less than proud of, trigger viruses may again be the culprits.

Amy, as it turned out, was taking a hypnosis certification course while she attended medical school. The instructor had installed a *temporary* thought virus in the form of a posthypnotic suggestion. The next three times she was served food, she was to walk across the room and verify the whereabouts of her keys. After that, this behavior would disappear. Amy did not consciously remember the suggestion. What is fascinating, though, is that when questioned about her unusual behavior, she *made up a reason to justify her actions*. This, in fact, is common with all thought viruses outside of our conscious awareness. Our thinking becomes noncoherent, because we invent meaning (as Amy did), or blame external circumstances for the triggered behavior, the limiting belief, or the internal conflict:

- "It's not *my fault* I get angry, it's because of the way you look at me."
- "I could never become fluent in a new foreign language, because it's too hard, and I never was good with high school Spanish thirty years ago."
- "I'd like to be wealthy, but it's okay that I'm not, because a lot of wealthy people are unhappy, and who knows, I might lose all my friends."

By observing the clear display of triggers and trigger viruses as they occurred with Amy and numerous seminar participants and clients, I have developed a model of what stands in the way of achieving our dreams and visions in life.

GETTING WHAT YOU WANT IN LIFE

To understand how the model works, it's useful to start with a simple exercise.

Exercise 6
What Stands Between You and Your Visions?

Think about an important goal, dream, or vision you have for yourself. Once you have one in mind, answer honestly the following questions:

- Are you making progress moving toward this vision?
- Is this something that you believe you will definitely achieve within a reasonable time?
- *Or* do you feel stuck and not really moving toward your outcome?

If any of your goals or visions have the least bit of possibility for success, yet you haven't achieved them or aren't even making reasonable progress toward achieving them, there are three possible reasons why.

1. *A trigger virus is creating a negative association with* having *the outcome.* Something about having the vision on some level feels more painful than not having it. As an example, we've probably all had the experience of being in a love relationship, being totally open to and trusting of our partner, when suddenly he or she did something to end the relationship. We were left brokenhearted. What often happens then is that feelings of love, openness, and trust toward an intimate partner get unconsciously *anchored* with the pain, grieving, and fear associated with losing the partner. A thought virus is installed. The virus then reproduces such that *any time* you start to get close with a potential love partner, that closeness triggers feelings of pain, grief, or fear.

2. *A trigger virus is creating a negative association with the* process of achieving *the vision.* Many of us could use more money, but the thought of what we might have to go through to get it creates a disempowering state. The thought of working a second job for a while might trigger a feeling of being trapped and not having enough time to have fun. The thought of developing an investment strategy to make your money grow might trigger feelings of confusion or frustration at not understanding the science of investment.

3. *A trigger virus is creating a positive association with* not having *the vision.* Not having what you want could be benefiting you in some

way. A woman with a condition similar to chronic fatigue syndrome once went to see the renowned physician and healer Milton Erickson. As it turned out, when she was most sick and least able to function, she received much attention from her family. In some ways her life was comfortable in that she was taken care of. Part of her was invested in remaining sick. Erickson quickly recognized that she didn't want to get better. He asked her to leave his office, and not to come back until she was ready to change. She never returned.

Not having what you want can be painful, but it can also be comfortable in that it is *familiar*. If you have never had what you desire, the unfamiliarity of having it might feel intimidating. When you think of some dream or vision you haven't achieved because you feel stuck, ask yourself these three questions:

1. What is it about the *process of achieving* your vision you'd do almost anything to avoid?
2. What is it about *having* your vision you'd do almost anything to avoid?
3. What's important about *not having* your vision?

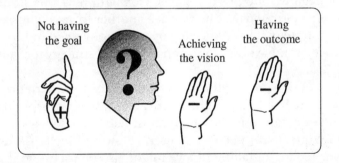

These questions are crucial because they reveal the positive intent of whatever is standing in the way of achieving your dreams in life—that is, the positive intent of potential thought viruses. You cannot cure viruses without maintaining the positive intent.

TYPES OF TRIGGER VIRUSES

Trigger viruses come in two varieties. One, the *simple trigger*, is the V/K, A/K, or K/K synesthesia discussed in chapter 2. This is also

commonly called an *anchor.* Here the visual, auditory, or kinesthetic (V, A, or K) trigger is *anchored* to a kinesthetic (K) state. A
person hears that certain tone of voice from his or her spouse and
automatically becomes angry. Most of the thought viruses we've
discussed in this chapter fall into this category. Simple triggers or
anchors give rise to phobias, compulsions, learning blocks, incongruent behavior, and disempowering states.

A second possibility, called the *complex trigger,* occurs when the
stimulus fires off a *sequence* of internal and external experiences
that ultimately lead to the undesirable state or behavior. This, as
discussed in chapter 1, is also called a *strategy* or a *program.* Remember that my strategy for procrastination was to *see* what
needed to be done (V^e); *hear* a stern internal voice telling me I
had to do the task (A^i); *hear* another internal voice (my rebellious
side) saying I don't want to do it (A^i); *picture* all the tedious details
to complete the task (V^i); and, finally, *feel* paralyzed (K^i).

To get into my state of procrastination, I unconsciously go
through several steps of external and internal experiences. Someone else might have an entirely different complex trigger that elicits the same state. A complex trigger or strategy is like a recipe or
a ritual. We all have individual, unique strategies to produce a variety of negative and positive states. We might have one strategy to
get highly motivated. Maybe we have another to get depressed. Yet
another strategy is necessary for us to be convinced to buy something. We even have a unique and individual strategy for falling in
love.

Consciously knowing the steps of a strategy to experience a *positive* state, such as being highly motivated or feeling inspired to act
resourcefully in the midst of apparent failure or setbacks, gives a
person control and personal power. Knowing the steps that trigger your feeling of falling in love might also be useful, so that you
don't wind up falling in love with an inappropriate person, just because he or she triggered your love strategy.

This was the demise of my past marriage. My former wife, an
artist, met an art agent who very powerfully triggered her love
strategy. She was swept off her feet and felt this person was her romantic destiny, her soul mate, so she had to leave our marriage. At
the time I was just learning about love strategies. I was convinced
this person had erroneously triggered her love strategy, and it
would be a mistake to end the marriage. Her experience with the
agent, however, had now evolved into a compulsion, so she felt she

had no choice. This is common with trigger viruses—the feeling that a person has only *one* apparent choice. Within a few months she realized she had made a mistake, but it was too late. The marriage was over. She now found herself enmeshed in a dysfunctional addictive relationship based in part on a barrage of inappropriate triggers.

Consciously knowing the steps we go through to experience a *negative* state, such as inappropriate anger, overwhelming feelings, or depression, provides opportunities to deactivate these viruses through the procedures of Thought Virus Therapy. This, again, gives us more control over the states we'd like to be experiencing.

SUBMODALITIES

Internal pictures, self-talk, and feelings are the three *modalities* of thought. *Qualities* of the internal experience are called *submodalities*.

Exercise 7
Visual Submodalities

Imagine someone you really care about. *Quickly* answer the following questions about how you picture this person. If you don't think that you visualize, then just imagine how you would answer each question if you could visualize this person.

- Do you picture this person in black and white or in color?
- Is the person moving or in still frame?
- Is the person close up or far away?
- Does the person appear clearly focused or slightly defocused?
- Where do you see this person in your field of vision? Do you picture him or her in the center of your field of vision? Up to the left? Down toward the right?

The qualities of your internal picture of this person are *visual submodalities*:

- black and white or color
- moving or still frame
- close up or far away

- location in your field of vision
- focused or defocused
- panoramic (all around you) or framed
- associated (you don't see yourself in the scene and picture it as you would looking through your own eyes) or disassociated (you picture yourself in the scene)

Exercise 8
Discovering Driver Submodalities

Next imagine someone you dislike. Again, *quickly* answer the same questions about how you picture this person. If you don't consider yourself particularly visual, imagine how you would answer the questions if you were.

- Do you picture this person in black and white or in color?
- Is the person moving or in still frame?
- Is the person close up or far away?
- Does the person appear clearly focused or slightly defocused?
- Where do you see this person in your field of vision? Do you picture him or her in the center of your field of vision? Up to the left? Down toward the right?

Which of the submodalities were most different between the person you don't like and the one you care for? The submodality or submodalities that are most different are called the *driver submodalities;* they allow the brain to store information in such a way that you can clearly distinguish between who you care for and who you don't.

Many pop-psychology books emphasize the value of positive self-talk. Probably equally important, if not more important, though, are *auditory submodalities*—the qualities of the internal voice being

- fast-paced or slow-paced
- inflected or monotone
- pitched high, low, or medium
- of a specific timbre
- your voice or someone else's
- apparently located in some particular place in your body

Kinesthetic submodalities are qualities of internal feelings. Feelings may seem

- warm or cool
- rough or smooth
- intermittent or steady
- sharp or dull
- hard or soft
- located in some particular place in the body

As we'll see in the next section, one powerful way to deactivate a simple or complex trigger is simply to change submodalities of key internal steps, and thereby change how we make meaning of whatever normally triggers the thought virus.

OVERCOMING ARACHNOPHOBIA

Karen was one of the foreign course participants in my NLP Certification Training. She told me there were some beautiful forest trails near her home in Germany. She very much wanted to take her young son out for walks on these trails, but she had a trigger virus, a compulsive fear of spiders. Whenever she thought about walking in the forest, she imagined spiders lurking under leaves and behind bushes, just waiting to jump out at her as she walked by.

"What is it about spiders that frightens you?" I asked.

"They're so dark and hairy and they have all those legs," she responded. "The thought of them just gives me the creeps." Her squinting eyes and gritted teeth were congruent with her words.

"Are you afraid of butterflies?" I asked.

"What? Why would I be afraid of butterflies?"

"Don't butterflies have dark bodies, a number of legs, and maybe even some hairiness?" I suggested.

"Well, I guess you're right, but butterflies are fine."

I was looking for a *counterexample*—something close to what what was causing the phobia, but without the negative emotional charge.

"Can you think of any way that having this fear is serving you— some way that you benefit from it?" I probed. "Thought viruses always have some seemingly positive intent or benefits."

"Well, if I discover a spider in the house, and if I scream loud enough, my husband comes to my rescue, and I feel taken care of." The benefit of feeling taken care of is called the *secondary gain.*

"If we could eliminate this fear, are there other things your husband could do so that you would feel cared for in the same way? Feeling cared for is certainly useful. I think it is important to maintain that with any changes we make." She thought about it, and suggested a couple of little things he would probably be willing to do.

"Before you allow this fear to disappear completely, might there be some situations in which it would be useful to maintain this fear?" I probed.

"Maybe it would be appropriate to keep enough distance from a potentially dangerous spider," she responded. "But I think a more useful feeling would be one of caution rather than the panic I feel now." I agreed that sounded more appropriate. This is another important consideration in change work. In some situations the change work needs to be *context dependent,* so you don't eliminate the behavior at times when it might be necessary and appropriate.

"If your husband is willing to do those little things so you feel cared for, and if appropriate caution can replace the panic, are there any other parts of you that would object to letting go of the fear of spiders?" I asked.

"No. I think that would be fine," she said. I then decided to approach the issue by helping her change her Internal Representations of spiders by changing the submodalities. I checked for the spider submodalities versus the submodalities of how she visualized butterflies. It turned out that the ones that were the *most* different, the driver submodalities, were closeness and color. She pictured butterflies close up and in color, while spiders were more distant, larger than lifelike, and a sinister gray-black.

Next I asked her to imagine a thick plate of Plexiglas sliding down in front of her to protect her from anything she visualized beyond it.

"Can you picture yourself out in front of the Plexiglas studying a butterfly the way you visualize it, in color and close up?" By seeing herself in the picture, this disassociated her from the experience. The Plexiglas provided a second level of emotional protection.

"Yeah, I can see myself looking at the butterfly. I'm studying it with a sense of curiosity and fascination."

"Good. Now remember the Plexiglas is as thick as it needs to be to protect you. Can you imagine Karen out in front of the Plexiglas looking at a *spider* with that same sense of curiosity and fascination . . . seeing it close-up, life-size, and in color, the same way she sees butterflies?

She thought for a minute, looked surprised, and said, "That's so strange. I really can see *her* doing that . . . *that* Karen out there."

"Good. Now *that* Karen knows something that might be really useful to you—how to look at spiders the way you look at butterflies. Is there any part of you that would not be comfortable with *you* having the same ability *that* Karen has?" I was doing another congruency check with other unconscious parts of her.

She paused again and responded, "No, I'm fine with that, as long as I'm cautious." I then had her imagine the Plexiglas sliding up and away from her. I suggested picturing *that* Karen walking toward her until she was close enough to draw *that* Karen into her heart. This metaphorically represents reintegrating *that* Karen, together with her new way of viewing spiders, back into herself.

I next tested to see if the integration was complete. "Go ahead and put the Plexiglas back in place and imagine a spider on the other side. What do you see?" She seemed comfortable picturing the spider, so I asked her to remove the Plexiglas and again picture the spider.

"This is bizarre. I really am fascinated and curious about it. It really is one of God's creatures, just like the butterflies." From there I *future paced* her by having her imagine herself in the future, back in Germany, walking with her son, and viewing a spider in this same way. She seemed fine with that. One last thing we could have done was to find a real spider to test the work. Unfortunately, as with the cats a few days earlier, the word must have gotten out among the spiders, and they all disappeared.

Antiviral Remedy 1
Overcoming a Phobia by Changing Submodalities

1. Identify the the phobia and ask yourself, "What is it about _____ [the phobia] that frightens me or makes me come unglued?"

2. Look for a *counterexample,* something as close to the phobia as you can think of with which you do fine and act resourcefully—for example, as with the butterfly for Karen.

3. Look for the *secondary gain,* any benefits you receive as a result of having the phobia. Ask yourself, "What benefit(s) do I get or *could* I get by having this phobia?"

4. Ask yourself, "How can I maintain this benefit when I let go of the phobia?" Allow enough time for the answer(s) to come into your awareness.

5. Check to see if there might be a *context* in which the fear would be appropriate. Ask yourself, "Before I allow this fear to completely disappear, would there be any situations in which it would be appropriate?" Notice what answers come up.

6. *Ecology check.* Ask yourself if any other parts object to letting go of the fear. If so, find the positive intent of the objecting part, and ask yourself, "How can I maintain _____ [the positive intent of the objecting part] while letting go of the fear?"

7. *Contrast the submodalities* of the phobia with those of the counterexample. In most cases it's easiest to work with visual submodalities—closeness of the image, moving or still frame, black and white or color, etc. (see Exercises 7 and 8). Find the driver(s)—the one or two that are most different for the counterexample versus the phobia.

8. For protection, disassociate yourself from your experience by imagining a thick plate of Plexiglas sliding down in front of you. Picture yourself out in front of the Plexiglas experiencing the counterexample with the driver submodalities (e.g., the butterfly close up and in color).

9. Now imagine looking through the Plexiglas, watching yourself experience whatever triggers the phobia with the same submodalities as the counterexample has (e.g., Karen seeing Karen looking at the spider close up and in color with a sense of curiosity and fascination). Make sure to keep the Plexiglas as thick as it needs to be for protection.

10. *Reintegration.* Now remove the Plexiglas. Imagine *that* other you out in front, with the ability to handle the trigger resourcefully. Imagine drawing that "you" into your heart.

11. *Test the change.* Put the Plexiglas back in place and imagine looking at the trigger, and notice your experience. If that feels okay, remove the Plexiglas and again notice the experience. If there is any remaining discomfort, go back to step 6.

12. *Future pace.* Imagine some future encounter with the trigger and your resourceful reaction.

After my NLP training in July, I didn't hear from Karen until December. She sent me a Christmas card thanking me for the session and saying she now regularly goes for walks in the forest with her son. She no longer fears spiders.

GETTING BEYOND MATH ANXIETY

Doris was a client who consulted with me on a number of issues over a period of a couple of years. One serious problem was that she wanted to pass a standardized teachers' exam in California to get her teacher's credentials. Part of the exam included algebra and geometry, but she had avoided taking these subjects in high school and college because of a trigger virus. She had math anxiety.

"Was there ever a time when you were good in math?" I probed, looking for a counterexample.

Well, actually, I think I was pretty good with math until the third grade. That year I had Mrs. Stonebreaker, and . . ." Her mouth suddenly dropped in a moment of recollection. As it turned out, whenever Doris made a mistake in math, Mrs. Stonebreaker would push her against a wood-burning stove, and Doris would get burned. Her unconscious connected doing math with getting burned. No wonder she had math anxiety! The positive intent of the thought virus was certainly worthwhile—to protect her, and keep her from getting burned.

It's worth noting here that Thought Virus Therapy differs from other forms of therapy in that it is not necessary to know what caused the virus in the first place; therapy can be just as effective without that knowledge. In Doris's case, the cause spontaneously emerged. The process I decided to do with Doris, to move beyond her math anxiety—a simple virus—is called *collapsing anchors.*

"I appreciate that this part of you is trying to protect you and keep you from getting burned," I said. "But each time you take the test and fail the math section, doesn't it just *burn* you that you are getting burned?" I was trying to point out to her unconscious the incongruence of continuing the phobia. She was getting burned academically, and this way of thinking was not protecting her career. I asked if, now that the danger of being physically burned was no longer an issue, any part of her would object to changing her way of thinking about math, so she could protect her career. When you let formerly obstructive patterns continue their "job" in a *constructive* way, they will work with you.

I next asked her to think about studying math. She took a deep breath, her jaws clenched, and she looked anxious and uncomfortable. I reached over and touched her left elbow to set up a negative anchor. I had her get up and walk around for a few seconds to change her state. I then tested the anchor by touching her left elbow the same way I had done before. Her face took on a similar expression.

"What do you feel?" I asked.

"Frustrated and blocked." It appeared that the negative anchor was set. My next step was to set up a *power trigger*—a stack of empowering states anchored on her *right* elbow.

"Can you think of a specific time when you felt a sense of unstoppable confidence?" She nodded. "Be back in that experience as if it were happening *now*. Now, seeing what you saw, hearing what you heard, and feeling what you felt, notice how your facial muscles are, and the expression on your face. What was your posture like? How were you breathing?" Having someone take on the physiology of the desired state is one of the quickest ways to cause the person to begin to associate into that state. She sat upright, breathed deeply, and relaxed her jaw.

"Now, feeling that sense of unstoppable confidence, allow the feeling to build, and let me know when it peaks for you." I carefully watched her facial muscles, and when I observed a shift that I thought might be the state peaking, I reached over and squeezed her right elbow. She verified that her state had peaked. I then asked her to allow the feelings to dissipate. I next repeated the steps of having her assume the physiology of the state and anchoring her when the state peaked. Again, I had her allow the feelings to dissipate.

"Do you smell the popcorn from next door?" I asked. She looked surprised and said that she didn't. I did this simply to interrupt her state. I then squeezed her right elbow. Her face lit up, and she smiled and said she felt strong. The most crucial key to the success of an effective anchor is to set the anchor at or just before the peak of the desired state. When I tested the anchor, if it did not produce the desired state, or if the state was present but weak, the anchor probably was not set at the right time. I would just go back and reset it.

Antiviral Remedy 2
Creating a Power Trigger

1. Find a quiet spot where you can sit comfortably undisturbed. Relax and breathe easily.
2. Go back to a time when you were powerfully experiencing the desired state. Be in that situation as if it were happening *now*. Notice the sights, sounds, and especially the feelings from that experience.
3. For *physiology*, notice, as you experience this empowering state:
   - your posture
   - your breathing
   - facial muscles and the expression on your face
   - most important, your gestures and movement
4. Decide on a *kinesthetic anchor* you can use to access this state systematically.
   - *You might touch or squeeze:*
      your earlobe
      your wrist
      your fists
   - *You might do a unique gesture with movement:*
      thumbs up
      clapping hands
      fist into the other hand
   - You might also include a *power word* (auditory component):
      "Yes!"
      "Boom!"
      a power word of significance to you
   - (The best gestures, touches, or sounds are ones that naturally occur when you are in the desired state.)
5. Intensify the feelings from this state.
6. When the feelings reach a peak, fire the anchor you have chosen. The most crucial part of the entire process is having the stimulus coincide with the peak of the experience or just before the peak.
7. Change your state by standing up, walking around, or drinking something for a few minutes.

8. Test the anchor by firing it; that is, experience the touch, sound, or both. If you do not go back into the desired state, redo steps 2 through 8 or use a different stimulus for your anchor.
9. Whenever you naturally find yourself in the desired state or other empowering states, you can *stack* your trigger by reanchoring these states at the peak of your experience.
10. You can create a power anchor by *stacking* a number of different empowering states using the same stimulus.

Another crucial piece here is that the positive anchor on Doris's right elbow needed to trigger a stronger positive emotional response than the negative state on her left elbow. I assured that this was so by *stacking* several more empowering states at the same location on her right elbow.

I then reached over and touched both elbows simultaneously. Initially she looked startled, and her face twisted asymmetrically. I expected her brain to short-circuit and to see sparks jumping out. Her brain was getting one message to feel math anxiety, and *simultaneously* getting another message to feel empowered. When the procedure works as desired, the negative anchor or virus will *collapse*. Triggers that once produced math anxiety will now produce a neutral state or possibly a positive one.

Antiviral Remedy 3
Collapsing Anchors

1. Set up an anchor, a particular stimulus, to trigger the undesired state by following steps 1 through 8 in Antiviral Remedy 2. Be careful not to make the negative state too intense, and by all means *do not stack* negative states. Firing the anchor, however, should clearly trigger the negative state.
2. Set up a power anchor with a different stimulus. Stack the anchor so that the positive empowering feelings are stronger than the undesirable state.
3. Fire both anchors simultaneously.
4. Test the work by firing the former negative anchor. If the anchors are collapsed, you should experience a neutral or slightly positive state.

I tested the change for Doris by reaching over and squeezing her left elbow (the old negative anchor). She didn't notice a change of state, either positive or negative. I asked her how she felt about the algebra and geometry she needed to learn to pass her test. She said she thought it would be a challenge, yet she looked forward to it. Having never had a course in algebra or geometry, she came within one point of passing the next test. We were both confident that with one more take she would easily pass. We didn't get a chance to test our belief, however, because before she could take it again, she decided to relocate back to Texas and move into a new career.

In helping Doris and others move beyond trigger viruses, I encountered another clue to how my friend Dana thought as she did.

CLUE NUMBER 3: INCORPORATE POSITIVE *REVERSE TRIGGERS* INTO YOUR THINKING.

REVERSE TRIGGERS

When I first recognized that triggers could be reversed—i.e., that a seemingly negative trigger could elicit a positive state or that a seemingly positive trigger could produce a negative state—I felt a sense of awe. As discussed earlier, a positive vision may have a negative trigger associated with it, and a negative circumstance may have a positive trigger. Notice the way that triggers color or distort the *meaning* we attach to getting what we want in life.

Exercise 9
Triggers and Reverse Triggers

Write down some of the positive *and* some of the negative emotions you experience when you think about or picture yourself

- being in an intimate love relationship
- having an abundance of money
- working at your present job
- actually doing those projects that you've been procrastinating

- finally working toward achieving New Year's resolutions or personal goals
- experiencing setbacks or failures along the way

Often people will say they want to be in a healthy, intimate love relationship, yet the thought of being committed to another person triggers a feeling of being stuck, or perhaps of suffocation. Another person may genuinely desire to follow through with his resolution to lose weight, yet the thought of dieting or exercise may trigger feelings of anxiety or fatigue. In each case a seemingly positive outcome triggers unresourceful emotions (a positive trigger, a negative state). These are examples of *negative reverse triggers.* Most of us have also been programmed throughout childhood that it is not okay to make mistakes. Apparent failures and setbacks can trigger such unpleasant emotions that we wind up not even trying.

Suppose that situations that now trigger negative states could be reversed; we'll call these *positive reverse triggers.* Suppose that when you think about that project on which you've been procrastinating, you can feel a sense of exhilaration. Suppose it were possible that when you thought about work, you could hardly wait until it was Monday morning so you could get started again. Suppose that whenever someone rejected you, you could experience a high sense of self-esteem or empowerment. Or suppose that when a waiter was rude to you, this could automatically trigger a sense of compassion, an awareness that perhaps he is having a bad day—or maybe a bad lifetime. If you could change the meaning that various conditions in life automatically trigger, how would life be different for you?

Exercise 10
Changing Meaning

Write down some areas of life, some behaviors, or some habits that, if you were to change the *meaning* of what was taking place, would radically improve the quality of life for you. Pick seven areas, behaviors, or habits in which changing the meaning would have the most impact and would most transform your life. What new emotions or behaviors would you like to have triggered to replace the old ones?

One way to iron out negative viruses associated with what we want in life is to collapse these anchors, as I helped Doris do with her math anxiety. Another, more subtle and powerful approach is to make use of the virus's energy, as you would use the energy of an opponent's blow in the martial arts. That is, create reverse triggers in the way that my friend Dana did unconsciously.

BREAKING THROUGH THE FEAR OF REJECTION

Leslie had a strong fear of rejection when approaching men. She was about 100 pounds overweight. She attended a seminar given by a colleague of mine who chose her to demonstrate in front of the audience how to get beyond fear of rejection. Her thought virus had "served" her in that if she didn't approach men, she was protected from the pain of being rejected. It also kept her out of an intimate relationship that might in any way resemble her painful memories from childhood and previous relationships. These intents are certainly worthwhile, but the trigger virus was, as usual, incongruent. Being overweight guaranteed lots of rejection, and staying out of a potentially healthy relationship ensured that her memories of childhood and failed relationships would continue to dominate her perception of what a relationship could be.

Making sure to maintain the positive intent of the virus, my colleague proceeded to have this woman establish a power trigger to elicit unstoppable confidence and personal regard for herself. He also had her imagine a role model of someone she knew who could flow with rejection and be untouched emotionally. He then set an anchor for rejection. He fired the rejection anchor and *immediately afterward* fired the power trigger. After doing this a number of times, he had reversed her trigger for rejection.

Antiviral Remedy 4
Setting Reverse Triggers

1. Set up an anchor for the undesirable state and a power trigger as you would for collapsing anchors.
2. When collapsing anchors, fire the negative anchor and positive trigger simultaneously. In contrast, when setting reverse triggers, fire the rejection anchor, *release* this anchor, then *im-*

mediately fire the power trigger. Repeat this until firing the former negative anchor by itself automatically triggers empowering states.

My colleague tested his work with this woman by having a man from the audience come up in front of the group. She was to try to get a date with him, and he was to reject her steadfastly. This reverse trigger worked. The more this man rejected and insulted her, the more confident and gently persistent she became in her quest for a date. This work was apparently transformational for her, because six months later she had reportedly lost more than half of her excess weight, and she was in a healthy relationship with a man.

Antiviral Remedy 5
Working with Intense or Phobic Fear of Rejection

In working with a client for whom the fear of rejection is too intense or even phobic, before setting the anchor and trigger, look for an emotional counterexample. The client might be able to resourcefully handle a feeling somewhat similar to rejection, such as disagreement or disapproval.

To neutralize the overwhelming emotional response of the trigger virus, proceed as I did with Karen and her fear of spiders. Remember, she visualized herself in front of the protective Plexiglas, changing the submodalities of her fear. She then reintegrated that person *out there* who now had the ability to resourcefully handle what was once terrifying.

From there, set up the reverse triggers.

Once I understood how triggers could be reversed, I realized this was one thing my friend Dana did unconsciously. Much of her experience, which would trigger resignation in most people, triggered humor, curiosity, and charm in her. I then recognized what had gone wrong with Dr. Chopra's heroin-addict patient. The old familiar setting on the train had simply triggered the urge to take heroin, because the thought viruses connected with the drug habit had not been dealt with.

I wondered what life would be like if all of those annoying trigger viruses that normally disempower us could be reversed to stimulate such states as confidence, motivation, exhilaration, or curiosity—states that would serve us. How much energy and power would this add to daily life?

Matter, like triggers, can be reversed. And like reversed triggers, reversed matter can release enormous energy. A form of matter composed of particles that have an electrical charge opposite to what they normally have is called *antimatter.* Antimatter, coming in contact with ordinary matter, totally annihilates the normally charged matter and itself to form pure energy. This is according to Einstein's famous equation $E = mc^2$. In fact, a chunk of anti-matter the size of a penny, coming in contact with matter, would produce an explosion comparable to an atomic bomb. Some have suggested that the Tunguska explosion I contemplated, while gazing at the meteor shower in the High Sierra, was caused by a chunk of antimatter. I wondered if reverse triggers might free up comparable emotional and mental energy.

4

LIMITING VIRUSES

FACED WITH A CHOICE
BETWEEN CHANGING ONE'S MIND AND
PROVING THERE IS NO NEED TO DO SO,
ALMOST EVERYONE GETS BUSY ON THE PROOF.

—JOHN KENNETH GALBRAITH

One crisp, frosty morning in November, I got up from bed and walked downstairs to get some juice and turn on the heater. I was barefoot, yet my feet felt comfortable as I walked across the carpet. When I reached the dining room, I noticed that my feet felt somewhat colder on the hardwood floor. Finally, when I reached the kitchen, I noticed the ceramic tile felt icy cold.

It seemed odd that these three floor surfaces should be different temperatures, so I grabbed a nearby thermometer and measured the temperature of each. To my surprise, they were all 48 degrees Fahrenheit, the air temperature of the room. Why, then, did I *believe* the tile was so much colder than the carpet? The three surfaces seemed to display a phenomena called *sequential incongruence;* despite being at the same temperature, they randomly felt different. Furthermore, whenever I talk with others who have walked across the similar cold surfaces, they share this erroneous or *limiting belief,* that different surfaces have different feelings of coldness. Some limiting beliefs appear to be universal.

LIMITING BELIEFS

What do all these people have in common?

- an overweight person who goes on and off diets
- a workaholic

- a person unable to sustain a career
- person in a codependent relationship

The answer is that they have limiting beliefs or values that fall into the category of thought viruses called *limiting viruses*. In chapter 3 we saw that triggers and trigger viruses occur automatically and unconsciously. Yet, even though they exist at such a deep level, they are the easiest of all thought viruses to cure. Limiting viruses occur at a slightly more conscious level of thinking, the level of beliefs and values. Here we create our internal map for understanding the world. Beliefs and values filter our perception of reality. At this level, we unconsciously decide which of the myriad stimuli bombarding our senses we will pay attention to, and which we will delete. Here we decide what provides pleasure and what we should fear as a potential source of pain.

To illustrate how powerfully limiting viruses can affect us, consider the story of a woman I'll call Susan, who had advanced breast cancer that had metastasized to other organs. She was quite fearful of her condition, and the pain throughout her body was so intense that she could barely walk. Since traditional treatment by itself offered little hope for her, she decided to try an alternative healing program that involved Ayurveda (an ancient form of medicine from India), massage, sensory therapy, and transcendental meditation. She felt so good with the treatment that on some deep level she didn't *believe* the fear and pain were necessary. They left her.

She excitedly reported to her doctor that she was now free from pain and could walk again. New X rays were ordered, and the cancer was still there. The doctor, bless his heart, assured Susan that the alternative therapy was all in her mind, and the pain would soon return. Susan believed him, so sure enough, the pain and fear did return. It took some time for the alternative therapists to undo the good doctor's work, but they were eventually successful. Even though the cancer persisted, Susan was getting the best of traditional and nontraditional therapies. As long as she was comfortable enough, and convinced on a deep enough level that pain and fear did not have to accompany her disease, she was free from these extra burdens.

When I heard Susan's story, I recognized that we all have limiting beliefs that color how we make meaning and that also hold us back. "I can't do _____," "I'm not very _____," "_____ is too hard for me or would take too much time." I wondered if there was a way we could change such beliefs. Furthermore, how do we decide whether we are successful or not? Why is it that some people have such a hard time with money, even though they are reasonably bright and well educated? Why do others have such a hard time with relationships or maintaining good health? Why is it so hard to stick to self-improvement programs, such as diet, exercise, and New Year's resolutions? What really motivates us in life?

Empowering beliefs and values are the basis of useful, flexible behavior and a workable understanding of life. They are the *foundation* for our highest ideals, and provide a way to measure how we are living up to those ideals. Limiting viruses are like termites that eat away at, weaken, and sometimes ultimately destroy that foundation. To understand limiting thought viruses, it is useful to have a better understanding of the level where they infect—beliefs and values.

BELIEFS AND VALUES

Beliefs form the fabric of our internal maps of reality, the canvas on which we paint life, the *rules* and *expectations* for how and why things happen as they do. They include such statements as these:

- "If _____ happens, it's because _____ took place."
- "People are _____."
- "I should _____," or "I can't _____," or "I have to _____."
- "When someone does _____, it means _____."

Values motivate us to do the things we do; they are the driving force of human behavior. What we fear will provide pain, and what we anticipate will bring pleasure. Our deepest core values are positive or negative emotional states. Values are more abstract than beliefs, and can usually be described in one or two words: relationships, freedom, rejection, peace of mind, humiliation, depression, security, adventure, and so on. Notice each of these words is a *nominalization,* something abstract that you can't see, touch, or put into a wheelbarrow.

A single value has a number of beliefs or rules connected with it, which measure whether or not we are getting the value. I asked Lynn, a dear friend of mine, what is important to her in an intimate love relationship. She said one important thing was that she *feels cared for.* That is one of her values. I asked further, "*How do you know* when you are being cared for?"

"Well," she replied, "my partner needs to be reliable in following through on things he promises to do; be willing to share his feelings, hurts, and desires; and reach out to and be patient with my young children."

Those were a few of the *rules* or *beliefs* connected with her *value* of feeling cared for. If a value were the gold thread for a necklace, beliefs would be the pearls we hang on that gold thread.

Most of us are convinced that we can't change beliefs, even if they disempower us. This is true on a conscious level, because disempowering beliefs, like other thought viruses, have a positive intent. Despite our best resolve to change, the unconscious will hold on to the positive intent and therefore to the virus itself.

The truth, though, is that beliefs are unconsciously changing over time without our trying. Aren't there things that ten years ago you absolutely knew were true, but that today you'd be embarrassed to admit you once believed? Thought Virus Therapy allows us to change beliefs by modeling the way they naturally change unconsciously. Changing limiting beliefs quickly is generally not as simple as changing triggers, yet it is still a relatively easy process. Often, however, changing the *values* connected with limiting beliefs is easier to do and produces more profound results. Since values exist at a more abstract level of consciousness, one changed value may carry the whole string of pearls—the limiting beliefs connected with the value.

TYPES OF BELIEFS

Beliefs fall into three categories, as listed below:

RULES OF UNDERSTANDING. We've gained these notions through our experiences in life. For example:

- It's hot in the summer and cold in the winter.
- Daisies are prettier than roses.
- If someone frowns at me, that *means* they disapprove of me.
- Eating too much saturated fat *leads to* heart disease.
- I *can't* dance, because I'm not coordinated enough.

Such beliefs may reveal holes or limitations in the internal map of
the person who believes such things. Obviously there are places
with cold summers and others with hot winters. Who says daisies
are prettier than roses? How do you know that a person frowning
at you disapproves of you as opposed to having a twitch in their facial muscles? Do you know for sure that your physiology does not
support the coordination to dance?

GLOBAL CORE BELIEFS. These are giant generalizations about
people, money, life, work, the opposite sex, and so on.

- Life is unfair.
- Men like to problem-solve, so they lack sensitivity to just listen
  to a woman's expression of her feelings.
- Money is the root of all evil.
- You can't teach an old dog new tricks.

Exercise 11
Limiting Core Beliefs

For each of these five areas (people, life, money, work, and the opposite sex) write down five of your core beliefs that may be holding you back or in some way limiting you. These statements
usually take the form of "People are _____," "Life is _____,"
"Women/men are _____," etc.

PEOPLE	MONEY
1.	1.
2.	2.
3.	3.
4.	4.
5.	5.

LIFE	WORK
1.	1.
2.	2.
3.	3.
4.	4.
5.	5.

MEN OR WOMEN

1.

2.

3.

4.

5.

Global core beliefs can be either empowering or disempowering. Since most of them are simply clichés or illogical statements that can't be proved one way or the other, why not choose ones that are empowering?

- Even though people don't always do what I'd like, they are doing the best they can.
- Money provides the freedom and choice for achieving my intellectual, material, and spiritual potential.
- Life is a gift and provides opportunities to make a positive difference here on Earth.

THRESHOLD BELIEFS. These are the rules for knowing that you are receiving a certain value. Suppose having financial abundance is an important *value* for you, the golden thread for your necklace. The question to elicit the pearls—your threshold beliefs—is "*How do you know* when you have financial abundance (or any other value)?" You might respond,

- "When I have an income of $_____ per year."
- "When I have $_____ in investments."
- "When I have $_____ in savings."
- "When I have a net worth of $_____."

Threshold beliefs are the scale by which we measure how successful we are in achieving the values and goals we want in life. Many people are highly successful in others' eyes, but they are unhappy because they are unaware of their own success. They have never established a clear, measurable standard to know when they are experiencing, or when they have achieved, what they set out to do. This is comparable to a pilot taking off in an airplane with no destination and no clear way of knowing where he is.

TYPES OF VALUES

Values have four primary categories:

MEANS VALUES. Many people will list such things as money, love relationships, and rewarding careers as values. These are not emotional states in themselves, but rather *means* to experiencing certain emotional states.

ENDS VALUES. When someone tells me having money is an important value, I agree that financial abundance is positive and worthwhile. I might ask him though, "Do you really just want a stack of green pieces of paper with pictures of notable deceased presidents?" Of course that's not what most people want.

If we ask the question, "*What's important to you* about having money (or any other means value)?" then answers such as "security," "freedom," or "power" emerge. They are the *ends values,* the motivation behind having money.

People don't really want relationships. A relationship is a means toward having a feeling of connection, feeling passion, not feeling lonely, or feeling in love—again, the ends values. A rewarding career is a means toward a state of feeling creative, not feeling financially strapped, or feeling empowered through the challenges work presents. Ends values provide the motivation, the emotional juice, behind any goal we have.

MOVING-TOWARD VALUES. These are values stated in the positive. They are the states or experiences that we anticipate will provide us with pleasure.

- I love *adventure.*
- I want *excitement* and *passion* in my love relationship.
- I enjoy *working with people* and *new learning* in my career.

MOVING-AWAY-FROM VALUES. These are what we *don't want* in our careers, our relationships, or our lives. These are states and situations we would do almost anything to avoid.

- I can't stand a rigid, overbearing boss.
- I'm not going to be poor.
- I'll never act the way my mother acted!

One problem with being motivated by moving-away-from values is that we are focusing on what we don't want, which is like trying to drive forward while looking backward. What we put our attention on grows in our awareness. The woman who insists that she'll never turn out the way her mother did has a good chance of turning out just like her mother. Moving-away-from values may signal unhealed significant emotional experiences from the past.

Limiting thought viruses, then, are glitches in our beliefs and values that lead to incongruent thinking and behavior.

HOW VALUES AND BELIEFS SERVE US

The positive values we think will bring pleasure, as well as the negative values we would do almost anything to avoid, filter what we pay attention to, and determine how we spend our time. In addition, values allow us to evaluate how well we manage our time. When we are not happy with the way we are spending time, it is because of conflicting values. Part of us thinks we should be doing *this,* and another part thinks we should we doing *that.*

Values provide the kinesthetic push behind motivation. Anything we are motivated to do comes about because we anticipate experiencing a positive state (value) or because we are trying to avoid a negative state (value).

Bob, one of my seminar participants, was having a hard time getting motivated at work. I asked him to remember a time when he was totally motivated in his job.

"Well, one time I went to work for the technical support department of a large computer firm, and I felt pretty fired up."

"Okay, go back to that time as if it were happening *now,* " I suggested. "Just as you began to feel motivated, what emotion or state did you experience?"

"I felt a sense of excitement with all the new things I'd be learning," he responded. *Excitement with new learning* was one value that provided the kinesthetic push at least one time when he was motivated. By having him remember a few more times when he was particularly motivated in the area of work, and what values were behind the motivation, we discovered some things that were missing in his present job. Sometimes knowing the motivating values in your career allows you to make simple logistic changes in your present job to provide more motivation. In other cases, a change of job might be the only option to get the satisfaction that only meeting your values can provide.

Exercise 12
Eliciting Values

1. Think of one area of your life that you feel could use improvement. It might be career, personal growth, relationship, finances, social or spiritual life, or some other major area. Think of one time when you were highly motivated in this area. What was the emotion or state just as you began to feel motivated? Put a label on it.

Keep in mind that it could be positive, like feeling connection, a sense of adventure, feeling creative, or it could be a moving-away-from value like fear of being fired, or fear of roughness in your relationship. Whatever it is, write it down. Don't judge right or wrong.

Next, think of another time you were particularly motivated in the area of life you have chosen. Again, what was the emotion or state just as you began to feel motivated? Write that down. Repeat this process until you run out of examples.

2. Ask yourself, "What would it take for me to walk away from or give up on this [the area you have chosen, i.e., the job, relationship, financial management scheme, or spiritual quest]?" Write down whatever comes up. This will provide you with more motivating values. If infidelity would make you leave a relationship, fidelity is an important value. If the possibility of losing $3,000 or more in investments would cause you to give up investing, then security or low risk may be an important value to you for investments over $3,000. Generate a list of values based on the question here.

3. For each situation that would make you walk away from or give up in your chosen area, ask yourself, "If this were to happen, is there anything else that could happen that would motivate me to return?" Write these values down. If nothing would persuade you to return, you have discovered one of your top values.

4. Prioritize the values you came up with in steps 1 through 3. Which is the most important value? Which is the second most important? And so on.

5. To expand your list of values, ask yourself, "What's important to me about _____ [your chosen area]?" Place these on your prioritized list according to their priority.

6. Are the four or five most important values on your prioritized list being met in your present circumstances? If not, what changes would be necessary to fulfill these values?

Beliefs serve us by providing understanding, meaning, and order from what otherwise would appear to be random and chaotic experiences in life. Making meaning in life (even if the meaning is erroneous) seems to be a fundamental part of being human.

Again, threshold beliefs provide the rules to know when we are meeting a particular value through the question, "How would I know when I am experiencing _____ [the value]?"

Exercise 13
Eliciting the Pearls

For each of your top four values from Exercise 12, ask yourself, "How would I know that I have _____ [the value]?" Or ask, "What would it take for me to have or experience _____?" List whatever rules (beliefs) come up.

Reflect on whether your threshold beliefs from Exercise 11 are serving you well. Do they make it easy to experience your most important values regularly, and hard not to experience them? If not, you might consider redesigning them through techniques presented in this chapter and chapter 15.

Beliefs and values together determine the meaning we attach to life, the clarity and coherence of our thinking, our direction through life, and ultimately our destiny. Empowering beliefs and values open up the floodgate of possibilities for a rich and fulfilling life. Disempowering ones can shut us down.

THE PROBLEM WITH BELIEFS

Tony Robbins asks, "Do you think our beliefs and values are part of a master plan, based on intelligent choices we have made as we move through life?" His answer is, "Hardly!" More than likely, our beliefs and values came about haphazardly from the random sequence of painful and pleasurable experiences primarily in childhood, and our attempt to make meaning out of these. For the most part we are living by beliefs and values we never consciously chose, moving us in a direction we don't know, toward a destiny about which we haven't a clue.

One particular problem with our usual way of thinking is that we often mistake our beliefs for our identities. To challenge someone's beliefs on politics, religion, or personal values may seem to that person like a challenge to who they are. In my Powerlearning seminars I demonstrate how stress-free and easy learning can be. I get my participants to do things they never believed possible, like memorizing Portuguese vocabulary words at a rate of eighty to one hundred words per hour, drawing with ease for the first time in their lives, or breaking boards with their bare hands. Interestingly enough, I occasionally get participants who are so attached to their learning blocks, they are actually offended by the prospect of doing things that shouldn't be possible *for them*. We have all gone through great pains to create understanding in life, including learning blocks. And holding on to that understanding, whether it is true or not, may feel much more comfortable than the perceived alternative—confusion.

Another problem with beliefs is that they are the basis of rules and expectations for social conduct. It has been said that all upsets in a relationship are rules upsets; you *expect* one behavior and get something different. Think of a time when you were upset with someone else. Wasn't the basis of the upset that they did or said something you believed or expected they shouldn't do or say? In my experience, there has never been an occasion when such an upset wasn't a rules or belief upset. Why do people get angry with the daily news? Isn't it because we expect people to behave more intelligently than they sometimes do?

The key to resolving upsets with someone you care about is to uncover the beliefs that are in conflict. From that point it's not a matter of whose belief is correct, but just that your beliefs are different. You can either accept the differences or redesign the beliefs.

I have an aunt who has the unspoken belief that whenever someone comes to stay for a visit, within one week they should send a thank-you note. That's how to *show* your appreciation. In my immediate family, though, whenever you visit someone, you simply *tell* them how much you appreciate their hospitality. A thank-you note is an unnecessary formality. After I'd visited my aunt once a year for a number of years, she became quite upset that I had never sent a thank-you note. Understand, we both had the same value—appreciation. It was only our rules or beliefs for how one communicates that appreciation that were different. Furthermore, when I talked with her about this, she was convinced that *everyone* shared her belief that you should send a thank-you note within one week. Anyone who didn't must be a clod. Once we each realized and accepted the other's belief, we were much more at peace with this issue. I didn't mind sending thank-you notes, and if I didn't, she knew from my verbal thanks that I still appreciated her.

This story illustrates another problem with closely held beliefs. We often think they are universal—any *reasonable* person would think as I do. If they don't, they are unreasonable and possibly a threat. Don't you normally feel in an argument that *anyone* (except the person you're arguing with) would support your point of view?

I heard an alarming statistic that 80 percent of violence is a consequence of revenge. Feeling the need for revenge comes from a sense of betrayal. Guess what betrayal is based on . . . that's right, someone has betrayed our *beliefs* and *expectations* as to what they should or shouldn't do. A measure of how violent a society is may equally be a measure of how inflexible people are with the thought viruses of limiting beliefs.

Beliefs provide the rules for measuring success and failure. Again, we can elicit these threshold beliefs with the simple question, "*How do you know* when you are successful?" or "*What does it take* for you to feel success?" Chapter 12 goes into more depth on the notions of success and failure. The problem for many of us, however, is that we've never consciously decided what it takes to be successful, or, worse yet, we've made our personal beliefs for success virtually impossible to achieve. Thus, many people who have financial, social, spiritual, and material abundance in everyone else's eyes may still not think of themselves as being successful.

A final thought on how beliefs limit us comes from the ancient Vedic philosophy of India. From a Vedic perspective, the fundamental need to hold fast to our beliefs is based on fear of the unknown. From experiences in life, especially in childhood, the unknown has sometimes dealt harsh and painful surprises. Beliefs, as they structure our internal maps of reality, provide the comfort *and* the illusion of knowing the unknown. We forget, however, the basic presupposition in NLP, that the map is not the territory. Each belief we cherish of how life *is* or *ought to be* is only an approximation of what truly is. The greater the gap between how we think things should be versus how they are, the more likely we are to experience disappointments and despair.

Again, from a Vedic perspective, the present moment contains virtually unlimited possibilities of what can be, and the present is completely unknown. To be spontaneously in the present, with a childlike sense of curiosity, joy, and wonder, as my friend Dana often was, is to embrace the unknown of the present. Each belief or notion that we rigidly *know* is true only projects boundaries and limitations on the unlimited possibilities of what is right before us in the here and now. Perhaps there are times when we should be more fearful of the known than of the unknown. Haven't some of the worst atrocities in war and social violence resulted from a difference in political or religious points of view, in which each side absolutely *knew* it was right?

LIMITING THOUGHT VIRUSES

"I'm never going to be like my mother!" snapped Dorothy. "My mother was a talented woman who could have had a great career. But in her time it was not acceptable for a mother not to stay home with her children. So she gave up her career, but made everyone in the family feel guilty for what she had sacrificed."

Dorothy was going to be different, so she trained for a variety of possible careers. The problem, however, was that she was still infected with her mother's limiting thought virus. Unconsciously she still accepted the erroneous belief that having a career, being a mother, and even having a successful love relationship were all mutually exclusive. Her motivation for having a career was based on a moving-away-from value, i.e., *not to be like her mother.* Dorothy had the first of three different forms that limiting thought viruses can take. Those three forms are as follows:

UNHEALED MOVING-AWAY-FROM VALUES. Dorothy's motivation was based on the fear of pain associated with unhealed emotional experiences involving her mother. By unconsciously trying *not* to be like her mother, her attention was on her mother. She only created a scenario that validated her mother's erroneous belief.

The consequence of this type of thought virus is called *sequen-*

tial incongruence or inconsistent results, as with the cold floor surfaces in my house. In Dorothy's case her career was a never-ending series of starts and stops. She trained to be a travel agent, but before even trying out the profession, she decided that it was not for her. She next decided to become a teacher, and got a four-year degree. Before starting her first teaching job, she came up with reasons not to be a teacher. When she finally started working in sales, she would work at a job for a few months, and then find something wrong with the company, the employees, or the product. Finally she would quit and move on to the next job.

How many people do you know who are continuously going on and then off diets or exercise programs? One day this person probably looked in the mirror, didn't like what he saw, and decided to diet or exercise. The motivating value was *not* to be fat, or *not* to be weak.

Again, the problem with motivation based on such a *moving-away-from value* is that you have to think about being fat or weak. Furthermore, the more successful your diet or exercise, the less you picture yourself being fat or weak, and the lower the motivation to continue. In contrast, if you are *moving toward* an image of being slender or healthy, the closer you come to your goal, the stronger the motivation.

You might check to see if any areas of your life show this pattern of alternating success and failure. There is a good chance that a moving-away-from value is driving the pattern. It's also important to be aware that even *moving-toward* values stated in the positive may have unhealed moving-away-from components behind them. When Lynn says she wants a man who will respect her values, she may still have painful memories of men who didn't respect them.

MISPLACED VALUES. A problem can occur when values are misplaced in priority. Has anyone ever complained about your need to be in control, to please others, or to be right most of the time? Is the need to be successful at work interfering with family life or your health? Or do you enjoy having fun so much that you rarely get anything done? These are all examples of values that are counterproductive because they are too important.

On the other hand, people who are always strapped for money, or always in poor health, inevitably do not have money or health within their top ten values. Properly ordered values allow life to flow naturally in the direction we'd like. Misplaced values create thought viruses. We wind up working against ourselves and attempting to swim upstream against life's current.

LIMITING BELIEFS OR DECISIONS. A presupposition in NLP is that if you believe something is possible for you, you're right, and if you believe the same thing is not possible, you're also right. If you believe that somehow, some way you can learn calculus, you are right, and if you believe you are not capable of learning calculus, you are also right.

Limiting beliefs—"I'm not very bright," or "I'm not very attractive," or "I'm not very coordinated" have a way of proving themselves to be correct even if they aren't. Here is a way of locating limiting viruses in the form of limiting beliefs that may be holding you back.

Exercise 14
Limiting Beliefs

Think of one area in your life that could most use improvement—career, relationship, finances, personal or spiritual growth, or some other area. In the context of that one area, think about what is holding you back or blocking progress. List those obstacles as statements in this form:

- "I can't _____."
- "I have a hard time _____."
- "I shouldn't _____."
- "I have to _____."

How would life be different for you if you could change each of these beliefs?

Like other thought viruses, limiting beliefs or decisions have a positive intent. Quite often this intent has to do with safety or "protecting" the experiencer from the sort of embarrassment, humiliation, or feelings of failure he or she has experienced in the past. Maybe my sister did outshine me academically when I was ten, so now, at age twenty-five, I still believe that I'm not very bright. Maybe ten years ago I had some negative experience or failure trying to set up my own business, so today it still feels safer to believe I am not capable of a business venture.

A limiting belief as a thought virus creates a hole or a blind spot, in that we *delete* perception or experience that might contradict the limiting belief: evidence that might suggest maybe I really am attractive, or maybe I could become wealthy, or maybe I could learn that foreign language. The positive intent is to protect us emotionally, and the negative behavior occurs because we act as if the belief were true, even though it may not be.

One of the things I admired about my friend Dana was that she was able to accomplish things other people would have not thought possible, simply because *no one told her she couldn't do it.* Even if someone did tell her that she wouldn't be able to find the cabin she wanted, or she couldn't get the therapy she needed, or she couldn't live on a tugboat, she would still find a way. I was surprised that it didn't seem to take much effort on her part to pursue what she believed in. In reflecting on this quality of hers, I uncovered another clue to her way of thinking.

CLUE NUMBER 4: WHEN VALUES ARE PROPERLY ALIGNED, WE *AUTOMATICALLY* AND *UNCONSCIOUSLY* MOVE TOWARD WHAT IS IMPORTANT TO US.

Aligning values is like precisely tuning the engine of a high-performance car. Conflicting values are like trying to drive a six-cylinder car on only two or three operating cylinders.

IMPROVING PERSONAL HEALTH

A fellow I'll call Richard came to see a colleague of mine whom I'll call Tim.[1] Richard said he was overweight, wanted to stop smoking, and was generally in poor health. His brother and father had each weighed as much as he did now, and they had each died younger than Richard was at present. Tim probed, "What's important to you about living?" since he figured that was what Richard wanted. Tim guided Richard through a process similar to what you did in Exercise 12 to elicit his top ten values about living. There was a gaping hole in the list of values. Health was not among them.

Tim showed Richard the list and asked, "Do you notice anything odd about your list?"

"No," responded Richard.

Tim probed, "Where's health?"

"Oops. I guess that's not one of my top ten values, but I think it should be." This was a classic case of a limiting thought virus in the form of a *misplaced value.*

As it turned out, Richard's top value was family. Tim and I share the belief that unless a person's number-one value is clearly disempowering or producing incongruence, it is best to leave that value in place. Since health was not even in the top ten values for living, Tim figured it would be useful to assist Richard to install health as his number-two value. How, then, do you go about installing or changing your order of values, given that the unconscious prioritizes them?

One approach is to elicit submodalities of the number-one value, elicit the same for a less important value, and find the one or two submodalities that are most different, i.e., the *driver(s).* The interview in a Thought Virus Therapy session would typically go something like this:

"Richard," Tim says, "when you *picture* your value for family [Tim prefers a visual representation], how do you picture it? In black and white or in color? Close up or far away? In a certain location in your field of vision?"

Tim continues quickly through the rest of the list of visual submodalities. He notes these submodalities, and repeats the procedure for another value farther down the list. He then questions, "When you contrast *how* you represent family against *how* you represent this other value, what strikes you as being most different?"

"That's odd. Family seems to be brighter, more in color, and located higher up toward my left. The other is lower down on my left."

"Good. Now how do you picture health?" Tim asks.

"Well, it's kind of vague and hazy."

"Good. Now go ahead and picture good health bright and in color, as you do for family, and in the same location, to your left. Once you've done that, move it down on your left, *just a little,* and make it just *a tiny bit* less bright and colorful than family. Do you have that now?" Tim questions. He has Richard back off from the submodalities for family just slightly, so that health will not replace his number-one value.

"Yes, that feels real different," Richard responds. Tim then does an *ecology check* to make sure Richard has no other parts that might object to this change.

Next he might *future pace* Richard with this change: "When you picture yourself in the future, making decisions on how you spend your time, what do you notice?"

"Well, my family and job are still most important, but it feels as if I am making changes in my routine to improve my health. I'm not sure what the changes are, but I feel motivated to make them."

Antiviral Remedy 6
Reprioritizing Values (or Beliefs)

1. Follow the guidelines in Exercise 12 (pages 72–73) to elicit values for *one particular area* of life: career, relationship, personal growth, finances, health, or to elicit values for life in general.
2. Look for values that might be causing problems for you:
   - *Values in conflict with each other,* such as security versus adventure, freedom versus commitment. You can resolve these using Antiviral Remedy 8 in chapter 5 for conflicting twin parts of a Gemini virus.
   - *Moving-away-from values.* These may indicate unhealed past emotional issues.
   - *Misplaced values,* i.e., one that is too important, or another that is not important enough. Follow the guidelines of this remedy to reprioritize them.
3. Elicit submodalities of how you *picture* your number-one value. This process can work with auditory or kinesthetic submodalities, but visual is generally easier. Elicit the corresponding submodalities for a less important value, and find the one or two submodalities that are most different, i.e., the *driver(s)*.
4. If you want to increase the importance of a value, picture it with the same driver submodalities as your number-one value, and then back off slightly—change the driver submodalities slightly, so you don't replace the number-one value.
5. If you want to decrease the importance of a value, change the drivers so that they are even more different from your number-one value than they currently are.
6. As a check, you might re-elicit your values to see where the formerly misplaced value is now.

More than likely, Tim's actual interview with Richard was similar to the above format. Some months after the session, Richard
called Tim and reported, "You have no idea how much that simple
change you helped me make has transformed my life and my daily
routine. At lunch I go for a walk, and after work, instead of going
to the bar, I now work out. I have stopped seeing friends who are
not into health, and am making new friends with people who are.
I am no longer *motivated* to do the unhealthy things I used to do."

This case also illustrates the principle that changing one value
can trigger changes in a multitude of beliefs connected with the
value. And as I observed with Dana, once the values were aligned,
changes took place automatically and unconsciously.

GETTING FREE FROM LOVE ADDICTION

Loni, an attractive and youthful artist in her early fifties, found
herself stuck in a verbally abusive and addictive relationship with
Evan. This relationship was draining so much of her time and energy that she had allowed her career and finances to tailspin. She
was now on the verge of bankruptcy and homelessness. For six
years she had been telling her therapist that she wanted to get out
of the relationship, yet something was preventing her. When she
contacted me, I felt that some thought virus might be at the core
of her reluctance to make the changes she wanted. She and her
therapist invited me to one of her sessions to see what we could
uncover.

"Loni, if this session were to completely transform your life,
what would you like to have happen?" I asked, putting out the presupposition that this might be a transformative session.

"I'd like to free myself from Evan and move on with my life, but
I need to do it in a way that's not hurtful to him," she responded.

"What's important to you about *not* leaving Evan?" I asked. I was
looking for the value that kept her in the relationship.

"Well, there really is a deep love there, at least at the times he's
not yelling at me, and we've invested an awful lot of time and energy into making it work. I keep thinking it could work, but it just
isn't," she said. As her thinking shifted back and forth between
staying with Evan and not staying with him, her body would tilt
one way and then the other. The words and body language indi-

cated to me a Gemini virus, where two conflicting parts, the one that wanted to leave and the other that wanted to stay, were literally tearing Loni apart. I sensed that mostly she wanted to leave, but for her to do that, we needed to know the positive intent or value of the part that resisted leaving.

"Given that you don't think it is working, what's important about not leaving?" I again probed.

"I don't want to hurt him and leave him unable to survive. He doesn't drive, so he depends on me to take him to his appointments. He's got a pretty rough personality, and I think I'm the only one who really understands him."

She provided a moving away-from-value ("I don't want to . . ."), so I suspected an unhealed emotional issue from the past.

"How do you benefit by not hurting him and not leaving him unable to survive?" I asked. "How does that make you feel?" I was looking for the *positive intent* of her value.

"I feel worthwhile and good about myself," she responded.

"How do you feel about yourself when you stay with him and he continues to be verbally abusive?" I asked.

"I feel pretty bad about myself, and unworthy. . . ." Her face took on an assymmetrical puzzled look as she began to notice the incongruence of the virus. The *intent* of not hurting him was to feel good about herself. On the other hand, the *behavior* was to maintain a relationship with someone who made her feel bad about herself, and unworthy. Sometimes gently bringing the incongruence of the virus to the person's awareness can begin to loosen the rigid pattern.

"Have you been in a similar situation in past relationships?" I asked.

"Well, Ann [her therapist] and I have traced through a number of relationships where I felt a need to save the other person. The earliest seems to be my grandfather," she responded. As it turned out, Evan bore a striking resemblance to her grandfather, who was a verbally and physically abusive alcoholic. When the grandfather was drunk and throwing a tantrum, little four-year-old Loni was the only one who could handle him and lead him to bed to sleep it off. It was up to her to *save* him and the rest of the family. The grandfather eventually developed cancer and was in so much pain that Loni couldn't touch him or sit on his lap, as she was used to doing. Part of her believed he was dying because she couldn't take care of him, and when he died it was her fault—a common limiting belief that young children of dying parents assume.

"Have you and Ann explored the connection between Evan and your grandfather?" I asked. My question really had nothing to do with the procedure for Thought Virus Therapy. I was just curious. The color drained from Loni's face.

"I think he is my grandfather—reincarnated," she blurted.

"Oh." Now, personally I have no idea whether such things as past lives and reincarnation really exist. As long as the client represents it that way in his or her map of reality, then I'll help him or her work with the map.

Connected with her unhealed limiting value, ("I don't want to hurt people and leave them unable to survive."), Loni had now revealed two limiting beliefs, two pearls. It was her fault for not saving her grandfather, and Evan was a reincarnation of him. I assisted her in removing those pearls and in snipping the strand that held those and other such pearls in place.

CHANGING BELIEFS

I prefer to change values rather than individual beliefs, because a changed value will carry a number of beliefs with it. Sometimes, though, a thought virus in the form of a limiting belief or decision may be particularly disempowering. Consciously, Loni realized the irrationality of her beliefs. Unconsciously, though, those beliefs were holding her back.

"If you were to change your belief about it being your fault for not saving your grandfather, what new belief would you want to have?" I asked.

"I know in my head this belief doesn't make any sense, but I don't know how to change my feelings about it. I was only a little girl. Beliefs are hard to change, aren't they?"

"I appreciate that you don't know how to make such a change *yet*. But if there were a way, what new belief would you like?" I asked.

"Well, I'd like to believe that I did the best I could as a little girl, and that he died because on some level he chose to, and that he is okay now."

"Think of something you absolutely know is true, such as that the sun comes up each morning, or that your name is Loni, or that two plus two are four. Just pick something you absolutely know is true," I suggested. She picked something, and I continued, "How do you know it's true? Do you picture it in a certain way, do you talk to yourself about it in a certain way, or do you have a certain feeling about it?"

"I talk to myself about it in a certain way," she said. I was looking for the most important modality she used to know that something was absolutely true. Normally a visual representation is easiest to work with. Loni, however, seemed clear that her internal auditory self-talk was what made it true for her. I found this especially interesting, since I knew she generally preferred visual and kinesthetic thinking.

"Now think of something you once believed was true and is now no longer true for you," I said. Once she had something, we checked the auditory submodalities for that belief. Then we contrasted those with the auditory submodalities for the belief she knew was true, to find the driver submodality or submodalities. The greatest contrast for her was the location of the voice and whose voice it was. The voice telling her the belief she knew was true was her own voice, centered in her throat. The voice telling her what she no longer believed to be true was a high-pitched, squeaky voice off to one side of her head.

"Is there any part of you that that would object to changing your old belief about your grandfather to the new one you'd like?" I asked. This was an *ecology check* to make sure there weren't other parts that might stand in the way of making the change.

Her facial muscles twisted asymmetrically, and she responded, "Yes. I don't know if it's right to make the change."

"What's important to you about not changing the belief?" I asked. I was seeking the positive intent or value of the objecting part. Once the unconscious recognizes how the change can take place, if there are objections, they will emerge.

"I don't want to lose my sensitivity to help people when I can," she said.

"That sounds important and worthwhile to me," I replied. "As an artist, you must have a part that is especially creative. I wonder if you could go inside and ask that creative part of Loni if she would be willing to help."

She nodded.

"Great. Now ask that creative part if she would be willing to come up with two or three ways that you can maintain sensitivity to help when you can, while changing your belief about the past. Take as much time as your creative part needs, and let me know when you have the ideas."

After a few minutes she responded, "I think the way I can most help others is by setting the example of helping myself. The other thing is to know clearly when I can help and when I can't, and to accept those times that I can't, as with Evan."

"Good job. Now ask that part of you that objected before, if you help yourself and if you distinguish between times when you can help and times when you can't, is it okay to change your belief about your grandfather?"

She nodded yes.

"Now check inside and see if there are any other parts of you that would object to the change."

"No, it feels okay now," she said.

"Good. Now change the voice that tells you it's your fault for not saving your grandfather. Change it to Mickey Mouse's voice, and put it to the side of your head."

She began to giggle. "That really changes it."

"Now I'm not going to suggest that whenever you think of that former belief, it will be in Mickey Mouse's voice off to the side of your head," I said, nodding, "but I'd like you to try to think of the old belief and *not* have it be in Mickey Mouse's voice off to the side." This is like asking a person not to think about a zebra, which they can't do without thinking about a zebra.

She started laughing. "How am I supposed to do that? Every time I think about that belief, I hear that squeaky voice. It's goofy—no, I guess it's Mickey." She continued laughing.

Gutting her old belief in this way left a vacuum. "Now imagine your own voice, centered in your throat, telling you that you did the best you could as a little girl, that your granddad made his own choices, and he is okay now."

Her eyes began to water. "That feels really good." The change in her former limiting belief was now complete. I then had her imagine going out to the future to check what happens in situations that would have triggered her former belief. She either laughed at Mickey Mouse's voice or appeared content with what she had done as a child, and she experienced a willingness to be sensitive to others and take better care of herself.

Antiviral Remedy 7
Eliminating a Disempowering Belief

1. Identify the limiting belief you would like to be rid of. Decide what new empowering belief you would like to use to replace the old one.

2. Pick a belief you absolutely know is true. Ask yourself, *"How do I know this is true? Do I picture it in a certain way? Do I talk to myself about it in a certain way, or do I have a feeling about it in a certain way?"*

3. Next, pick something else that you once believed was true, but now no longer do. Find the driver submodalities—the one or two that are most different between the belief you know is true and the one you no longer believe.

4. *Ecology check.* Ask yourself, *"Is there any part of me that would object to changing the old belief to the new one?"* If you experience an uneasiness, an unpleasant sensation, a *gut feeling* of *"No,"* then part of you may be objecting. Ask that part what is important about *not* changing the belief. There must be some positive intent, otherwise your intent to change would be congruent, and no part of you would be objecting. Once you have the positive intent(s) of what is important about not changing, be creative. See if you can devise a way to maintain the positive intent of not changing, while changing. Make sure the objecting part is satisfied with the idea. Once no part objects to the change, proceed.

5. Now change the submodalities of the belief you want to get rid of to those of the thing you no longer believe is true. When you think of that unwanted belief, notice what happens. There should be a noticeable change.

6. To install the new belief, imagine the new belief with the submodalities of the belief you absolutely know is true. Now when you think of this new belief, what do you feel?

7. *Future pace.* Test your work by projecting yourself into the future to check what happens in situations that would have triggered your former belief. If the change is not clear and obvious, repeat the process.

I repeated this whole procedure for the other belief that Evan was Loni's grandfather and she needed to save him. We again worked with auditory submodalities. She came to the belief that even if Evan was her former grandfather, it was up to Evan to take care of himself. For Loni to intervene was disempowering Evan and would deprive him of the opportunity to learn to be self-sufficient. Now that the limiting beliefs were changed, the rest of our session was devoted to working with the moving-away-from value, i.e., "I don't want to hurt people and leave them unable to survive."

After working with Loni, I wondered to myself what life would be like if the rest of us could let go of all those limiting beliefs that are holding us back. What if we each followed the steps of Anti-viral Remedy 7 to eliminate any limiting beliefs holding us back? What if we could eliminate sequential incongruence, so that it would be easy to stick to diets and exercise programs, and progress toward our goals and highest ideals? In fact you might ask *yourself,* "What would life be like, if my beliefs and values *automatically* took me in the direction I want, toward the destiny I desire?" Properly realigning beliefs and values is one step in that direction. Chapter 15 will provide more practical insight on how to accomplish this lofty vision.

The shift in thinking that Loni made came about because unconsciously she no longer believed she was responsible for saving her grandfather, either in the past or the present. Her unconscious then took care of producing changes that have transformed her life, like Susan, the cancer patient, who, when freed from the belief that the pain was necessary, felt no pain.

Susan's story also has a happy ending. Sometime after her pain disappeared, the cancer vanished. As far as I know, she is still in good health. All along, Susan had wanted good health, but thought viruses had led to incongruence in her physical well-being.

The cancer, like the apparent incongruence of the cold surfaces beneath my bare feet, was born of the illusion of faulty thinking. Just as unhealed moving-away-from values create incongruence, heat *moving away* from my feet created my experience. The kitchen tile is simply a better *conductor* of heat than the carpet. My feet more quickly lost their heat to the tile, and it felt colder. In the same way, money, love, good health, and other important values can be quickly lost along a pathway laden with thought viruses.

5

GEMINI VIRUSES

October 19, 1900, Berlin, Germany. A thought virus in classical physics—thought viruses also can infect scientific thinking—has led to a breakdown in our understanding of the emission of radiant energy. This breakdown, known as "the Ultraviolet Catastrophe," has just been explained today, in a paper published by the theoretical physicist Max Planck. However, he explains it in a most peculiar way.

One of the great mysteries in physics is how the opposite *twin parts* of creation work together. All of reality, as we know it, has only two basic forms, or parts: waves and particles. These complement each other, yet have opposite qualities.

A pure *wave*, such as light, sound, or even a water wave, has no location, and mathematically can extend an infinite distance to the left or to the right. It does, however, have a precise rate of vibration or frequency.

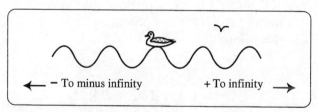

$\longleftarrow$ – To minus infinity   + To infinity $\longrightarrow$

A *particle,* such as an electron, a virus, or a baseball, has a definite location, but certainly no frequency, because there is nothing to vibrate. Planck implied that light *waves* can behave as if they were *particles*. Other physicists later discovered situations in which *particles,* such as electrons and protons, can behave as *waves*. The twin parts of creation are apparently interchangeable.

This is truly remarkable because waves, which have *no location,* behave as if they had location. Meanwhile, particles with *location* but *no frequency* behave as if they had no location, but do have a frequency. How can something have location yet *not* have location, or have frequency yet *not* have frequency? This fundamental philosophical dilemma lies at the foundation of that branch of twentieth-century physics called quantum mechanics. Yet, in spite of such apparent paradoxes with twin-part opposites, quantum mechanics has been enormously successful in explaining the physics of atoms and molecules.

I first heard of Planck's ideas from Dr. Simms, one of my physics instructors. Dr. Simms was a fascinating character, with many interests. After he graduated from high school, he went into the army and became a helicopter pilot. I remember his asking me one day if I knew why helicopters had two sets of blades. They really only need one set to fly, yet they always have two sets. In a sense these work together, yet work against each other, like two conflicting parts.

This was characteristic of Dr. Simms himself. His primary love in life was playing jazz on his saxophone. He had wanted to live an artistic, bohemian lifestyle, and play jazz professionally. His parents, however, had insisted that he be practical and train for a career in which he could make a decent living. After his stint in the army, he decided to pursue a degree in physics. He was quite gifted in both mathematics and science, yet he found himself doing things to sabotage his studies, such as avoiding studying, not showing up to class, or occasionally blowing midterms and tests. Part of him still wanted to be a professional jazz musician, and part of him wanted to please his parents and be practical, so he was at odds with himself.

CONFLICTING PARTS

Have you ever had an experience like this? Part of you wants to do one thing like working on the income taxes, while another part of you wants to get enough sleep so you can be fresh the next day.

Maybe yet another part wants to go out and party. Each part has a positive intent, and each is in conflict with other parts. Maybe at times you didn't act like yourself, or you experienced an emotional state such as anger or jealousy that embarrassed you later on. Afterward, you wonder how you could have possibly acted that way. In fact it may have felt as if it *wasn't really you* acting like that.

Parts in conflict are thought viruses in that they result in inner conflict and incongruent behavior. The viruses are twins, like the astrological sign Gemini, seeking balance through harmonizing opposite sides (twins)—hence the name "Gemini viruses." Any mental part that is involved in inner conflict must have an opposite part to oppose. Yet, strangely enough, the two conflicting parts of a Gemini virus generally have the same positive intent for the experiencer, so they are mirror-image or reverse twins.

In chapter 2, I pointed out that a thought virus occurs when a portion of the nervous system becomes functionally detached owing to significant emotional experiences. Such a part is a virus because the behavior it generates is incongruent with its positive intent. Again, the simplest of these mental glitches, the trigger virus, results when a V, A, or K stimulus automatically triggers a kinesthetic (K) response (simple trigger) or a strategy leading to a disempowering state (complex trigger). Limiting viruses, resulting from moving-away-from values, misplaced values, or limiting beliefs, are somewhat more evolved and complex as a pattern. As we noted before, moving-away-from values can result in sequential incongruence—an alternating path of success and failure.

The third category, Gemini viruses, are even more evolved, functionally detached, and complex. They can have their own beliefs and values that may be quite different from those we normally entertain. Thus, when the opposite part of a Gemini virus takes over our behavior for a while, we may have the feeling afterward of not having been our self. These viruses bridge the entire range from simple internal conflict to multiple-personality syndrome. They cause the general incongruence of working against yourself through self-defeating patterns, such as fear of success, inability to make decisions, and procrastination.

The Bhagavad-Gita, a story from the spiritual tradition of India, gives a classic account of the human condition in which these viruses can incapacitate us. In ancient times, the army of good and the army of evil were lined up on a battlefield. Arjuna, the greatest archer and warrior of the time, was set to lead the army of good into battle. As he looked at the opposing army, he was shocked to see many of his relatives—uncles, brothers, cousins. It would be a sin to kill his kin, yet it would be a sin not to support righteousness, and to allow evil to prevail. Arjuna became emotionally paralyzed and sank into despair.

We all experience this in life. When we have difficult decisions, it's not that one choice is obviously right and the other obviously wrong. Rather, each side presents positive merit.

HOW GEMINI VIRUSES BREED AND FUNCTION

What do you want in life that you don't have now?

- more money?
- a more rewarding career?
- a love relationship that inspires you?
- being slender or being in top-notch physical shape?
- having a more rewarding family or social life?

If any of these is at all possible for a person in your circumstances, yet you don't have it, there is a good reason why. Most likely, part of you feels it is not possible or appropriate to have what the other part of you wants; you are afflicted by the opposing twins of a Gemini virus.

Some NLP researchers have suggested that the ingredients of a Gemini virus, *dissociated parts,* come about from emotional experiences too intense for us to handle consciously. It's an emotional counterpart to the experience in which physical pain is so intense that we pass out. With sufficient emotional pain, we may "pass out" of being associated. "That's not really me having that experience. I am someone other than that." As a means of protection, part of me then becomes dissociated from me and from what I am experiencing.

This unconscious coping mechanism can indeed provide protection and some measure of comfort. Furthermore, having parts in conflict—two opposing viewpoints—can provide a means toward objectivity. This is Gemini's ideal of achieving harmony by balancing opposite viewpoints.

The problem with having separate parts, each with its own purpose and behavior, is that it fragments our sense of wholeness and leads to nonintegrated and incongruent behavior. Suppose that one day you went to work and found that your company had reorganized, and now you had two different bosses. One boss asks you to complete a certain project, and is careful to let you know why you are doing it. You follow her instructions exactly, yet the completed project sabotages its intended purpose, so your boss is upset with *you*. The second boss then gives you a project that seems to work against the first project, but it also works against its own intended purpose. The instructions from one boss often contradict instructions from the other, so you are caught with indecision about whom to please. If that were the scenario at work, I'm sure you'd think the company had gone haywire, and you would immediately seek employment elsewhere. Yet when we are in the grip of Gemini viruses, this is the way most of us live our lives.

Some authorities believe that having more internal parts is better than having fewer. The problem here is that each separate part, being incongruent itself, adds to the overall incongruence of the individual. Many psychologists and spiritual traditions believe that we are born into a sense of wholeness or oneness. Before long, however, that wholeness is shattered on the hard rocks of significant emotional experiences. Part of the spiritual quest is to integrate conflicting inner parts and return to a state of wholeness or oneness. Milton Erickson and Fritz Perls, who had a profound influence on the development of NLP, and Richard Bandler, who was a codeveloper of NLP, all believed that fewer parts are better than more parts.

TYPES OF GEMINI VIRUSES

Gemini viruses fall into several types, although the distinction among them can be fuzzy. Categorizing the virus as this type or that type is not always clear.

SIMPLE INTERNAL CONFLICTS. Part of you wants to exercise. You know it's good for you, and you feel great when you do it. Yet another part of you finds all kinds of reasons not to exercise. It's too cold outside. There's not enough time, and let's face it, exercise is hard work! Who wants to subject himself or herself to pain and discomfort? Both parts want you to feel good, one part through the vigor of exercise, and the other through the comfort of avoiding hard work. When it comes to deciding whether to exercise, the opposing parts are likely to produce a state of indecision or emotional paralysis. This results in procrastination, which means you probably won't exercise.

Exercise 15
Identifying Twin Parts

Do you exercise regularly and sufficiently to be in really good shape? If you do, then think of some other area of your life where there is a deficiency, such as getting enough sleep, eating the right foods and avoiding the wrong ones for good health, or spending enough time with your kids or significant other. You can do this process with that area in mind, or if you're not working out enough, use exercise. I'll word it as if you had chosen exercise.

1. For that twin part of you that believes in the value of exercise and that you should be doing more exercise, ask that part what's important to you about exercise. How do you benefit from exercise? List whatever reasons come up for you.
2. For the opposite twin part that is somehow getting in the way of regular exercise, ask that part what's important to you about *not* exercising. How do you benefit from not exercising? There must be some benefit, otherwise you would be exercising regularly. Again, list whatever comes up for you.

The first step in resolving the twin differences of internal conflict is to become aware of the positive intent of each twin.

Opposing twin parts may be due to values that are in conflict. Maybe you value a love relationship, but freedom is also one of your top priorities, so you have a hard time with commitment. Maybe you love adventure, but security is also a high value, so you are at odds with yourself. Conflicting values result in conflicting parts.

SIGNIFICANT OTHER PARTS. A client I'll call Gwen, who lived in Hawaii, once came to Dr. Tad James.[1] She said that her marriage had ended a few years before, when her husband had abruptly left and gone back to the mainland. She had no contact with him, and no idea where he was. However, she now felt the need to clean things up with him emotionally, so she could move on with her own life.

"Let me talk to that part inside of you that is your ex-husband," Tad requested.

"What?" she responded.

"Just play along with me for a minute. Suppose there were a part of you inside that was your husband. Would it be okay if we could talk with that part?"

"Well, I guess so." Gwen looked a bit surprised.

"If that part of you that is your ex-husband were present with us right now, what do you need to tell that part to completely clean things up emotionally?"

Gwen then proceeded to say what she needed to say.

"Good. Now have that part who is your ex-husband say what he needs to say for him to clean things up emotionally for himself." She then said what she imagined he needed to say.

After the session she reported that she felt much better about her ex-husband and moving on with her own life. Two days later, however, she got her first call from him in two years. He said he had been thinking about things, and thought they should get together to clean things up emotionally.

Some psychologists feel that we carry each significant person in our life—a parent, a caretaker, a deep love relationship—with us inside as an unconscious part. If the beliefs or values of that part are in conflict with another part of us, we have a virus. The conflict may correspond to unresolved issues we have with that person. If the person is deceased or unapproachable for therapy, then a workable therapy is to work with the part of you that represents the significant other, as Tad did with Gwen.

MINOR PERSONALITIES. Holly, a bright, quiet, mature eleven-year-old girl, had a close relationship with her single mom. However, whenever her mom's boyfriend was around, she was a completely different person—whiny, clingy, throwing tantrums, and occasionally violent. When the boyfriend left, she would usually return to her normal self, and would sometimes feel embarrassed about how she had acted.

Holly with her two sides, "Mr. Milquetoast" who is a terror on the highway, and the polite and admired sports hero who beats his wife, all illustrate Gemini viruses which have evolved to minor personalities.

When I first became aware of the power of Gemini viruses to pull us in opposite directions and in some cases tear us apart, I was dismayed because I, like most people, have been infected by my share of them. I wondered what hope there was to get beyond such deep and habitual thought patterns. I got my first clue to a way by again observing my friend Dana's congruence in doing things she had never done before. What I learned from Dana was stated more succinctly in my NLP certification.

❧

CLUE NUMBER 5: ALL THE RESOURCES WE NEED, TO SOLVE A PROBLEM OR INTERNAL CONFLICT, ARE ALREADY THERE WITHIN US. ALL WE NEED TO DO IS LOCATE THEM, INSIDE.

GETTING MOTIVATED TO CHANGE CAREERS

Jim, one of my seminar participants, was dissatisfied with his job and the limited work options he had with his limited education. For several years now he had wanted to go back to school and train to be an accountant, but something was holding him back. I was about to demonstrate in the seminar a process called Six-Step Reframing. I thought this might prove effective in helping Jim reintegrate the resistance and collapse the virus.

"Jim, do you sense there is part of you that is resisting going back to school?" I asked.

"I never thought of it that way, but it must be true, because I just can't seem to get going," he responded.

"I'd like you to go inside and ask that part of you that is resisting going back to school if it would be willing to communicate with us," I suggested.

Now, in asking questions of parts, we mentally put out the question, and let go of any preconceived idea of what the answer will be. We innocently trust that whatever comes up is the answer from the part. The answer can be in any of the three modalities. A person might mentally

- *see* the words *yes* or *no,* or see someone nodding or shaking his head
- *hear* a verbal yes or no
- have a *feeling* or *sense* of the response

"I get that the part is willing to communicate," Jim reported. Now if a part indicates that it doesn't want to communicate, you can thank it for communicating, because it just has. An unwillingness to cooperate generally means lack of rapport with the part. In such a case you can create the necessary rapport by assuring the part that you appreciate that it is wanting to serve you, and you will respect and maintain its highest purpose.

"Now go back inside and ask the part if it would be willing to let us know how it is trying to serve you, or what it wants that is positive for you as a result of not going back to school," I said.

"It doesn't want me to be successful and just wants me to be stuck in this lousy job I have," he said. Now, in putting myself in Jim's place, communicating with such a part inside of me, this didn't feel like the sort of answer I would have gotten. I suspected this answer was coming from the part's twin, the part that this present part was in conflict with.

"Go back inside and check. The part that is resisting your going back to school, is that what *this part* wants for you, or is it something else?" I asked.

"No. What I sense is that if I go back to school, I won't have time to work out, or watch TV, or just have time for myself." That answer felt more congruent to me.

"So this part wants you to have time for working out, watching TV, and having time for yourself?" I checked.

"Yeah. That's right," he said.

"Well, that sounds pretty important and worthwhile to me. I'd like to thank this part of you for serving you in this way. Now, Jim, you seem to me to be a creative person, so you must have a creative part. Why don't you ask your creative part if it would be willing to come up with two or three ways you could go back to school to change careers, yet be able to work out, watch TV, and have time for yourself."

He paused for a few minutes and responded, "I could limit the TV to a few of my favorite programs as a reward for my study. I could also break up my workouts to a number of short ten-minute segments that I could do between study sessions. I could also take less than a full-time load, so I would still have some time for myself."

"Great! I think your creative part has done a nice job in coming up with these ideas," I said. "Now why don't you ask the part that *had* resistance toward your going back to school if it would have any objections to your trying out these new ideas?"

"No. I think this is fine." If the part objected to one or more of his ideas, we would just go back to the creative part and have it generate more creative alternatives that maintained the positive intent of the part, yet would allow him to go back to school. The last step was to make sure the rest of his unconscious was congruent with these ideas for change.

"Now go inside and ask if there are any other parts that might object to going back to school and trying out these new ideas, of limiting TV, working out between study sessions, and not attending school full-time so that you can have some time for yourself." Jim indicated there were no other objections. Again, if any other parts objected, it would just be a matter of going back to the creative part for more alternatives.

"How do you feel about going back to school?" I asked.

"It feels good. I really think I can work with myself now," Jim responded.

In my mind, resolving internal conflicts, making peace among conflicting internal parts, and reintegrating fragmented parts is one of the most heartful and even spiritual parts of Thought Virus Therapy. We are taking what we formerly regarded as internal resistance, discovering its positive intent, and using that intent to achieve what we want. It's like using the energy of an opponent's blow in the martial arts to neutralize the opposition. Here is an outline of the process I did with Jim:

Antiviral Remedy 8
Six-Step Reframing

1. Identify the internal resistance, fear, or unwanted behavior. Ask yourself, "What is the resistance or behavior I want to change?"
2. Establish communication with the internal part that is responsible for the behavior. Go inside and ask the part, "Are you willing to communicate with me? Please give me a signal."
3. Separate the positive intention of the part from the unwanted behavior. Tell yourself with congruence, "I'd like to thank you for communicating with me, and can you let me know what you are you trying to do that is positive for me with this resistance or behavior?"

4. Find two or three other choices that satisfy the positive intent of the part, but do not have the negative implications of the unwanted behavior. Ask your most creative part, "Would you be willing to come up with two or three other ways to satisfy the positive intent of the part, even though we change the behavior? Let me know when you have the new choices." Allow enough time for the new choices to come into your awareness.
5. Check back with the part to make sure the new choices are acceptable. Ask, "Would you be willing to try out these new choices? Please signal me." If you get a "no," go back to step 4 and have the creative part generate some new choices. The other option would be to ask the part if it would be willing to try out the new choices for some specific time period, such as two weeks or a month. Assure the part that you can always return to the old behavior if it is not satisfied with the results.
6. *Ecology Check.* Ask yourself if any other parts object to the new choices. If so, go back to step 4.

In Jim's case, he was *mostly* congruent with the idea of changing careers, and one objecting part had been holding him back. In such a case Six-Step Reframing worked quite well. What about a situation, though, in which the person is more evenly divided between the two conflicting sides of a virus?

COMMITTING TO COMMITMENT IN A LOVE RELATIONSHIP

Juan, a client of mine, and I were having lunch in a restaurant, when he noticed an elderly bachelor spending this Friday afternoon just hanging out, reading, and drinking coffee.

"You know, when I get to be his age, I don't want to turn out like that," Juan said. "I see him in here often. He isn't married, I don't think he has many friends, and he seems pretty lonely to me. I really want the passion and excitement that a love relationship can give while I'm younger, and companionship and friendship when I'm older."

I could certainly identify with what he was saying, yet with such a strong moving-away-from value of not wanting to be like this gentleman, I wondered if Juan might not turn out that way. Juan

seemed reasonably attractive and had had several short-term marriages and a number of short-term relationships. He assumed that
these had not worked out simply because he had chosen the wrong
people, or that in some cases the timing wasn't right. He told me
that Maria, his most recent lover, complained that he seemed to enjoy competing with her, that he was too independent and seemed
incapable of being really committed in a love relationship.

"Have you ever heard those complaints before?" I asked.

"Oh, I guess so, but what do they know?" he responded. "They
were just looking for something to complain about." I had a feeling that he might be experiencing conflicting values in his past relationships, and asked if he would be interested in clarifying his
values. Maybe something was working against him. He agreed that
whatever he had done in the past clearly had not worked. He was
willing to try anything.

I then guided him through the steps from Exercise 12 in chapter 4 to elicit what was important to him in life and what was
important in a love relationship. As it turned out, being in a passionate intimate relationship was one of his top five values, and
having independence and freedom (these felt connected to him)
was another. Those two values could certainly conflict, causing or
at least contributing to incongruence in his previous relationships. He had also grown up the youngest of four children. Being
the youngest, he felt dependent and at the mercy of the older siblings. He had learned to compete to get attention from the parents. I decided to help guide Juan through a process called the
visual squash. This can powerfully and cleanly bring about an integration of equally balanced conflicting values.

"Can you go inside and be in touch with that part of you that
wants to be in a committed, passionate, and intimate relationship?" I asked. He nodded, and I continued, "If that part were to
come out and stand on one of your hands, which hand would it
stand on, the right or the left?"

"I think that part would be on my right hand."

"Good. Now which hand would that part of you that values independence and freedom like to stand on?" I continued.

"That feels like the left hand," he said. I put my two hands,
palms up, in front of me, tacitly suggesting that he do the same.
He did.

"Good. Now that part of you on your right hand that wants to be in a passionate, committed relationship—if *that* part were to look at the part on your left hand that wants independence and freedom, what would the part on the right hand admire or appreciate about that part over there on the left hand?" I asked.

"Well, I guess in a relationship a certain amount of freedom and independence means you won't lose your own identity. You can still develop your own uniqueness." Juan looked surprised at the words that had just popped out of his mouth.

"And that part on your left hand that wants freedom and independence—what does that part admire or appreciate about the part on your right hand that wants a committed relationship?"

"Hmm. I guess a relationship would allow me the freedom to develop and express sides of me that I couldn't without a relationship," he answered.

I decided to suggest a way he might reframe his notion of independence. "If you *always* have to be independent, doesn't that make you *dependent* on being independent?" I probed. He stared blankly, and I could sense the gears inside his head beginning to grind.

"Yeah, I think you're right. Being in a relationship gives me more choice of sometimes being independent and sometimes being dependent, and I guess that *is* more independent," he said. My next thought was to look for deeper values beyond independence and freedom. To elicit deeper values, we can follow a procedure called *chunking up*. Ask, *What is important to me about* _____ (the value)? or *How does* _____ *serve or benefit me?* The answer will usually be another value. Ask the same question about this new value. As you keep repeating this process, you are getting larger chunks of your pattern of thought—deeper and more abstract values.

"Great. Now that part of you on your left hand that wants independence and freedom—ask that part what's important to you about independence and freedom," I suggested. I was encouraging him to "chunk up" on this value.

"Well, when I have more independence and freedom, I feel more self-sufficient," he responded.

"Good. Now, what's important to you about feeling self-sufficient? How does that serve you?" I asked.

"I feel a greater sense of wholeness," he said, as he unconsciously gestured a bigger feeling by spreading his hands farther apart.

"Okay. Now ask that part on your right hand what's important about being in a passionate intimate relationship," I suggested.

"Well, with the right person, I'd probably feel more love and friendship," he said.

"What's important to you about feeling more love and friend-ship?" I asked.

"Well, that makes me feel more complete as a person." His face relaxed and his eyes softened.

"What's important to you about feeling more complete as a per-son? How does that serve you?" I asked.

"I feel more wholeness." His hands again spread apart.

I scratched my head, "Oh, that's interesting. So both parts want more of a feeling of wholeness?"

He looked surprised. "I guess that's true."

"Do both parts remember having once been part of a single whole?" I asked. I rarely have a client who does not respond yes. In such cases I ask if they can *imagine* having once been part of a single whole.

"Yes. I don't remember specifically, but I get a sense that may have been true," he said.

I again put my hands palms up in front of me, and suggested, "Before you allow these parts once again to join together to be-come a single part that can work toward having a passionate, com-mitted relationship *and* maintaining appropriate freedom and independence—before you do that, I'd like you to go inside and see if it's okay with the parts to join together." If either part ob-jected, or if some other part objected, I'd use one of the steps of Six-Step Reframing. I'd ask his creative part to come up with two or three ways to satisfy the objection, yet allow the integration to take place. In Juan's case, there were no objections.

"I'm not sure how you might want bring these parts together," I said as I began moving my hands together. I noticed his hands be-ginning to move together as well. "That's right, now only allow your hands to come together as fast as your unconscious can join these parts to become one super part that can blend all these val-ues harmoniously in a way that really works for you." I moved my hands at about the same pace his hands were coming together. Once his hands joined, his face and body took on a more sym-metrical appearance. He said he felt more at peace with the no-tion of a committed relationship.

Antiviral Remedy 9
The Visual Squash

1. Identify the two competing values or parts and what each part wants for you.

2. Ask one of the parts, "If you were willing to come out and stand on one of my hands, which hand would you like to stand on?" Ask the other part if it would be willing to come out and stand on the other hand. You might place your hands in front of you, palms up, as if you were holding each part.

3. Ask the part on your left hand, "What's important to you about _____ [what it wants for you], or how does _____ benefit me?" Continue to chunk up by asking, "What's important to you about _____ [the answer to the previous question], or how does _____ benefit me?" Repeat this questioning until you have the highest intention of the part. You might in fact ask the part if this *is* its highest intention.

4. Repeat the process in step 3 for the part on your right hand. Again, chunk up until you get the same or a similar value to the highest value for the opposing part. Ask the parts if they notice that they each want similar or identical outcomes for you.

5. Ask the two parts, "Do you remember once having been part of the same whole?" If not, then ask if they can imagine once having been part of the same whole.

6. Ask the part on the right hand what it admires or appreciates about the part on the left hand. If it says, "Nothing!" ask what it *could* appreciate if it wanted to. Ask the part on the left hand the same question about the part on the right.

7. *Ecology check.* Ask yourself, "Before I allow these two parts to join together again to become a single part that can work toward having _____ [highest intention of one part], while maintaining _____ [highest intention of the other part], is this joining-together okay with these parts and all my other parts?" If yes, then continue; if no, go to the creative part, as with Six-Step Reframing, and have the creative part come up with two or three ways to satisfy objections, while allowing the conflicting parts to reintegrate.

8. Allow your hands to move together only as fast as your unconscious can comfortably reintegrate these parts to work together harmoniously as one super part.

As I pointed out earlier, The Visual Squash provides a way of integrating competing parts or values of a Gemini virus when each carries nearly an equal amount of weight. It also provides a workable visual and kinesthetic representation of the parts integrating together.

The session with Juan must have had an impact, because Maria reported that Juan's attitude was transformed, and within four months they married.

Juan had been torn between committing to a passionate intimate relationship and a need for freedom and independence, just as my physics instructor, Dr. Simms, was torn between being a professional musician and pursuing his academic studies. I wasn't aware of thought viruses or Thought Virus Therapy when I knew Dr. Simms, but he finally resolved his dilemma on his own. He concluded that one value shouldn't exclude the other. He continued his studies, and rewarded himself during study breaks by practicing his saxophone. On weekends he would play jazz professionally, not so much for the money as for the fun of it. The money, however, did help pay his tuition.

Einstein once pointed out that the solution to difficult problems cannot be found in the thinking that produced the problem in the first place. Thus, when Arjuna stood on the battlefield, the conflicting values of fighting for righteousness versus killing relatives and loved ones emotionally paralyzed him. He could not solve his dilemma on that level of thought. Einstein implied that we must transcend that thinking, i.e., *chunk up* to higher levels of thought and more-abstract values. Arjuna's charioteer, Krishna, had this same wisdom. In the Bhagavad-Gita, he had Arjuna transcend thought altogether through meditation. He then guided Arjuna to a state of enlightenment. From this perspective he could act in freedom, without being attached to his normal expectations, judgments, and the illusion that life is made up of opposites: good versus evil, right versus wrong, light versus darkness, life versus death.

From a Vedic perspective, life just *is*. Labeling and judging it in terms of opposites is an illusion, just as when Max Planck and other quantum physicists looked at physical reality, they saw either location (particles) or nonlocation (waves). They soon realized, however, that reality is neither location nor non-location. This is similar to looking at a coin. We see heads or we see tails, and we may forget that heads cannot exist by itself, separate from tails, and is an illusion, just as tails cannot exist by itself and is also an illusion. Heads and tails are a result of our perception being limited to looking at just one side of the coin or the other. The coin, of course, is neither heads nor tails, yet it contains these opposite qualities.

Certain experiments show the "heads" side of reality (location), while other experiments show the "tails" side (nonlocation). We certainly cannot see both sides at the same time, just as we can't for a coin. Reality itself, however, is neither location nor nonlocation, just as the coin is neither heads nor tails.

As the story goes, once Arjuna reached enlightenment, and was free from the illusion of opposite values and the limiting expectations and judgments these produce, he could act in harmony with natural evolution. By knowing the spirit of each relative would transcend the opposite values of life and death, he was able to act in attunement with "divine will," or nature seeking to balance herself, and wipe out the forces of evil.

In the same way, the apparent separation of twin parts in a Gemini virus is an illusion. They derived from an original oneness, and became opposite sides of that wholeness. Maintaining the illusion of separation causes the opposite parts to work against each other, just as in a helicopter, the main blades rotate in one direction, but those blades would cause the helicopter body to spin the opposite way, if this were left uncorrected. Integrating twin parts allows opposite qualities to work together, just as adding a second set of blades to the helicopter provides an opposition to the main blades, and keeps the helicopter body from spinning.

6

KILLER VIRUSES

AFTER AN INCIDENT IN CROYDON
INVOLVING A POLICE VAN AND A CONCRETE MIXER,
POLICE ARE LOOKING
FOR EIGHTEEN HARDENED CRIMINALS.

—"THE TWO RONNIES," BBC-TV

Karl, a former student of mine, was racing to the hospital to see his aunt Peg, maybe for the last time. Unfortunately he failed to notice a highway patrol car parked at the entrance of a hazardous curve. The officer wasted no time in pulling Karl over.

"Are you going to a fire or the hospital?" asked the officer sarcastically.

"I really *am* going to the hospital," Karl responded. "My aunt is dying!" The officer looked skeptical.

"Do you know how many accidents happen at this curve, because of speeding motorists who skid off the road?" asked the officer.

"None," Karl said, remembering a discussion on the laws of motion in my physics class. "It's actually *not* possible for a high-speed car turning a curve to skid off the road." Karl remembered his physics, but not his rapport skills. The officer figured Karl was a wise guy or on drugs, and went for his book to write a ticket.

"Wait!" said Karl. "If I can prove to you that what I'm saying is true, will you give me a break?" Karl's eyes began to water as he remembered the last time he had seen his aunt Peg.

She was in an oxygen tent on an emphysema ward in Marin County, California. Karl was shocked to see how frail and bluish white she appeared, as each breath seemed a struggle. She could barely utter a sentence or two without losing her breath. At the time, Karl was thinking how unfair it was, that such a warm and gentle spirit as she was dying at only forty-seven. Suddenly she climbed out of the oxygen tent, walked out into the hallway, and did what she had done once every half hour for the past thirty years. She lit up a cigarette. A doctor's poster on the bulletin board proclaimed this ward "Marlboro Country."

"There *is* value in what I'm going through," whispered Aunt Peg.

Karl couldn't imagine what that might be. It seemed so senseless, like his mother who died from liver sclerosis after years of alcoholism, and his cousin who had been killed by a stray bullet in a gang-related drive-by shooting. How could the twisted thinking that led to such tragic consequences have any value?

DEADLY THINKING

Biologically, we have classified humans as *Homo sapiens,* which means "man the wise," yet the number-one cause of death and suffering in this country is *not* heart disease. It's not cancer, strokes, AIDS, or even the IRS. It is *faulty thinking* caused by killer viruses. To understand the hidden epidemic of killer thought viruses in our country, consider the following:

- In recent American history, the Vietnam War stands out as a national tragedy—59,000 soldiers killed in nine years. Yet, during that same time, more than twice as many people died in this country from accidents involving drunk drivers.
- More people in the United States die in *one year* from smoking—500,000 from first- and second-hand smoke—than all the Americans killed in World War II.
- We are the most violent of Western developed countries, with 26,000 murders per year—five times the rate of violent crimes per 100 people in Europe and four times the rate in Canada.
- The incidence of violent crimes here is about four times what it was in 1960, and has grown nine times faster than the population.
- The number of reported child-abuse cases has tripled since 1980, to 3 million per year, with one third of those cases involving babies under one year old, and one baby out of ten is born addicted to illegal drugs.

Plagued with addictions and compulsions, how can we understand why we indulge these behaviors? Why has noncoherent thinking increased so much in the last twenty years? What positive intents do these killer thought viruses have for us? How can we as a society move beyond the noncoherent thinking that causes such destruction?

THE ADDICTION VIRUS

Most of us have experienced negative or positive addictions of one form or another: coffee, smoking, running, chocolate, sex, or foods that are too rich or fatty. For me, even though I've eaten a generally healthy low-fat vegetarian diet for twenty-five years, my addiction was chocolate. Until a few years ago, I had to have chocolate almost every day. My positive addictions have been meditation and running.

I've discovered that negative addictions which harm us mentally or physically are based on distorted thinking in the form of an *addiction virus*—a combination of trigger viruses, limiting viruses, and Gemini viruses. Since most killer viruses involve addiction, it is useful to understand how the three basic viruses function together.

TRIGGERS. In many cases the addiction begins with an erroneous trigger or association. For a child, smoking may be anchored with feeling grown up, like her parents; for an adult, it may be associated with thoughts of relaxation or having a head that looks like a camel. Being in a gang means being accepted by one's peers or protected from other gangs. Gambling is anchored to thoughts of wealth and freedom.

Violation of our beliefs and expectations can *trigger* a violent reaction.

- "A wife *should* appreciate her husband and *should never* talk to her husband like that. I'll teach her—the way Dad taught Mom and me."
- "I can't believe you [the baby] are still screaming and keeping me awake. I've fed you, and changed your diapers twice. You better shut up, or I'll give you something to cry about!"
- "Willy knew better than to sell drugs in our territory. We're going to have to drive by, and show him and his gang what happens when you break the rules."

The thought viruses here, besides being triggers, are limiting viruses—the expectations are inflexible and erroneous. Inflexible, erroneous beliefs of how things *should be* are bound to lead to a mismatch with the way things are. The resulting disappointment or feeling of betrayal is the breeding ground for depressed or violent individuals. Violent individuals make a violent society.

Once a destructive addiction or behavior takes hold, certain triggers evolve to elicit that behavior. Completing a meal, having a drink, a stressful moment at work, each triggers the need for a cigarette. Paying the monthly bills or hearing the lottery commercial may trigger that irresistible urge to gamble. A nasty encounter with the boss may trigger the need for a drink.

LIMITING BELIEFS. Justifying the addiction or behavior to oneself and others involves more limiting beliefs.

- The smoker rationalizes that smoking is necessary to control stress, or to keep weight under control. And besides, there was this woman who smoked all her life and lived to be 112!
- The gambler who has lost almost all of his money mistakenly believes he is more likely to win if he keeps going. The long losing streak increases the chance to win now. Unfortunately, probability is independent of past history. If I flip a coin, and it lands tails twelve times in a row, there is still a 50-percent chance of getting tails the next time I flip it.
- The person who can murder with no remorse generally regards the victims as *not human*. In fact, the viewpoint that the enemy is less than human may be psychologically necessary for soldiers in combat.
- The student thinks, "I'd better bring a gun to school to protect me from all the other kids who might have guns."

THE GEMINI COMPONENT. In spite of attempts to justify a self-destructive behavior, the person indulging in it is likely to be incongruent and at odds with himself or herself—the victim of a Gemini virus. One part recognizes the destructive nature of the pattern, while the other part is committed to maintaining the perceived positive benefit of the killer virus.

Furthermore, most addictions alter brain chemistry in the production of neuropeptides and neurotransmitters connected with pleasurable states. It has been suggested that these internal neu-rotransmitters can be as addicting as external drugs.

When an addiction, based on trigger viruses, limiting viruses, and Gemini viruses works toward our demise, the result is called a *killer virus*. Strangely, even when such destructive, noncoherent thinking is doing us in, the virus still has a positive intent. Quite often the intent is simply to change our state.

THE TOBACCO VIRUS

Despite assurances of our friends in the tobacco industry, medical and scientific evidence clearly indicates that smoking *is* addictive and causes emphysema, chronic obstructive pulmonary disease or COPD lung cancer, and kills more than a half-million Americans per year. Nevertheless, nearly 46 million people, or one quarter of our adult population, still smoke. How come?

Biochemically, nicotine increases levels of acetylcholine and norepinephrine—brain chemicals that control memory, mood, and attention. It also appears to stimulate production of dopamine in the pleasure center of the brain, as cocaine, alcohol, and heroin also do.

From a behavioral perspective, when you took your first puff on a cigarette, did you think to yourself, "Mmm, boy, does this ever taste good!" Not too likely. More likely you coughed, gagged, choked, and your lungs wondered what in the world you were doing.

To get us beyond the initial discomfort, tobacco companies and advertisers associate pleasure with smoking. As a thought virus, smoking gets connected with being a real man (the "Marlboro Man"), being "Kool" and sexy, and with the evolution of women's rights ("You've come a long way, baby."). Peer pressure on us as children may connect smoking with the pleasure of being ac-cepted and the thrill of getting away with something forbidden. We associate the periodic ritual of long, slow, deep breaths with re-laxation, yet have never thought of long, slow, deep breaths with-out the smoke. The positive intent, at least initially, behind the tobacco virus is to be cool, a real man, sexy, liberated, relaxed, glamorous, accepted.

For the seasoned smoker, smoking does provide pleasure through production of brain chemicals. Smokers also believe that smoking eases pain, helps regulate moods, and alleviates loneliness, boredom, and anxiety.

An estimated 80 percent of smokers would like to quit, and each year 30 percent try. Only 2 to 3 percent are successful. Yet in spite of this difficulty in quitting, 45 million Americans are now ex-smokers.

ALCOHOL AND DRUG VIRUSES

Again, when you drank your first beer or your first shot of whiskey, did it taste delicious? More likely you made a sour face and wondered why people drank this stuff. But if your friends were drinking, you knew you could cultivate a taste for it, to be accepted by them. If you were a teenage boy, educated by the beer commercials shown during televised football games, you knew all these sexy women clad in bikinis would flock around you when you drank beer. And when you popped open a beer, the world would be a very cool place. But how sexy, really, is a man drinking a beer?

While medical research goes back and forth regarding the possible cardiovascular benefits of light alcohol consumption, especially red wine, my point is that the erroneous associations connected with drinking, together with possible genetic predisposition, can lead to destructive addiction, the alcohol virus.

Statistics show that 18.5 million Americans, or 10 percent of our adult population, are victims of the alcohol virus—alcoholics. More than one hundred thousand people in the United States per year die prematurely from liver damage, heart damage, drunk driving, violence connected with drinking, and the higher risk factor for chronic degenerative diseases connected with excess drinking. Even more people die the emotional death of being out of control in life.

Among illegal drugs, cocaine is particularly devastating, because it powerfully does the two things people want most: It eliminates pain and provides pleasure. When people are experiencing such unpleasant states as despair, worry, guilt, or emotional or physical pain, they have learned that a quick and reliable way to change the state is through drinking, taking drugs, overeating, or smoking. Cocaine produces one of the most pronounced immediate changes of state, apparently by flooding brain receptors with dopamine. Unfortunately, when the drug is withdrawn, either less dopamine is produced, or fewer dopamine receptors are available. As a result, the user is increasingly less able to feel pleasure and more apt to experience pain without the drug. Consequently, cocaine has grown to be a $10 billion industry in the United States, with more than 1.3 million users.

SOCIAL THOUGHT VIRUSES

Addictions to violence, gambling, and sex may not kill outright, but certainly can destroy dreams, careers, and home life. The common element with these thinking disorders is likely trigger viruses that erroneously connect the habit or behavior with a *state* of excitement, thrill, vitality, or euphoria.

Deepak Chopra has pointed out that each emotional state we experience results in the brain producing neuropeptides and neurotransmitters. As an example, when we feel powerful and invincible, our brains produce a substance similar to interleukin 2, one of the most powerful substances known to destroy cancer cells. When we feel depressed, the brain produces substances that inhibit the immune system. When we feel calm and settled, we produce a natural tranquilizer similar to Valium.

A fascinating characteristic of such states is that it is not only the brain that experiences the state, but the whole body. Each cell in the body has neuroreceptors for receiving the chemical "signals" (neuropeptides and neurotransmitters) put out by the brain. Further, there is evidence that cells throughout the body also produce these same substances. From a biochemical perspective, then, the whole body experiences the emotional state. Very likely, *addiction* to a particular state—excitement, thrill, vitality, euphoria (erroneously linked with the *trigger* of violence, gambling, or sex)—is, in fact, a physical addiction to the natural substances the body produces. The states are certainly useful to experience, but *without* the destructive negative triggers.

THE SUICIDE VIRUS

How can some people, like my friend Dana, lose virtually everything they have in life, be dying of cancer at age forty-two, yet manage to cheer up the people around them, while someone else commits suicide because he or she flunked a calculus midterm? How can a wealthy, successful, and well-liked movie star die from a drug overdose, while a Mother Teresa goes to India with virtually nothing and gives to the poorest of the poor? In observing and reflecting on Dana, what occurred to me was that people do *not* commit suicide because of loss of money, a job, a lover, a home, or flunking school. They commit suicide because of the *states* they experience as a result of the loss. The faulty thinking—i.e., the virus—is to escape the way they feel by escaping life.

One feature of killer viruses in general is that they provide an erroneous and destructive way for us to manage or escape from our states. From what I knew of Dana, she seemed relatively free of such behavior. When thinking of how she managed her states, I recognized . . .

CLUE NUMBER 6: TO MANAGE YOUR STATES IN A CONSTRUCTIVE WAY, CULTIVATE THE ABILITY TO BE IN THE HERE AND NOW.

Thought viruses connected with regret cause us to be preoccupied with the past. Thought viruses associated with worry lead to preoccupation with the future. Discomfort with what we are feeling at this moment moves us away from now. All of these rob us of our experience of the present moment.

Dr. Chopra suggests that we can enhance our experience of the here and now by simply putting our awareness on sensations in the body. If we are experiencing a pleasant state, body awareness will ground us in the moment and enhance the experience. If we are experiencing an unpleasant state or a craving, easily putting attention on how the body is experiencing the discomfort will allow the brain naturally to produce endorphines and neurotransmitters that allow the state to dissipate. All too often we attempt to escape what we are feeling by some destructive means, rather than facing it straight on.

Sometimes, when Dana called me on the phone, I would ask where she was. She would respond, "I'm here!" When I asked her what time it was, she would say, "It's now!"

THERAPY FOR KILLER VIRUSES

The essence of most killer viruses is an addiction—to tobacco, to gambling, to alcohol or drugs, to sex, or to violence. The addiction is a destructive way to change our state, to move away from pain or to move toward perceived pleasure.

What works best,[1] from the perspective of Thought Virus Therapy, is *brief* intervention to deal with

- *positive intents* of the underlying virus
- *depression,* which accompanies many addictions
- *dietary factors,* which may be fueling depression, lack of clear thinking, or hyperactivity—missing trace minerals, toxic processed oils and fats, too much sugar, etc.
- *practical tips,* for understanding the particular addiction and triggers that elicit the addictive behavior
- *limiting erroneous beliefs* such as denial with addictions, and feelings of betrayed expectations that lead to violence
- *state management* for cravings, mood shifts, maintaining energy levels, and feeling good about oneself during the process of recovery

One particularly powerful antiviral remedy to alleviate addictions is to elicit and make use of the person's *motivation strategy*: the unconscious sequence of steps the person goes through to become highly motivated. The next case study illustrates this approach.

FREEING YOURSELF FROM SMOKING

Barbara had been smoking for three years and trying unsuccessfully for a year to break the habit. She and her children were unhappy with her smoking; she knew all the reasons why she should quit, yet something was keeping her hooked. She knew one problem was that she loved to play darts and was quite good in dart competitions. Unfortunately, of course, most competitions take place in bars, with lots of smoking and drinking.

In Barbara's case she was too busy with her job, her kids, and her social recreation to be depressed. She had much energy, and as she told me, she just didn't have the time for depression. Since she had originally quit smoking nine years ago, I figured that unconsciously she already knew how to quit.

"When you successfully quit before, how did you do it?" I asked. I sought to uncover her *strategy*—the sequence of external and internal experience that *motivated* her nine years ago to stop smoking and to follow through.

"I just decided to stop, and I stopped," she said.

"Can you go back to that time when you made the commitment to stop? Be in that experience as if it were happening *now*. *Seeing* what you saw, *hearing* what you heard, and *feeling* what you felt, what was the *very first thing* that happened to *trigger* your motivation?" I asked.

"Well, I was pregnant with my youngest, and I thought about how the smoking would affect her," Barbara responded.

"When you first thought about how it would affect her, did you *picture* how it would affect her, or *talk* to yourself about it?" I probed. "Again, be there as if it were happening now."

"I pictured the fetus being poisoned, and suffering from the smoking," she said.

"Okay, once you pictured the fetus and the effects of the smoke, what was the very next thing that happened for you to feel motivated to stop smoking? Did you say something to yourself, make more pictures in your head, see something on the outside, talk to someone, or immediately have feelings?" I continued.

"Well, I had been coughing a lot. Because I was pregnant, the coughing was painful. I remember asking myself, 'Am I really enjoying this?' I actually felt my body respond, 'No,'" she answered.

"At that point, did you feel motivated to quit?" I asked. She nodded. Her strategy or program to successfully motivate herself was:

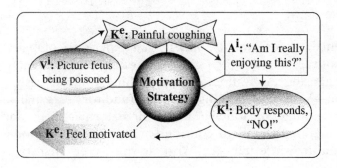

To further refine knowing how she did her strategy, I elicited submodalities of how she pictured her fetus being poisoned, and the qualities of the voice asking if she really enjoyed smoking. She pictured the fetus in full color, uncomfortably close up, moving, and right in front of her. She described the voice as being soft, inflected, located inside her head, and her own voice. It was caring and compassionate, as opposed to blaming or judgmental.

Next I asked her to imagine her heart, lungs, and other internal organs being poisoned, and directed her to use the same submodalities she had used to picture her fetus. I also had her picture her future life and her relationship with her children being poisoned in the same way. Finally she used that same voice, with the same inflections, softness, location, and sense of caring and compassion, asking her if she really enjoyed smoking. Barbara winced, shuddered, and said, "No." She said she felt her body answer her the same way it had nine years ago.

Antiviral Remedy 10
Eliciting Your Motivation Strategy

To discover your own motivation strategy in any area of life, begin with physiology. When you are totally motivated to do something, how does your body feel? What sensations do you notice with your facial muscles? What is your posture like? How are you breathing?

The next step is to uncover the sequence of steps—the strategy—you unconsciously use to motivate yourself. You can do this by thinking of a specific time when you were totally motivated and consequently completely effective in what you were doing. Be in touch with all the feelings, sights, and sounds from that particular experience. It is crucial to be in touch with that experience as if it were happening *now*. Here is a seven-step process to construct your strategy:

1. Once you feel yourself back in that experience of being totally motivated, notice the *very first thing* that must happen to begin triggering motivation. Is it something you see (visual external—V^e), or something you hear (auditory external—A^e), or something you touch (kinesthetic external—K^e)? Maybe it's something you picture inside (visual internal—V^i) or self-talk (auditory internal—A^i). Write down this very first step.

2. Next notice what happens on the *inside* once you have seen, heard, or touched what started your motivation. Do you now visualize something inside, hear some words or self-talk inside, or have some internal feelings (V^i, A^i, or K^i)? Once you are aware of this step, write it down.

3. Once you have seen, heard, or felt something inside, does something else internally or externally need to happen for you to be completely motivated? Write down that step. Continue the process until it feels complete; a typical strategy may involve two to five steps.

4. After you have listed each step, you might conjure up another time when you were totally motivated. Put yourself back in that situation as if it were happening now, and see if that experience involves the same sequence of steps. This may lead to some refinement in your strategy.

5. Often the first step in your strategy will be in your dominant modality. If you are primarily visual, the first step is likely to be something you see; if you are auditory, it may be something you hear; and so on. The first step, however, is the one most likely to change from situation to situation. The last step in your strategy is a kinesthetic internal feeling of being motivated. Notice how you feel the motivation in your body.

6. Once you are convinced you have the correct sequence of steps, write it down. This is your recipe for getting yourself motivated.

7. To refine your strategy, check for submodalities of the internal steps.

Once I had Barbara apply her past motivation strategy to the present task of quitting smoking, I had her imagine in the future triggers that would normally activate her craving for a smoke. Even visualizing the triggers and sensing the craving, she expressed determination not to resume smoking.

Beyond that, I shared some practical tips on smoking cessation with her.

Antiviral Remedy 11
Tips To Free Yourself From Substance Addictions[2]

- Smoking, alcohol, and drugs can be powerfully addicting as long as you have the substance in your system, which in some cases can be up to a year. The most difficult period is usually the first couple of months. Beware. Relapses usually occur within three to four weeks.

- Know that you *can* quit on your own, but if you want to improve your chances of success, seek a counselor who specializes in addictions. One trained in Thought Virus Therapy* would be especially useful, so that you can uncover and maintain the positive intents of thought viruses connected with the habit. A counselor can be indispensable in helping with the depression that often accompanies these addictions.
- Aim for total abstinence. A single relapse puts the substance back into your system, and is a powerful trigger itself to resume the habit.
- Energize yourself with exercise, walking, swimming, sports— whatever you enjoy doing that increases your pulse rate and gets your brain's natural endorphines going. This will help neutralize depression, and you'll notice increased endurance as your physiology begins to clear and heal.
- Avoid situations and routines that are strongly anchored to the addiction.
- Avoid or minimize, for a few weeks, other substances that might be a depressant and a natural trigger for your past addiction. In the case of smoking, beware of coffee intake. Reduced nicotine can make you more sensitive to caffeine.
- Be easy on yourself if you aren't successful the first time. People sometimes try to stop six or more times before they are successful. Learn from your experience.

Barbara's one session was brief, about one and a half hours. She felt confident she could quit, and has now been smoke-free for more than a year.

The First Law of Newtonian physics states that an object set in motion will continue the motion, undeviating, *along a straight line*, unless there is a force to change it. In the same way, a killer virus, once set in motion, carries us unimpeded on a straight line toward a destiny we may not be proud of. Barbara was able to change her course; Karl's aunt Peg, unfortunately, was not.

The changes Barbara made came about simply because of the way she now made meaning about smoking, a meaning that was

* See Appendix 2.

aligned with her unconscious motivation strategy to stop. Her unconscious then *automatically* produced changes that allowed her to vary her direction and keep herself on the road of life.

When Karl told the highway patrolman that cars don't slide off of curves, he was right. The highway patrolman knew enough physics to accept Karl's explanation and had enough compassion to forget about the ticket and let Karl make it to the hospital to see his aunt for the last time. Aunt Peg whispered that the *value* of her demise was learning for her, but it was more important for the people around her, who could see the *consequences* of faulty thinking that maintains destructive addictions.

Without enough force *to change its direction,* a high-speed car simply proceeds in a straight line, obeying the law—Newton's First Law. The car doesn't skid off the road; rather, the *road* curves away from the *car*—just as life curves away from those of us who continue the noncoherent thinking of self-destructive behavior.

PART TWO

THOUGHT VIRUSES AND HEALING

7

THOUGHT VIRUS THERAPY

A MOMENT'S INSIGHT
IS SOMETIMES WORTH
A LIFE'S EXPERIENCE.

—OLIVER WENDELL HOLMES

W hen someone comes to me for a consultation, usually there is only one reason. He or she wants to feel good. Some pattern of thinking or physical ailment is blocking the experience of pleasurable states, or providing painful ones. The states he or she experiences are interfering with health, relationships, career, personal growth, finances, or enjoyment of life.

Have you ever noticed that when you are upset, frantic, or wound up emotionally, your thinking lacks clarity or coherence? Then, when you cool down emotionally and mentally, it's as if some sort of internal shift or *phase transition* takes place. Perhaps you then find a new way to make meaning out of whatever is taking place, and your thinking is much more powerful and directed. Maybe you asked yourself one or two key questions that allowed you to look at things in a new light, and you felt better even in the face of adversity.

On the physical level, matter takes on more coherence or orderliness at lower temperatures. Such qualities as electrical resistance and random thermal vibration reduce. At certain key temperatures, orderliness increases dramatically with what's called a *phase transition*. For example, on a crisp autumn morning, disorderly, noncoherent water vapor forms orderly crystals of frost on blades of grass at the freezing temperature. Even more dramatically, electrical resistance suddenly disappears entirely at a few degrees above absolute zero, when certain materials become superconductors.

One of the most inspiring qualities of a great athlete like Joe

Montana was his ability to maintain his *cool* even under the most trying circumstances—the *heated* battle of a football game. In fact, when his team was down, he stepped up his performance and was even more effective.

Up to this point we have demonstrated Thought Virus Therapy as a means to reintegrate various thought viruses, and have illustrated a number of antiviral remedies. What, specifically, is Thought Virus Therapy? What can it do, and what situations in life are most helped through its procedures? How can we use it to cool mental and emotional temperatures and thus increase the coherence and power of our thinking? Are phase transitions limited to physical phenomena like water freezing and electrical resistance changing, or is there a mental counterpart?

THE PURPOSE OF THOUGHT VIRUS THERAPY

The antiviral remedies presented so far can help people to deactivate or even reverse triggers that would otherwise stimulate phobias, compulsions, and emotional states and behavior we may be less than proud of. Other remedies help us reprioritize values so that they work together more smoothly to move us toward our visions in life or eliminate disempowering beliefs that are holding us back. Six-Step Reframing and The Visual Squash (explained in chapter 5) allow us to make peace among conflicting parts of Gemini viruses and thus eliminate internal conflict. Bringing to conscious awareness the normally unconscious steps we go through to motivate ourselves can begin the process of eliminating destructive habits—killer viruses. Conscious use of our motivation strategy can also provide the spark for completing projects and goals, and for setting new directions in life.

In considering, then, what this therapy really means, I thought about what my friend Dana did unconsciously when things weren't going her way.

CLUE NUMBER 7: TO CHANGE THE WAY YOU FEEL ABOUT ANY-THING THAT HAS OR HASN'T HAPPENED TO YOU, CHANGE OR *RE-FRAME* THE MEANING.

This seemed to me a common denominator and bottom line of virtually any therapy. For the woman who was one hundred pounds overweight, being rejected meant the humiliation of feeling bad about herself. With therapy using a reverse trigger, she reframed rejection to trigger feelings that empowered her. Being at peace with herself also meant she could lose the weight she had carried for so many years. For Richard, who did not have health within his top ten values, exercise meant unpleasant, hard, tedious work. With his values reprioritized, he unconsciously reframed exercise to mean feeling strong, feeling lots of energy, and feeling good about how he spent his time. To a woman who was raped or sexually molested, the experience may have meant feeling violated, feeling dirty, or not trusting men. With appropriate therapy, the same memories might mean that she survived the ordeal and she is stronger because of it.

There are four approaches for changing meaning through Thought Virus Therapy:

- factors affecting physical well-being (physiology)
- a power questioning technique
- the antiviral remedies explained in this book
- an ancient Vedic technique for lowering mental temperature and instilling coherent thinking and functioning

WHAT THOUGHT VIRUS THERAPY IS, AND WHAT IT ISN'T

Although Thought Virus Therapy contains a number of methods and techniques, the heart of the approach is the *attitude* of the person administering the therapy. Properly, the attitude is one of care, compassion, and, above all, *curiosity:* "How is it that this person could think like this or create this condition?" Milton Erickson, one of the foremost hypnotherapists and healers of the twentieth century, approached each client as if he were a detective, trying to piece together the puzzle of how the client could have created the condition that now afflicted him or her. He was also a master of observing the subtle.

Once a lovely young woman came to see Dr. Erickson. The woman complained to Dr. Erickson about being depressed, and the doctor noticed something subtle about the way the woman moved her arms when she made gestures to accentuate her points. Dr. Erickson then asked her, "How long have you been dressing as and pretending to be a woman?"

His client looked shocked, and asked, "How did you know?"

"A woman never moves her arms to gesture the way that you do," he responded.

A therapist who has mastered the art of this therapy is as interested in *how* someone says something—posture, breathing, eye movements, gestures, and voice inflections—as in what he or she is saying. The therapist notices visual, auditory, and kinesthetic references and mannerisms as well as language patterns that point toward limitations in the client's internal map of reality. In fact, the therapy can be relatively content-free. It really doesn't matter *what* the phobia is, *who* did what to whom in childhood, *what* part is conflicting with what other part inside. All of that can cloud the real issues: *how* the person created the phobia or the internal conflict, and *how* the person's thinking continues to perpetuate the emotional effects of childhood trauma or internal conflict.

The therapist's attitude is also one of trust that the client already has all the internal resources he or she needs to solve the problem. Maybe the client has an intense fear of rejection, but if she has had even one experience of being resourceful in the face of rejection or something similar, unconsciously she already knows how to handle it. If another client habitually procrastinates, but had one experience of being focused and motivated to act, on some level he already knows how to move beyond procrastination; he just hasn't gotten around to it yet. The therapist's job is not to fix things, but rather to guide the client through his or her own internal resources to handle the problem. I like to think of a thought virus as a tangled knot in the line of life. The therapist's job is to help the client unravel the knot. The bottom line though, is that the client is an invaluable expert here. Because the client created the knot, he or she knows best how to untangle it.

Some of the methods of Thought Virus Therapy and the antiviral remedies can be done on your own. Most, however, are considerably more effective if done with another person, especially a therapist who is trained in the methods. (See Appendix 2 for information on resources.) Even if you just have a friend who is interested in learning the methods with you, doing many of the techniques and processes with your friend is an excellent way to begin mastering them.

WARNING: Thought Virus Therapy is *not* a substitute where there is a need for psychiatry or medical attention, or where the client presents a physical danger to himself or others.

GAINING THE SUPPORT OF YOUR PHYSIOLOGY

What states would you like to experience on a more regular basis?

- more energy
- more creativity
- more physical vibrancy
- more enthusiasm and passion for what you do each day

A major key to how we make meaning is how we feel physically and emotionally. The truism "the world is as we are" is valid. One of the quickest and most reliable ways to get leverage over how we feel and the states we experience is through the physiology. Five key factors make a difference.

EXERCISE. Proper exercise can be a great rejuvenator and a key to youth, and can provide leverage for energetic, empowering states. Research repeatedly shows that exercise strengthens the heart and lungs, protects against high blood pressure, and lowers cholesterol and the risk of cancer. Not exercising causes widespread damage to the body, including reduced vital capacity, reduced oxygen availability to cells and organs, elevated triglycerides, and loss of muscle mass. The Surgeon General of the United States has gone so far as to issue warnings that lack of exercise may be hazardous to your health.

During the 1980s, aerobic exercise—running, swimming, cycling, speed walking, and so forth—became fashionable as a means to improve cardiovascular fitness, strength, and endurance, and to extend youthfulness. Unfortunately, by itself, aerobic exercise is not particularly effective to accomplish any of these. A key to understanding why this is so comes from the field of biochemistry. An amino acid called glutamine is a key to immune cell reproduction—a measure of the strength of the immune system. Glutamine, however, is not produced in the immune system, but in muscles.

Unfortunately, though, as we age we typically lose muscle mass. The average man from age twenty to age eighty loses 25 percent of his muscle mass.[1] A typical woman between twenty and forty years of age loses eight pounds of muscle and gains twenty-three pounds of fat. Such muscle loss seriously compromises the immune system's ability to slow down aging.

The present thinking, then, is that a three-sided *balance* of exercise works in synergy to promote a sense of physical exhilaration and emotional well-being.

- *Stretching or yoga* promotes flexibility and reduces chances of injury in sports and other exercise.
- *Weight-bearing exercise* with *moderate* weight improves strength, endurance, and cardiovascular capacity.
- *Aerobic exercise,* especially in combination with weight-bearing exercise, also improves endurance and cardiovascular capacity.

WARNING: Consult with your physician before beginning any new exercise program.

DEEP-BREATHING EXERCISES OR MASSAGE. The body has two major circulatory systems: the system of veins and arteries to circulate blood, and the lymph system, into which cellular wastes are deposited, to be carried off by lymph fluid. Unfortunately, the lymph system does not have a pump like the heart. Lymph fluid moves as a result of body motion. With no movement, the body begins to drown in its own toxins.

Tony Robbins[2] recommends deep-breathing exercises a couple of times a day as a means to enhance lymph circulation and energy. Breathing exercises, which are an integral part of many yogic and spiritual traditions, may thus have a physiological basis for their effectiveness.

Another effective and pleasant means to enhance lymph movement is massage. The fundamental human need for touch appears to also have a physiological basis.

DIET. Obviously, what we put into our bodies has a profound effect on the states we experience. Some foods naturally promote energy and a sense of well-being. Other foods are natural cancer preventers. Still others promote lethargy, and increase our chances of

contracting heart disease and cancer. We will take a closer look at
the connection of diet and mental states in chapter 8, on depression.

POWER MOVES. Think about the word *emotion*. Contained within
that word is the word *motion*. This is no coincidence.

Exercise 16
The Physiology of States

1. Think of a *specific* time when you experienced an empowering
   state, such as feeling high energy, exhilaration, joy, intense enthusiasm, or unstoppable confidence.
2. Placing yourself back in that experience as if it were happening *now*—seeing what you saw, hearing what you heard, and
   feeling what you felt—notice how you naturally move your
   body, or the gestures you make to express the feelings. In particular notice what happens to
   - your facial muscles
   - your posture
   - your breathing
   - gestures you make with your arms and hands
   Write down what you observe. These are part of your recipe
   for experiencing this state.
3. Change your state, and imagine you are in a state of lethargy
   and total boredom. Again notice
   - your facial muscles
   - your posture
   - your breathing
   - gestures you make with your arms and hands
   Anytime you want to feel lethargy and total boredom, this is
   the physiology you need to assume.
4. While in this lethargic state, *suddenly* change to the breathing,
   posture, gestures, and so on that you had in the empowering
   state. In fact, *exaggerate* these changes. For most people this
   change in physiology quickly pulls them out of the lethargic
   state. What is your experience?

Knowing the physiological qualities of any empowering state, particularly the gestures, provides a powerful key, a *power move* to access that state. The power move can be used either by itself or,

even better, as the first step in a power trigger (Antiviral Remedy 2, pages 57–58) designed to set up that state. There is, however, one thing to remember if you have desirable empowering states that you are not experiencing on a regular basis. You may have an opposing part of you—a Gemini virus—that on some level objects to experiencing the desired state. In this case, Antiviral Remedy 8 or 9 (pages 98–99 and 103) would be in order.

LISTENING TO THE BODY. Part of the process of becoming intuitive is learning to trust "gut feelings." When you are faced with a difficult decision, as you weigh each alternative, simply notice how your body feels. If you have some misgivings or uncertainty, you will feel some discomfort in the body. The physiology has not learned to lie about or to cover up feelings. If one alternative elicits bodily discomfort, that doesn't mean you shouldn't pursue it; it simply means you are incongruent and need to deal with the parts of you that feel misgivings.

Aside from decision making, listening to the body also provides clear indications of the need for rest, for movement or exercise, or perhaps that you have eaten something inappropriate which is producing a tired state.

THE ANTIVIRAL THERAPY SESSION

Specific interventions for phobias, limiting beliefs, negative anchors, internal conflicts, and so on are explained in detail in the antiviral remedies presented thus far. Beyond these instructions, which are specific to various problems, some general components are common to any therapy session designed to reintegrate a thought virus.

1. *Establish a well-formed outcome.* From the point of view of Thought Virus Therapy, knowing clearly what you want, and having the desired outcome well formed or organized, is half of what it takes to reach the outcome. A well-formed outcome has three key characteristics:

- *The vision.* Make sure that the outcome or change you want is stated in the positive—what you want to move toward, as opposed to what you *don't* want (moving away from): "I want to be around cats and feel normal," as opposed to "I *don't* want to have allergic reactions to cats." When someone rejects or abandons me, "I want to let go and feel good about myself," as opposed to "I *don't* want to feel devastated when someone rejects me." "I want to be free from migraine headaches," as opposed to "I don't want to have migraine headaches."

- *The signpost.* How, specifically, will you know when you have achieved the desired outcome or change? This should be specific, measurable evidence that lets you or your client know when you have accomplished the change: "I would like to have a cat living in my house and have dry eyes and clear sinuses." "If people reject me, I might feel some initial disappointment, but I still want to feel good about myself." "I'd like my head to be free from the pain of migraine headaches."

- *Feasibility.* Is the outcome something you feel is possible for people in general to achieve? Is it possible for you *and* within your control? Is it something you feel you deserve for yourself? If I'm five feet two inches tall and I want to move beyond my fear of failure of not becoming a star basketball player, I might have a problem. If I want others to accept me and stop rejecting me, that's not within my control. An alternative approach would be to learn to react resourcefully in the face of lack of acceptance or rejection.

2. *Check for secondary gains.* Is there some way that you benefit— perhaps some attention or sympathy you get from others—as a result of having the allergies or the migraines or being rejected? Look for alternate ways of maintaining secondary benefits while alleviating the problem. Maybe you just don't like cats, so being allergic provides a good reason why your husband, who would like a cat, can't have one. Perhaps having migraines gets you out of having to mow the lawn, since the loud noise aggravates the headache.

3. *Check the* context *of the problem.* Be aware of when and where desired changes are appropriate, and any possible *consequences* of change. Might there be certain situations in which the problem serves an important purpose? An allergy to chemical vapors might be useful if the vapors happen to be toxic chemicals. The allergy provides a warning of their presence. You might not want to eliminate *all* headaches, since their presence might indicate a potentially dangerous medical condition. Before I work with someone

who has migraines, I want to be absolutely certain he or she has been thoroughly tested by a physician, and that the physician is aware of our working together. I ask the person's unconscious mind to allow a headache, if there is some condition present that needs medical attention.

4. *Check for* ecology. Do you have any internal parts that object to the desired changes? When you ask yourself this question, listen to your body. If part of you objects to the change, more than likely you will experience some anxiety or discomfort. This simply means you need to communicate with the objecting part, discover how it is attempting to serve you, and find ways to maintain the positive intent(s) while changing the problem. Without dealing with objecting parts, your impetus to change is incongruent and noncoherent, and your best intentions to change are doomed to failure.

If fear of rejection keeps you from venturing out to meet attractive singles, there's a good chance part of you is trying to protect your self-esteem. Migraine headaches may indicate an internal conflict that must be resolved before the headaches can leave for good. Some therapists and consultants prefer to do the ecology check near the beginning of the session. Others prefer to do it just before completing the intervention. Once the unconscious knows *how* the change will take place, if objecting parts are present, they will readily emerge.

5. *Apply the antiviral remedy or remedies.* Keep in mind that any given problem may result from a combination involving two or more forms among the trigger, limiting, and Gemini virus species. Be spontaneous and flexible to see where solving the problem will lead. In some of the remedies, I have already indicated the need to check for secondary gain, context, and ecology. Regardless of whether or not they have been mentioned, be sure to include them.

6. *Future pace.* Imagine being in a situation in the near future that in the past would have triggered the problem state. Picture and feel how you now *automatically and unconsciously* react resourcefully. You might see yourself picking up the cat and remaining free of the allergic response. You might see yourself being cruelly rejected, and, with a reverse trigger, feel your confidence and self-esteem building. Imagine encountering some stressful trigger that in the past would have brought on the migraine, but

now your head feels fine. Project yourself into enough future situations that you feel *convinced* of the changes you've made.

THE POWER QUESTIONING TECHNIQUE

Back in chapter 1 we discussed how deletions, distortions, and generalizations filter and limit the ways in which we make sense out of things. Because, consciously, we cannot possibly pay attention to all of the myriad stimuli and thoughts bombarding our awareness, we select a small portion of them to consciously address. But what determines where we put our attention? How do we evaluate our experience to determine what is important? How do we unconsciously decide what is important and what isn't?

What we pay attention to is determined by our values, especially core values—those emotional states we most anticipate will bring pleasure and those we most fear will lead to pain. If I am single and value being in a relationship, I'll be especially aware of good-looking women around me. If a core value for me is security, I'll probably be acutely aware of situations and people that might make me feel insecure. If my car has broken down, and it's urgent that I get a new car, and if I've been considering, say, an Acura Legend, what cars am I likely to notice out on the highway?

Beyond values, a major component of evaluating and making meaning from our experiences is asking ourselves questions about them. When I see an attractive woman, I'll probably think

- "Is she single, or does she have on a wedding ring?"
- "How old is she?"
- "Is she my type?"
- "How can I meet her without embarrassing myself?"

Of course, these are all questions. When I see an Acura Legend on the highway, I might first wonder if it is an Acura, then what year it is. I might ask myself if that is a color I like, how reliable the car has been for its owner, and so forth.

Tony Robbins has made a unique contribution toward eliminating and reintegrating thought viruses through a process of empowering self-questions.[3] We ask ourselves questions all the time to evaluate experience. Some of those questions can empower us; others are neutral and simply provide information; and still others can shut us down.

Exercise 17
Disempowering Questions

1. Think of some mistake you made in the past, when as a result you were particularly embarrassed or humiliated—some mistake you'd rather not admit having made.
2. Ask yourself the following questions about that mistake:
   - "*Why* in the world did I do that?"
   - "How could I be so stupid?"
   - "Why do I do dumb things like that?"
3. Notice how you feel.
4. Quickly erase all of this from your mental chalkboard.

In some ways the brain is like a computer—designed to answer whatever questions we pose to it, even if the questions make no sense. Almost any question we ask ourselves that begins with the word *why*, such as the first question in Exercise 17, will be disempowering. It has no reasonable answer. The brain, however, will still search its memory bank for an answer and perhaps come up with, "It's because you're always doing dumb things like that." Notice the disempowering presuppositions in the second and third questions. There is no way to answer these without buying into the presupposition that you are stupid and do dumb things.

Exercise 18
Reframing Past Mistakes

1. Think of that mistake from the past which you worked with in Exercise 17.
2. Ask yourself the following questions about that mistake:
   - "What did I learn from that mistake that is of value to me now?" If you can't think of anything, ask, "What could I learn if I wanted to?"
   - "What was funny about making that mistake, or what could be funny?"

- "What changes have I made or could I make as a result of that mistake that would make me feel proud of myself? What *in particular* about these changes makes me proud? How does that make me feel now?"

3. Again, notice how you feel.

When you contrast feelings from the last two exercises, Exercise 17 is a good way to beat yourself up for making mistakes, while Exercise 18 is a good way to empower yourself. Unfortunately, I think too many of us choose the strategy of Exercise 17.

If you would like a way to start each day with inspiration and enthusiasm, try the following:

Antiviral Remedy 12
Power Questions[4]

1. List ten questions for yourself that have empowering presuppositions, for example:
   - What am I excited about in my life now?
   - Who loves me? Whom do I love?
   - What am I proud of in my life now?
   - What am I grateful for in my life now?
   - What am I learning now that makes me feel good?
   - How could whatever is happening to me now be moving me toward my highest dreams?

   List whatever questions feel most relevant to you. When you ask such questions with a sincere interest in receiving answers, your brain will search out answers that will make you feel good.

2. When you wake up each morning, begin the day by asking yourself two of the questions in a certain format. Let's say you choose the above question, "What am I grateful for in my life now?" For each answer you think of, expand on that answer with two more questions:
   - What about *that* makes me feel grateful?
   - How does that make me feel?

3. Repeat the process in step 2 for the second question and each answer that comes up. Again, notice how you feel.

4. Do this for twenty-one days, and see if the quality of your daily life, especially your start in the morning, isn't transformed.

HOW TO SYNCHRONIZE YOUR BRAIN WAVES[5]

One of the most powerful methods to enhance clarity of thinking and to put yourself into a more mentally coherent state is also one of the simplest. It is an ancient mental relaxation and stress-reduction technique to reduce mental activity and thereby lower your emotional and mental temperature. This ancient technique has recently been "rediscovered."

The brain puts out weak electrical signals called brain waves, or, more technically, EEG waves. These vary in frequency. The right and left sides of the brain each put out a mixture of frequencies; the side more involved with the activity at hand puts out a stronger signal; the less involved half puts out a weaker signal with more alpha waves, indicating it is more relaxed.

Brain Wave Types

TYPE	FREQUENCY	ASSOCIATED WITH
Delta	.5–4 Hz*	deep sleep
Theta	4–7 Hz	deep meditation and reverie ("twilight" level of consciousness)
Alpha	8–14 Hz	relaxed state or daydreaming
Beta	14–22 Hz	wakefulness; wide awake or engaged in mental activity

* One Hz is one vibration per second.

A common characteristic of the signals is that brain waves on one side of the brain are very different from brain waves on the other. This indicates that the two halves of the brain are relatively unsynchronized or noncoherent.

During practice of the mental relaxation technique mentioned above, as mental activity or "temperature" lowers and reaches a certain critical level, something extraordinary occurs—a phase transition in brain functioning. Dr. J. P. Banquet observed that the brain waves become purified in frequency and synchronized between left and right.[6]

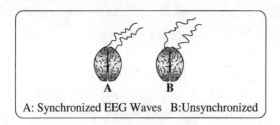

A: Synchronized EEG Waves B:Unsynchronized

The synchronized waves are not identical, but are much more alike than normal. This would seem to indicate more of a balanced functioning between left and right, with a level of coherence and synchrony never before seen. Furthermore, when people practice this technique over a period of time, some of the brain-wave synchrony begins to carry over into activity.

You might wonder what the advantage would be of sitting down, relaxing, and allowing your brain waves to synchronize. More than 600 scientific studies done on people experiencing this state of awareness have demonstrated some far-reaching benefits for emotional well-being, creativity, and intelligence.

Researchers have observed that when a person takes up this practice, he or she becomes less prone to anxiety, hostility, and depression.[7] Self-esteem and self-actualization improve.[8] Long-term and short-term memory immediately improves.[9] Comprehension, ability to focus, and creativity are enhanced.

Later studies have shown a synchrony among the back, center, and front of the cortex, as well as vertical synchrony within the brain. Synchrony between the back and center of the cortex would suggest improved perceptual motor activities, such as sports and dance. A number of studies have indeed shown this to be the case, and many professional athletes now practice the technique. Vertical synchrony may also account for autonomic changes such as blood pressure, respiratory rate, and pulse observed to be considerably lower than in deep sleep.

At this point you are probably wondering what technique I am talking about. I've been describing a form of meditation called *transcendental meditation* or TM for short. I am very familiar with this form of meditation, since I have practiced it for about twenty-five years. If you meditate for fifteen or twenty minutes twice a day, you begin experiencing better memory, clearer thinking, increased physical well-being, synchronized brain waves, and empowering states.

Aging and Meditation[10]

From the viewpoint of physics, aging results from an increase in entropy or disorder in the body as time goes on. If TM increases coherence in the mind and body, you might wonder if that wouldn't also reduce the body's entropy and affect aging. Biological aging *can* apparently be slowed as a result of meditation. Dr. Keith Wallace and others have discovered that people practicing TM for five to ten years frequently have a biological age that is five to ten years less than their actual age.

We have known for a long time that aging is very individual. It is as though we each had an internal biological clock, each running at a different rate. Now we have a way to slow down our clocks.

Other forms of meditation may produce similar benefits, but TM is the most researched form, and is the only technique I am aware of that produces brain-wave synchrony and coherence to this extent.

TOWARD A THOUGHT VIRUS IMMUNE RESPONSE

As I became aware of and studied various antiviral remedies, it occurred to me that these came about as a result of *modeling* certain people—the ones who have the uncanny knack of unconsciously freeing themselves of distortions in thought. In other words, just as a few people naturally develop biological immunity to the worst of plagues, a few people naturally develop mental-emotional immunity to thought viruses. By studying the blood and immune responses of survivors of biological plagues, we have the potential to develop cures and vaccinations for diseases. In the same way, by studying those few people who naturally free themselves from the effects of thought viruses, such people as Milton Erickson, Virginia Satir, Fritz Perls, John Grinder, and Richard Bandler have developed antiviral remedies that can work for the rest of us. The bottom line for most of these remedies is that they change

the way we feel about disturbing situations and events, by changing or reframing the meaning we attach to them.

Using the antiviral remedies in a therapy session with a therapist, a friend, or, in some cases, on your own, can quickly produce
results that are truly magical and transformative. Keep in mind,
however, that if you undergo a session for a particular virus, and if
the problem returns at a later time, it doesn't mean that the remedy didn't work. It just means the work wasn't quite complete. You
may need some more work to recondition your mind to get used
to more-congruent thinking. If you have spent years being out of
shape physically, you can't exercise just once and then think,
"Great, I'm glad that's over. Now I'll be in good physical shape for
the rest of my life." Antiviral remedies may in some cases require
follow-up and periodic emotional conditioning.

What about the *preventive* quality of an antiviral immune response? It seems to me that constructively managing states is the
key. When we experience resourceful states and our action is in
line with our highest values, this provides the foundation for un-
tying the twisted knots of thought viruses and establishing coherent thinking to prevent new ones from forming. The three pillars
that support the platform of resourceful states are mind, body,
and spirit.

MIND. Empowering self-questions are a great way to start the day
and provide a way to put our attention on things happening in life
that will empower us if we just think about them. Dana started
each day with a calendar page that had an uplifting quote or an af-
firmation for that day. I believe her way of changing or reframing
the meaning of whatever was happening to her was that she unconsciously asked herself empowering questions. Some, in fact,
may have connected with her daily quotes.

BODY. Taking care of the physiology through appropriate exercise,
life-supporting diet, breathing exercises (or massage), and power
moves provides a foundation for feeling vibrant and experiencing
empowering states.

SPIRIT. Most religious and spiritual traditions talk of the value of
prayer or meditation as a means of growth and self-actualization.
Now scientific evidence supports that notion. Meditation *is* an ef-

fective means to lower our mental temperature and bring about a
phase transition in coherence, just as lowering the physical temperature in certain materials allows them to become superconductors.

The current epidemic of thought viruses is related to the fact
that so many of us haven't been taking care of our minds, bodies,
and spirits. Poor breathing and eating habits, the lack of power
moves, the sedentary epidemic, habitually asking ourselves poor
questions, and allowing family, religious, and spiritual values to
slip away are the causes.

Thought Virus Therapy lowers emotional temperature, and
leads to more-coherent states of awareness, just as lowering physical temperature leads to more-coherent states of matter such as
the phase transition that produces superconductivity. Higher-
temperature superconductors now provide the means of producing the most powerful electromagnets made—four times
more powerful than conventional electromagnets. Superconduct-
ing magnets may provide the means to levitate 300-mile-per-hour
trains above their tracks, so that they can glide along the rails with
a minimum of friction just as virus-free coherent thinking resulting from Thought Virus Therapy may one day allow us to glide
through life with a minimum of emotional friction.

8

DEPRESSION

I SAT
EVALUATING MYSELF.
I DECIDED
TO LIE DOWN.

—PETER MCWILLIAMS

"What the #@*$? How could this apple go bad so quickly?" I had left an apple sitting on my dashboard that morning, only five hours ago, when my friend Satch and I left to go job-hunting. At only twenty-six years old, with an advanced degree in physics, but without a job, I felt myself to be a failure. I was experiencing symptoms of what has been labeled "the common cold of mental illness"—depression. It is not contagious, but 17 million Americans catch it each year. Even when the symptoms are obvious, and 80 percent of cases are curable, two-thirds of its victims go untreated, because they are unwilling to admit having it or simply don't recognize the symptoms.

At that time I didn't understand what I was experiencing. Why was it so hard to get up in the morning? Why would I stare at three identical sets of underwear, and not be able to decide which one to wear? Why did I feel as if I were walking through quicksand just to do routine daily tasks and to look for a job? Why had I lost my first engineering job since graduating from college only ten months ago? Why did I keep asking myself all these "why" questions?

My apple tree produces the best apples I've tasted. I don't know what variety they are, but they are both sweet and tart. They are great for eating and for baking. Each morning when they are ripe, I pick two as I leave home. One I eat right away, and the other I save for a late-afternoon snack. Why did this stupid apple turn completely brown on my dashboard in only five hours?

The radio talk show, on environmental dangers of the green-house effect, didn't cheer me up, but it reminded me of my friend Kathy who was also going through depression. Hers was even more frustrating than mine, because she had no idea why she was depressed. I had been out of work for six months, and had received nearly two hundred rejections of my employment applications. Kathy, in contrast, had just begun a change in lifestyle she had desired for two years—to quit work so she could stay home with her two-year-old daughter, take one college course per semester, and bake bread, cakes, and cookies. She loved to bake. Unlike me, she sought help for her depression. She was undergoing therapy and taking antidepressants. Unfortunately, four months of therapy had made no difference for her, and she was even more depressed each time she got the therapist's bill. Maybe she was undergoing the wrong kind of therapy. Maybe something was going on that the therapist was missing.

WHAT IS DEPRESSION?

What did Mark Twain, Winston Churchill, William Faulkner, Georgia O'Keeffe, and Abraham Lincoln have in common? Most people would recognize creativity, leadership, a great sense of humor (for Mark Twain and Winston Churchill), and pioneering spirits. Unfortunately, these and other well-known historical figures were also dogged with major bouts of chronic depression, which goes to show that depression can strike anyone regardless of fame, fortune, power, or how much admired.

No one knows for sure what causes depression, but it is commonly associated with major life transitions—the loss of a loved one, a marriage, a job, moving, or even such positive changes as winning the lottery. Sometimes, however, there is no obvious cause. Women are twice as likely to be depressed as men, and people over sixty-five have four times the incidence of younger people. Depression is the most common complaint physicians hear.

Depression has traditionally been attributed to weakness of character and self-indulgence, something a person should simply snap out of. Recent research, however, has shown it to be something quite concrete and real. Brain scanning tomography has identified two parts of the brain that function abnormally during major depression.[1] The left prefrontal cortex has an abnormally high blood flow; this may be associated with the constant flow of negative thoughts that typically accompany this state. The amygdala, a small inner brain structure, thought to regulate emotional reactions, also has a high blood flow both during and between bouts of depression. From a biochemical perspective, depression is connected with reduced levels of the neurotransmitters serotonin, norepinephrine, and dopamine.

As a result of reduced levels of these neurotransmitters, especially serotonin, people experience two major symptoms: a feeling of depression, and anhedonia—the diminished ability to enjoy things that normally bring pleasure, such as food, sex, or favorite hobbies. Indicators of depression include

- fatigue and weakness

- slowed body motion
- changes in sleep
- moodiness and irritability
- weight loss or gain

- inability to concentrate and make decisions
- sad, empty moods
- changes in eating patterns
- feelings of failure and worthlessness
- preoccupation with thoughts of death or suicide

Aside from the immediate discomfort these symptoms produce, a depressed brain also produces neurotransmitters and neuropeptides, which inhibit the immune system, so we are more prone to getting sick.

PHYSICAL CAUSES OF DEPRESSION

Phil, an accountant in Portland, Oregon, had lived a charmed existence. He had received scholarships for his university studies; he was happily married to the woman of his dreams; he had a rewarding job with a prestigious accounting firm; and he loved Portland and his new home. Lately, however, his body ached with fatigue. He could hardly motivate himself to get out of bed in the morning, much less go to work. Recreation that used to excite him no longer seemed to matter. It made no sense that he should be so down, and he thought he must be losing his mind.

Finally his wife dragged him into therapy with a psychiatrist who just happened to have training in biopsychiatry—the understanding of medical and physical conditions that can mimic depression. After listening to Phil's complaints and running him through a series of medical tests, the psychiatrist discovered that Phil's condition was caused by sunlight deficiency, a condition that affects 5 million to 25 million people per year in the United States and is easily correctable with light therapy.

The good news about depression is that about one-third of all cases result from physical causes, rather than emotional causes or thought viruses.[2] Like Phil's, most of these are easily treatable. Here are some of the most common physical contributors to depression:

UNSATURATED OILS. The current epidemic of depression in our country began about the same time we began a mass dietary shift from saturated fats to unsaturated fats. Reduced saturated fats have in fact lessened the occurrence of cardiovascular disease and heart attacks. In 1995, however, *Science News* reported a study that linked low-cholesterol diets (presumably higher in unsaturated fats) with increased rates of depression and suicide.[3]

In the category of unsaturated fats, only two oils are considered "essential": alpha linolenic acid, referred to as Omega 3 and linolenic acid, referred to as Omega 6. Omega 6 *by itself* has some toxic effects that may include promoting cancer growth and depression. Fortunately, Omega 3 can balance or neutralize these toxic effects. Unfortunately, the average American diet is very low in Omega 3 and very high in Omega 6. Most vegetable oils contain little or no Omega 3. To make matters worse, the commercial processing of vegetable oils, including heating, bleaching, and partial hydrogenation, disrupts the molecular structure of Omega 6 to convert it from its natural structure to an even more toxic twisted *trans-fat* configuration.

The most commonly used products containing partially hydrogenated fats, and trans-fats are margarine, shortening, and shortening oils. Anyone who is serious about maintaining health and avoiding depression should avoid entirely all fried and deep-fried foods and all products containing hydrogenated or partially hydrogenated oils. Unfortunately, these are pervasive in such products as cookies, breads, cakes, and candies.

The healthiest course of action is to minimize your consumption of all fats and oils. Supplement your diet with a tablespoon of flaxseed oil twice a day. It should be organic, cold-pressed, refrigerated, stored in a light-tight container, and used within a month or two of the date it was pressed.

DIET. A shortage of certain minerals and other nutrients can lead to depression. Much of our food is so highly processed, loaded with sugars and fats, and depleted of essential vitamins, minerals, amino acids, and phytonutrients, it's a wonder more of us aren't depressed. Minerals as supplied by many multivitamin pills are largely ineffective, because they are not chelated—bound into an organic molecule, as they naturally are in mineral-rich foods. A recent congressional study concluded that 93 percent of Americans have diets that are deficient in essential minerals. Unfortunately, modern practices of industrialized agriculture have stripped the soil of many essential minerals, especially zinc, magnesium, selenium, and chromium.

PHYSIOLOGY. A depressed mind is intimately linked with a depressed body. Whatever we can do to improve functioning of the physiology can help alleviate depression. The symptoms of fatigue, lethargy, and lack of energy in some cases may be due to lack of exercise. Because of the lack of energy, depressed people may have a more difficult time *motivating* themselves to exercise. Studies show, however, that when depressed people do start exercising regularly, depression diminishes and, in some cases, disappears altogether. Weight-bearing exercise and aerobics promote the strength and endurance that the depressed individual so desperately needs. Massage and deep-breathing techniques that promote lymph circulation also promote a feeling of well-being.

PRESCRIPTION DRUGS. A number of drugs used to treat high blood pressure, glaucoma, irregular heartbeat, arthritis, and a number of other conditions can trigger depression. If you suffer depression and are taking prescription medication, consult with your physician to see if depression is a possible side effect.

SMOKING AND HEAVY DRINKING. Smoking and depression are clearly connected, as are excess drinking and depression. Depression triggers the urge to light up, and smokers are more prone to depression than are nonsmokers. By definition, alcohol is a depressant—it slows down or depresses the physiology. Excess alcohol pickles the brain.

THYROID PROBLEMS. Seven million Americans suffer from thyroid problems, which can produce depression.[4] Ten to fifteen percent of depressed people have some form of thyroid malfunction.

DIABETES. Another 7 million Americans, who have diabetes, don't even know it. Untreated diabetes can bring on symptoms of depression.

FEMALE HORMONAL IMBALANCE. This occurs naturally during times of premenstrual syndrome (PMS), menopause, and the first few months after giving birth (postpartum depression).

ALLERGIES. Allergies activate the immune system much as a low-grade flu might do, and may give rise to similar symptoms—lethargy and achiness. Many people have mild food allergies they aren't aware of that can trigger depression.

SUNLIGHT DEFICIENCY. An estimated 5 million to 25 million Americans suffer from seasonal affective disorder (SAD). Interestingly, 83 percent of these people are women between the ages of thirty and fifty.

THE DEPRESSION VIRUS

Once depression has begun, we require a certain way of thinking for it to continue. If the depression is not due to a physical or dietary cause, more than likely it starts with some initial trigger: the loss of a spouse or a job, a financial setback, or moving from one's community. The loss can be more subtle and abstract, such as loss of confidence, of face, or of youthfulness. This is the initial part of the trigger, the external part. Beyond this, becoming depressed depends on only one thing—how we *make meaning* of what has happened.

If there is enough emotional shock or pain associated with whatever happened, the result may be a complex trigger virus. Just thinking about what has happened becomes emotionally anchored with the painful state. All you have to do is *picture* the circumstances in a certain way, or indulge internal self-talk in a certain tone of voice, and—whammo!—you trigger the feelings. The submodalities of *how* we picture the circumstances or *how* we talk to ourselves about them, and the *sequence* of what we experience (the strategy), is as important as, or more important than, the actual internal pictures or words.

Exercise 19
Submodalities of the Depression Virus

Many of us beat ourselves up emotionally when we make mistakes by using a highly critical, stern, scolding internal voice. If the internal message is critical enough, we may wind up feeling depressed. Others *picture* mistakes and the prospect of failure in a way that makes them feel bad.

1. If you are aware of a critical internal voice, imagine that voice attacking and criticizing you, but change it to Donald Duck's voice. Notice how you feel with Donald Duck criticizing you.
2. If you picture mistakes and potential failures in a disempowering way, notice the submodalities of *how* you picture them (color versus black and white, up close versus far away, moving versus still-frame, having a certain location in your field of vision, sharp focus versus unclear focus, and so on). Experiment with changing the submodalities of how you picture them, to find which most dramatically reduce or eliminate your emotional reaction.

When we make conscious the normally unconscious submodalities and strategy of the complex trigger required to maintain depression, we can interrupt or reprogram the steps to achieve a more empowering state.

Aside from the trigger, a limiting virus (limiting beliefs) usually comes into play. Remember the presupposition that any emotional upset is a *rules* upset. We expect that things *should* happen in a certain way, and they don't. In fact, the thinking and language patterns of depressed people are often riddled with words like *should, must, have to, supposed to*—a reflection of rigid thinking and beliefs that is bound to lead to feeling disappointed or betrayed. When a person's beliefs or values concerning *what ought to be* have been violated, this leads to endless loops of rehashing the experience. Self-talk is also likely to involve blaming oneself or others, together with unending questions and commentaries such as *why, how come,* and *if only*.

THERAPY FOR DEPRESSION

When Ron first came to see me, he was emotionally devastated. He was a talented biology professor and a dedicated, focused researcher at a nearby college. Recently he could barely make it through his lectures without bursting into tears. He cried in his office between lectures; he couldn't concentrate, eat, or sleep. He had been happily married for six years, convinced that he and his wife would be together for the rest of their lives. Out of the blue, his wife had announced she was having an affair with the man of her dreams, and wanted to end the marriage.

Such chronic states as grieving and depression have a natural sequence of healing—a beginning, a middle, and an end, just like a physical wound. For the healing to be complete, it is necessary to go through all three phases. Nevertheless, some people seem to move quickly through loss, grieving, and the accompanying depression, while other people take years to recover. What is the difference? It boils down to how different people think. To understand the difference, NLP researchers have studied people who are "skilled" at quickly moving through the different stages of grieving, and have contrasted their strategies with those of people who get stuck in depression.

Ron had recently seen his doctor for some unrelated physical complaints. He told the doctor about the marriage breakup and what he was going through emotionally. After talking with Ron for only ten minutes, the doctor told Ron he was clinically depressed, and gave him a prescription for Prozac. Ron, like many victims of depression, was reluctant to take drugs, and wondered if therapy or just "toughing it out" might be a better approach.

With the development of a new category of antidepressant drugs called *selective serotonin-reuptake inhibitors* or SSRIs, such as Prozac and a number of others, a major controversy has arisen regarding depression. For most people, the drugs appear to have few if any side effects, and many people have benefited greatly from taking them. Especially in cases of severe or long-term chronic depression, people who take them feel they have been given a new lease on life. The controversy centers on whether it is better to treat depression by treating the body with drugs (tolerating possible side effects) or to treat the mind through appropriate

therapy and counseling. Does the body, through reduced levels of
serotonin, norepinepherine, or dopamine, cause the brain to be
depressed, or does the brain, through faulty thinking, cause the
body to become depressed? This question is similar to the old rid-
dle of which came first, the chicken or the egg?

Clearly, alleviating biochemical imbalance in the body does improve thinking. Many people who have suffered severe and
chronic depression have found that an appropriate antidepressant could restore emotional balance and clarity of thought. The
medication also doesn't make you euphoric, and doesn't reduce
daily stress.

On the other hand, improved thinking can have a profound
impact on the biochemical balance of the body. For mild to moderate depression, therapy to change how the person thinks seems
to work as well as, if not better than, drugs in restoring body chemistry. Depression likely involves a vicious cycle in which negative
thinking upsets the biochemistry, which then leads to more negative thinking, which further imbalances the biochemistry. One
way or another, the cycle must be broken.

As a society, we generally prefer the "magic bullet" approach to
quick and easy solutions for sometimes complex and difficult
health problems. If you have a headache, take aspirin; if you have
a heart condition, pop a few nitroglycerine capsules; if you can't
believe you ate the whole thing, take Alka-Seltzer. The problem
with the drug approach is we are masking the symptoms, much as
we do with pain relievers. We don't take the time to get to and resolve the emotional core of what is causing the depression. For a
number of people, drugs do have some side effects, such as difficulty in reaching sexual orgasm. Therapy proponents argue further that depressed patients are less likely to have relapses if they
learn thinking strategies to ward off future depression. In a recent
study at the University of Minnesota, researchers found that
within two years, 50 percent of a medication group relapsed into
depression, while only 20 percent of the therapy group did.

One of the more popular therapies for depression, called Cognitive Psychotherapy, was developed in the 1960s by Aaron Beck,
now at the University of Pennsylvania. Based on the notion that
thought *patterns* create feelings, the cognitive therapist assists the
client to identify distorted destructive perception and beliefs
caused by the depression, which in turn fuels depression.

THOUGHT VIRUS THERAPY FOR DEPRESSION

The corresponding approach in Thought Virus Therapy typically involves handling both the complex trigger virus and the limiting viruses.

THE COMPLEX TRIGGER VIRUS. The internal pictures and self-talk that keep triggering depressing feelings normally take the form of a strategy. What is the particular *sequence* of external and internal perceptions the person must run through to *re-create* the feelings of depression? Once you know the strategy, you can alter it by

- reprogramming it with different steps to lead to a more resourceful state
- interrupting it repeatedly as you run through it, so the strategy becomes scrambled and you can no longer do it
- changing submodalities of the strategy

A useful metaphor for *interrupting the pattern* of a strategy is as follows: Think of a negative state as an old vinyl record in a jukebox. If you press the right button, the record emerges and plays. Suppose each time it plays, you scratch over it with a knife. Soon you'll never be able to play the record again.

THE LIMITING VIRUS. The key question to elicit limiting beliefs connected with loss is, *What does it mean to you that _____ happened?* (You lost your job, your husband left, or you forgot to take out the garbage.) Statements of blaming either yourself or others are likely to emerge.

- "If only I didn't screw up so much at work, I'd still have my job."
- "Why did he leave me for that woman who's thirty years younger than he is? I must be getting old and ugly."
- "Why does that stupid garbage man always show up on time? Doesn't he know it's socially fashionable to be a little late, so I can get out the garbage?"

By asking the further question, *What's important about believing or thinking that way?*, you can elicit the value or positive intent behind the belief. Then it's simply a matter of changing the value or beliefs using Antiviral Remedy 6 or 7 from chapter 4 (pages 81 and 87).

Ron was still in the first stages of grieving—emotional shock. He could not even think about what had happened without experiencing debilitating emotions.

"What do you think about that really intensifies the depression?" I asked.

Tears began streaming down his face. "I see myself all alone in our home," he responded, as he looked up toward his right and then down. One fascinating discovery in NLP is the notion of *eye accessing patterns*.[5] We each have a habit of looking in one direction to remember something we've seen before. We'll look in another direction to remember something we've heard before, and still others for things we have felt, are picturing for the first time, or ideas we are just putting into words. For most people, looking up to the right is the direction to visualize something they've never seen before. Looking down, as Ron did, was either to access self-talk or feelings. Those two steps were apparently part of his strategy to create his feelings of despair. I decided to use a process called the Eye Movement Scrambler to interrupt the pattern of how he was producing such intense feelings of grieving, to interrupt his strategy.[6]

I put my index finger about six inches in front of Ron, up to his left (see position 1 in the illustration). I asked Ron to again picture being alone in the house as he followed my index finger. I moved back and forth between position 1 and position 2 at various speeds for about twenty seconds.

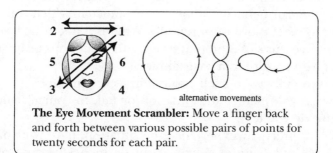

alternative movements

The Eye Movement Scrambler: Move a finger back and forth between various possible pairs of points for twenty seconds for each pair.

"When you think about being alone in the house, what do you experience now?" I asked.

"Well, I don't know. It does feel a little different. It doesn't have quite the edge to it," he said. I asked him to again think about being alone in the home, and to follow my index finger as I moved it between positions 1 and 3 for about twenty seconds, again at various speeds.

"Now what do you experience as you think about the house?"

"As I picture it, it has more color. It's a little closer, and the emotions don't seem to have quite so much charge," he said. I repeated this process for various other combinations of two points, and checked after each to see what changes were taking place. Each time there was some slight shift in *submodalities* of how he pictured his future. Toward the end of this process he began to picture having a new roommate, so he was no longer alone in an empty house, and he seemed to experience much emotional relief. I later repeated the process for other images and self-talk Ron found especially depressing.

Antiviral Remedy 13
The Eye Movement Scrambler

You can do this process on your own, but it is easier with a partner, so you can just focus on your experience. All the partner needs to do is to move his or her finger back and forth between pairs of points at various speeds for fifteen to twenty seconds for each pair. Then pause and reflect on your experience and insights that may have emerged.

1. Think of some situation in life that triggers disempowering emotions or behavior, some circumstance in which you would like to react more resourcefully. What is it about how you experience this situation that triggers the emotions or behavior?
   - Do you picture it in a certain way?
   - Do you talk to yourself about it in a certain way?
   - When you picture the situation or talk to yourself about it, how do you feel?
2. As you internally experience the situation, have your partner put his or her index finger about six inches in front of your eyes, and move back and forth between points 1 and 2 at various speeds for about fifteen to twenty seconds. Pause for a few seconds and describe any shift in how you perceive the situation, or any insights that occur.

3. Repeat this process for various other pairs of points. If you notice that a certain pair feels particularly awkward or uncomfortable, ask your partner not to do that combination, at least
for now. Again, pause between pairs of points and notice insights and shifts in submodalities of your experience.
4. Experiment with figure eights and infinity symbols (∞). (See
the illustration on page 151.)

The Eye Movement Scrambler does more than scramble unproductive strategies. Moving the eyes to different accessing positions can bring in constructive resources from each position that
aren't currently being utilized, i.e., constructive self-talk, putting
new ideas into words, picturing memories of times when you handled trying situations resourcefully. These neurological connec-
tions happen spontaneously and unconsciously.

From here I moved to the next step of therapy with Ron. "When
you picture your ex-wife, how do you see her?" I asked. As it
turned out, she was slightly defocused, she was more black and
white than color, and her image was located slightly to the left of
the center of his visual field. Picturing her this way elicited feelings of sadness, loss, and emptiness.

"Now think of someone who is no longer in your life, but when
you think about this person you feel really good," I said.

"Oh, that would be my uncle Bud," he responded. Color returned to his face, and his facial muscles relaxed. As it turned out,
the image of his uncle had a clearer focus and was more in color
and located higher and more to the left in his field of inner vision.
The primary driver submodality seemed to be *where* the memory
was stored.

"Would any part of you object to picturing your ex-wife in the
same way as you picture your uncle?" Ron did have objecting parts
based on the way his ex-wife had treated him. We used Six-Step Reframing (Antiviral Remedy 8, pages 98–99) to work with issues of
trust, forgiveness, and emotional safety for him in the future. He
finally decided he would like to carry with him the positive memories of what he and his wife had shared. He also wanted to maintain learning from things that hadn't worked, and to let go of
unresourceful feelings. He shifted the image of her *and* images of
some of their happiest moments together, and put them close to
where he thought of his uncle.

Beyond that, we worked with changing some of the negative beliefs about himself that the incident had stirred up. The several sessions we did to accomplish those changes were not a magic bullet, and didn't replace the natural steps of grieving, depression, and healing that the body and mind must pass through. Ron still experienced some ups and downs over the next couple of months. He did report that, after our work, he was able for the first time in a month to sleep through the night and to start regular exercise and running. His appetite returned, and he felt he would be fine without antidepressants.

I also didn't think I needed antidepressants back when I was twenty-six and experiencing depression from losing my job and not being able to find another. Like many people in this country, I was too embarrassed to admit my depression; I erroneously believed it was a weakness of character. This unfortunate attitude is what gets in the way of many people getting the help that can make a difference in enjoying life once again. I just toughed it out.

My friend Kathy, with no apparent cause for her depression, went through four months of unsuccessful therapy and antidepressants before she finally went to another psychiatrist who happened to have some knowledge of environmental science and indoor air pollution. He had read an article about problems that can be associated with gas stoves, and was tipped off by the amount of baking Kathy did. It turned out that Kathy's kitchen had poor ventilation. With the amount of unburned hydrocarbons, nitrogen oxides, and carbon monoxides her oven put out, her kitchen often had worse air quality than downtown Los Angeles during rush hour. Once she replaced the stove with an electric model, her depression vanished. To me this underscores the need for expertise to check out possible physical, medical, or environmental causes of depression, before rushing off to get Prozac.

I also learned a valuable lesson from my bout with depression. It turned out to be a major gift and a turning point in my life. As a result of losing the engineering job, I eventually started substitute teaching part-time, then teaching part-time at a local college. Within two years I was a full-time physics instructor and chairman of the department. Almost everyone I talk with who has experienced major loss tells me that eventually they get to a point where they can look back and see something valuable that came from their experience. It's too bad we can't look at it that way while we are going through it, but things are not always the way they initially appear.

Tony Robbins suggests that appropriate power questions, such as the following, can reframe the meaning of what has happened and move us toward looking at it in a more positive light.

- "What does ——— [the loss, changes, etc.] mean to me?" (To elicit possible limiting beliefs). "How does this way of thinking benefit me?"
- "How specifically do I manage to get myself depressed?" (To elicit your strategy)
- "How might I one day be able to look back and see how beneficial this change has been for me or for the people around me?"
- "What am I willing to do to have things be the way I want them to be?" (Problem-solving experts suggest spending 80 percent of your time on the solution, and only 20 percent of your time on the problem.)

Cultivate a sense of curiosity, as if you were a detective trying to figure out how you depress yourself, what the events mean to you, and how the changes might be moving you in a more positive direction in life.

After my initial annoyance when I picked up the brown apple from my dashboard, when I realized I would not have my afternoon snack, curiosity got the best of me. It was really hot inside the car, the way it gets with the windows rolled up on a hot summer day. I had just learned that this is an example of the Greenhouse Effect. Carbon dioxide and other gases trap radiant ground heat, prevent it from escaping, and cause global warming. The glass in a greenhouse or a car lets in sunlight, but also blocks radiant heat from escaping. It can get up to 150 degrees Fahrenheit inside a parked car, on a hot, sunny day, so I assumed heat had accelerated the decay of my apple. I was puzzled, though, that the brown apple had a pleasant smell to it. I bravely took a bite. To my delight, I tasted my first solar-baked apple.

Things aren't always the way they appear to be. Now, if you walk by my car, parked at my college on any workday in September or October, you will see an apple baking on my dashboard for my afternoon snack.

9

ALLERGIES

Janet was gasping for breath, just barely clinging to life, as she arrived at the hospital emergency room. At only seven years old, her allergic reaction to a honeybee's sting—anaphylactic shock—was close to ending her short childhood. Dr. Lu rushed to administer epinephrine, the one medication that might allow her swollen throat muscles to relax so she could breath again. "If Janet recovers," Dr. Lu predicted, "she will have to carry epinephrine with her the rest of her life, for whenever she might get stung again."

Ironically, our immune systems, while serving the purpose of protecting us, can also *mistakenly* bring on detrimental symptoms, and in rare cases can wind up killing us. And so an estimated 35 to 50 million Americans have immune systems that overreact to mostly harmless substances and produce allergies. Symptoms include sneezing, runny nose, itchy, watery eyes, excess swelling, and occasionally shock and even death. Allergies account for about 10 percent of all doctor visits. In one study of 4,000 allergy sufferers,

- 86 percent experienced chronic rhinitis or hay fever, i.e., allergy to pollen
- 77 percent were allergic to dusts and dust mites
- 54 percent were allergic to animal fur and dander
- 10 percent were allergic to insects and insect bites or stings

Others include food allergies, allergies to perfumes and toxic chemicals, and recently a rise in allergy to latex gloves among

156

physicians and dentists who must routinely wear them to protect against the possible spread of AIDS.[1]

ALLERGIES AND TRIGGER VIRUSES

Stress is known to aggravate allergies. It may also be that certain stressful situations or environmental stimuli other than allergens actually trigger allergic responses. In one experiment, guinea pigs were given a foreign protein that produced allergies. At the same time, they were exposed to a certain odor. After doing this procedure on only five separate occasions, the odor by itself was enough to induce the allergic response.[2] In another experiment, rats were given egg whites, which produced allergies, and they were simultaneously exposed to blinking lights and a humming sound. Again, after doing this several times, the blinking and humming was sufficient to induce the allergic symptoms.[3]

Researchers have also demonstrated that stressful situations can compromise immune system functioning. When we feel sad or depressed, the brain produces neuropeptides and neurotransmitters that inhibit the immune system, so we are more prone to getting sick. Deepak Chopra describes an experiment in which one group of rats was given substances to inhibit immune system functioning, while simultaneously being exposed to the odor of camphor. A second group of rats was given a substance to enhance immune system functioning, while again being exposed to the smell of camphor. After repeating the process several times, the smell of camphor by itself was enough to suppress the immune systems of the first group of rats, and enhance the immune systems of the second group.

Some have suggested that if we are naturally in an emotional state that has suppressed our immune system, or we are experiencing some flu-like sickness, and *simultaneously* we experience the pollen, the cat, the food, the odor, or the dust mites, the unconscious may erroneously link or anchor the two together. The allergic response may be more the result of how we *think* than a purely physiological reaction. This point of view is certainly supported by studies of people with multiple personality syndrome (MPS). It is not uncommon for one personality to have allergies and another to be free of them. Here we have the same person, and the same allergens. What is the difference? The only possible difference is in the way the personalities *think*.

THE ALLERGY VIRUSES

From the viewpoint of many people in the medical community, an allergy is caused by a mistake in the immune system. I suggest it is a thought virus involving a deeply unconscious limiting belief and a trigger—i.e., the allergen. The immune system has white blood cells whose job is to remove foreign particles, such as pollen and cat dander, from the system. The body generates these white blood cells in the bone marrow, and can produce millions in a few minutes. You might say, then, that in reaction to foreign particles, the immune system *learns* very quickly. In many people the immune system can also produce a specific antibody, *immunoglobulin E* (IgE), that appears to have no function except to produce allergic symptoms. IgE attaches itself to receptor sites, called mast cells, in our connective tissue. The mast cells in turn release histamine and other substances that can give rise to allergic symptoms. From the perspective of Thought Virus Therapy, the limiting belief is that the immune system misidentifies allergens as invading viruses. It then responds inappropriately with IgE, inflamed sinuses, runny nose, swelling, watering eyes, and so on.

Some people lose days from work as a direct result of allergies. For almost everyone else, having allergies compromises the immune system's ability to do its proper job, to ward off disease. The immune system is mobilized by the false alarm raised by the presence of allergens, so the individual is more prone to colds, flu, and other diseases. In one study of children who experienced multiple middle-ear infections, 81 percent turned out to be allergic to certain foods. When they were taken off the offending foods, 70 percent of them experienced improved health over the four-month study while they avoided the foods. After returning to the foods for several months, 60 percent of them again had clogged ears.[4]

The fact that, physiologically, the allergic reaction is as complex as it is leads some researchers to speculate that it wouldn't have survived evolution if it didn't have some positive purpose. Some have suggested the allergic response helps fight off parasites, such as worms, ticks, chiggers, and lice. Others believe it is a backup defense or a warning system against toxins. The price we pay for the system's false alarms is allergies.

Some years ago, Robert Dilts developed a simple mind/body technique designed to retrain the immune system to react appropriately to allergens. Tim Hallbom and Suzi Smith, major NLP trainers, modified the technique and presented it in my Practitioner Certification course.[5] One of my colleagues told the story of what happened shortly after Dilts developed the technique. My colleague had just learned of it, and got instructions on a pay phone, so he wrote them down on a napkin. He was attending a hotel conference, so he started back to the meetings.

On the way back he encountered a man in the elevator who was allergic to most foods. In fact, this man had only a few foods left that he could eat without getting sick. My colleague quickly ran through the technique with this man, and warned him to be very slow and careful in testing his response to the offending foods. The appropriate test was to take just a few bites of something that, in the past, had produced only a mild reaction. With success, the man could gradually try out small quantities of other foods. The man agreed, shook my colleague's hand, then proceeded straight to the dining room, where he ordered wine and steak with mushroom sauce—probably the worst possible foods for his former condition. The man could easily have gotten quite sick, and possibly died, but fortunately the technique worked. The man was well on his way to enjoying a variety of foods.

WARNING: Certain allergies can be life-threatening. If your symptoms are severe or have the potential to be severe, consult your physician, work only with a professional trained in these methods, and make sure your physician is present at the therapy session.

Therapists and medical doctors using the technique have reported it to be completely effective in 80 percent of cases in which the allergy is specific and known to the client—that is, in which the allergy is to a specific animal, a specific odor, a specific plant, or a specific food. In the case of such nonspecific allergies as hay fever, the technique can work, but is much less reliable. This may be because the specific allergen is unknown, and possibly because it is more difficult to find a counterexample—something similar to the allergen, but without the allergic response. It is also important to note that this, as well as any other mental technique, cannot claim to be a *cure* for any health condition. Providing "cures" is the domain of the medical profession. All the practitioner or consultant does is to guide the client through processes whereby the client's unconscious mind can begin the healing or at least become free of the symptoms.

FREEDOM FROM HAY FEVER

Marie was a client I consulted with on a number of issues. Her sinuses were partially blocked most of the time from allergies caused by various pollens and dusts, which can be found most times of the year along the central California coast. I had not thought to work with her specifically on the allergies, because the technique is less reliable with the nonspecific and mostly unknown allergies that Marie experienced.

I was vacationing one summer at an isolated and remote valley resort in a coastal range in central California. Even though we were only about thirty or forty miles from the coast as the seagull flies, the climate was considerably different and the air had a different feeling to it. The days were warmer, the nights were balmy, and the air was drier than at my home on the coast. Still, the valley was lush with vegetation owing to creeks and streams that flowed through it.

One day I met Marie there. I asked how she was doing, and she said, "Great." She wasn't experiencing her allergies at this little oasis.

"Would you like to add an allergy session to your vacation plans?" I asked. I wasn't sure how well it would work, given how nonspecific her allergies were, but I saw a window of opportunity during these few days when she was free of the symptoms.

"Well, I don't normally mix vacation and therapy, but I sure would love to get rid of the allergies if there is a chance," she said. I began to help her set up a well-formed outcome following the guidelines on pages 130–33 of this book.

- *The vision.* Marie wanted to experience clear sinuses and dry eyes even in the presence of high levels of pollen or dust.
- *The signpost.* The specific evidence of achieving her outcome in her case was the same as the vision—clear sinuses and dry eyes.

- *Feasibility.* She believed that it was possible for people in general to get beyond allergic symptoms, that it was possible for her, and that she deserved the results. Her body language indicated to me that she was congruent in her beliefs.

From here we checked for possible *secondary gains.* When she experienced allergic symptoms, she continued with her daily life, and was not aware of any sympathy from others or any other benefit for having the allergies; it was simply an annoyance. The pollen and dust that triggered her allergies were benign and presented no health threat, so there didn't appear to be a *context* in which the allergies would be useful.

A crucial piece in the allergy technique is to identify a *counterexample,* something that produces no allergic response, yet is similar to the allergic trigger. If the person is allergic to cats but not to dogs, dogs would serve as a good counterexample. The person may be allergic to beestings, but maybe not to wasp stings or ant bites. In Marie's situation, we had the perfect counterexample all around us.

"Did you notice all the flowers and blossoms here at this facility?" I asked. She nodded. "You know what that means, don't you? The air here is loaded with pollen. It's probably different from the pollen at your home on the coast, but there is probably just as much here. Your immune system must already know how to handle pollen appropriately, at least the kind that's here." That hadn't occurred to her, so she looked surprised. I then began the antiviral remedy.

"I'd like you to imagine a large, thick plate of Plexiglas sliding down in front of you to protect you from whatever is happening on the other side. Can you do that and picture yourself on the other side of the glass?" Again she nodded. "I'd like you to see yourself out in front of the glass, being here at this beautiful retreat facility, surrounded with all this pollen, yet your immune system is responding appropriately. Notice how good it feels to have clear sinuses and dry eyes."

"That's easy, because I'm already here, experiencing this. It does feel good not to have the allergies," she said.

"While you are noticing how that feels, let me touch you here on the elbow to stabilize your experience." I reached over and touched the back of her left elbow to set up a trigger for her resourceful way of handling pollen. While continuing to hold her elbow, I said, "Now, I'd like you to imagine *that* Marie, out there in front of the Plexiglas, back at your home on the coast, handling the pollen in the same appropriate way you are handling it here. Can you see her doing that?"

She paused a few minutes and said, "Yes. I can see *her* doing that, but I'm not sure about *me*."

"Good. Now, *that* Marie, out there, has something that could be very useful for you. Her immune system knows the right way to handle pollen back home. Is there any part of you that would object to your being able to handle pollen in the same way?" I asked this to do the ecology check. Once the unconscious knows how the desired change can take place, if objecting parts are present, they will emerge. She assured me no parts objected, and again her body language seemed congruent.

"Good. Now imagine the Plexiglas sliding back up, and *that* Marie out there walking toward you with the gift of an immune system that reacts appropriately to pollen. Allow her to merge back into your heart only as fast as you can integrate her gift for you." I continued holding her elbow as she allowed internal feelings and sensations to settle. She smiled and said the process felt good.

I future-paced our work by letting go of her elbow and having her imagine, without the Plexiglas, being back home.

"That feels okay, just like being here, but is that all there is to the process?" Her skepticism was typical of people experiencing this technique.

"Not everyone is successful with this technique, and I can't guarantee that you'll be among the 80 percent of people who experience complete freedom from the symptoms by simply doing what we just did. The process *is* quite simple, and often the people who get the best results are the ones like you, who question the process. It will be clear when you go home, whether or not this process has worked for you," I said.

When she returned home, she was completely free from the chronic hay fever. Furthermore, when she traveled to other parts of the country that have different and likely higher concentrations of pollen than California, she remained free of the allergies. I have a feeling that an important piece, when working with nonspecific allergies like Marie's, is to be able to work in an environment where the client is temporarily symptom-free, yet you can locate a good counterexample. In our case, things just happened to work out that way. Marie's results continued for about six months, until she began experiencing stressful personal circumstances. At that point the allergic symptoms started reappearing.

Some might say, "See, the method didn't work." I would respond, "What do you mean, it didn't work? It worked for six months! All she needs is more conditioning and follow-up." I did another session with Marie, and the allergies again disappeared.

Without this simple technique, Marie would have been sentenced to a lifetime of antihistamines and various drugs to mask her symptoms, just as seven-year-old Janet would be sentenced to a life of carrying epinephrine, were she to live.

Dr. Lu did manage to save her, and she carried the epinephrine with her until, as an adult, she went to see a major NLP trainer in Colorado to experience the allergy technique. Afterward she was skeptical, just as Marie and many others are. She did become more lax about carrying the epinephrine with her, and one day, while not carrying it, she was stung by another bee. She felt a surge of panic, not knowing whether the technique would work, and immediately called her doctor, who asked her to calm down and simply observe the symptoms before she called 911. The only reaction she had was the normal one for beestings—some redness and swelling in the immediate vicinity of the sting. Janet still carries the epinephrine with her, but is optimistic she will never again need to use it.

10

CANCER

Lhasa, Tibet—the "rooftop of the world." A French pilgrim, Alexandra David-Neel, secretly enters Tibet to see what some of the world's leading experts on mind/body control can do, and is astounded at what happens. She reports observing monks sitting naked in the snow, drying water-soaked sheets with mere body heat.[1]

Many years later in the early 1980s, Robert Benson, a Harvard cardiologist and author of *The Relaxation Response*, was encouraged by the Dalai Lama to see for himself. He wired up monks with electronic sensing devices to monitor physiological changes, while they dried sheets in the frigid cold of the Himalayan landscape. Soon the sheets began to steam as the monks' skin temperatures rose by as much as seventeen degrees. No doubt, if an ordinary person tried this, he would shiver uncontrollably and quite possibly die.

If the mind is capable of such miraculous feats as this, what might it be able to accomplish in other areas of life, such as healing? After all, healing does take place unconsciously. You don't have to think about how you are going to heal a cut, or how you are going to rid yourself of a cold. Occasionally a person's unconscious mind even finds a way to rid the body of a life-threatening, "incurable" disease such as cancer through a spontaneous remission.

Is there an unconscious connection between how we think and the likelihood of either contracting or avoiding cancer? Does this disease only happen because of unhealthy lifestyles, environmental factors, and bad genes, or can a *cancer thought virus* play a part? If certain personalities *are* more prone to cancer, could Thought Virus Therapy reduce one's chances of getting the disease or enhance one's chances of recovery? And if healthy or unhealthy thinking can play a part in cancer, why did my friend Dana, who was congruent and powerful in so much of her thinking, die from this disease?

AN OUNCE OF PREVENTION

Dana was one of a half-million Americans per year who now die from cancer. The form she contracted, ovarian cancer, is particularly deadly, with only about 15 percent of its victims surviving. The two-decades-old "war" on cancer, heart disease, and other degenerative conditions initially sought to seek a cure for those afflictions. More recently, however, research has turned toward finding defective genes. Ovarian cancer did run in Dana's family, and genetic researchers have now isolated a gene that predisposes women to getting the disease. It is likely she had the gene. No doubt, genes do play a part, but what genetics doesn't explain are facts like these:

- Not all of the most damaging cancers are inherited. The vast majority of victims begin life with healthy genes.
- Remissions from cancer can and do occur.
- The occurrence of all cancers except lung cancer has increased 35 percent since 1950.
- Not all people with genetic predispositions to certain cancers get them.
- Americans are five times more likely to develop certain cancers than are people in some Pacific Rim countries, and up to *fifty times* more likely than in some "less developed" countries.[2]

Modern medicine seems better equipped to deal with acute illness, injury, and infection than with diseases that progress slowly, over years and sometimes decades. Such chronic degenerative diseases as cancer are doubly tragic, because for many people they are preventable. When Dana finished having children, she even went so far as to have *one* of her ovaries removed as a precaution, since her mother and other family members had died from ovarian cancer. Unfortunately, the other ovary spawned the cancer years later.

We now know that many of the general risk factors—smoking, a fatty diet, a sedentary lifestyle, toxic dusts and chemicals, and genetic predisposition—increase the likelihood of contracting cancer. However, finding a cure and the real cause still eludes us. Over a decade ago, John Cairns of Harvard pointed out the folly of spending hundreds of millions of dollars on chemotherapy while doing little if anything to protect the population from smoking, which by itself accounts for about 30 percent of all deaths from cancer.

Knowledge is there. If we know how diet and lifestyle affect health, then why do people continue to smoke, or eat a poor diet, or continue to postpone physical fitness? The answer is that it feels good, it tastes good, and exercise may feel like too much work. Like any other thought virus—refusing to accept reality in the face of extensive scientific research, *or* feeling that "I am an exception; those other people might get sick, but that could never happen to me"—these glitches in thinking have a positive intent.

Making any real headway in reducing or eliminating cancer needs to be on the level of *prevention*. We need the courage to discover and face up to all those factors that increase our chances of contracting these diseases. We need mass educational programs and effective methods to *motivate* ourselves and our children to get rid of distorted thinking and to make appropriate changes, even if special-interest lobbies object. We need to teach and learn *healthy* ways to feel good, and to seek life-supporting recipes that satisfy our need for good-tasting food.

Powerful as her thinking was, Dana was not entirely free from thinking that could impair her health. A year before the cancer was discovered, Dana went through a traumatic breakup of an engagement to a man she dearly loved. She left the West Coast, moved to Florida, and went though nearly a year of grieving. Sometime during that period, the cancer began. Some researchers suggest a strong correlation between the onset of cancer and a significant emotional experience happening one to two years before. In Dana's case the genetic predisposition was lurking like a time bomb, but was it mere coincidence that the emotional trauma immediately preceded the cancer, or did the experience trigger the disease?

SPONTANEOUS REMISSIONS

One of the most spectacular examples of the unconscious mind applying itself to healing is spontaneous remission—those rare situations in which the body, for no apparent reason, suddenly heals itself of some incurable disease. Spontaneous remissions have been documented in all types of cancer, and in most other diseases from diabetes to warts. Only a few of the half-million Americans who contract cancer each year have the good fortune to experience a spontaneous remission, and in my life I have met several such people.

Five years ago I was attending a weekend training session in NLP as applied to health issues and healing. About one-third of the participants were medical doctors. I had the pleasure of meeting the mother, whom I'll call Roberta, of one of our trainers, whom I'll call Jeffrey. Ten years prior to this workshop, Roberta had been diagnosed with a terminal case of leukemia and a cancerous tumor. Treatment of either condition would aggravate the other, so the doctors had given up on her. They told her she had about six months left to live, so the best advice they could offer was to decide how she wanted to spend her last six months.

When she told her son Jeffrey about her prognosis, he began Thought Virus Therapy and questioned her in detail about her beliefs and values. Prior to discovery of her condition, she had been a bit of a workaholic, working long hours and complaining constantly that she was "dying to take a vacation." As you might imagine, Jeffrey was concerned about her language pattern and what her unconscious might be saying. He discovered that part of her unconscious did want her to heal. Another part of her, however, felt that healing herself would be an insult to her own mother, her grandmother, and other women in her family who had died from cancer. This was a deeply unconscious belief she had never been aware of. She was suffering from a killer virus that had conflicting parts (a Gemini virus) and limiting beliefs as major components.

Shortly after my training, I heard Deepak Chopra tell the story of a young Indian woman with advanced breast cancer that had metastasized. When she came to see Dr. Chopra, she was undergoing chemotherapy even though her condition seemed hopeless. Understandably, she was quite nervous and frightened by her condition and prognosis.

As she continued both traditional and nontraditional healing methods, her fear and nervousness disappeared. Furthermore, her outlook on her situation greatly improved. Unfortunately, her physical condition continued to deteriorate. One day, when Dr.

Chopra called her home to see how she was doing, her parents said she had gotten quite sick and was in the hospital. Fearing the worst, Dr. Chopra went to visit her. She had a very high fever and her vital signs were slipping. After some time, however, the fever broke, and her vital signs signs normalized. Shortly after this sickness, she received X rays to monitor the progress of her tumors. The doctors were astonished to discover that the tumors had completely disappeared. Hers was another rare case of spontaneous remission.

Experiencing a high fever just prior to a remission is not uncommon. Some researchers suggest that the immune system suddenly "recognizes" cancer cells as being foreign. It then kicks into high gear, producing the fever and destroying malignant cells, much the way it would destroy cells infected with viruses.

MIND/BODY HEALING

Four thousand years ago the great Indian sage Mahabarata defined two types of disease, those that affect the body and those that affect the mind. Each type arises from the other and cannot exist without the other. Bodily diseases arise from faulty thinking, and diseases of the mind arise from physical disorders. Until recently, such thinking was likely to draw loud protests and skepticism from the medical community, who typically would even dismiss miraculous cancer remissions as diagnostic errors. However, the discovery of neurotransmitters and neuropeptides has changed that.

Neuropeptides and neurotransmitters are messenger molecules produced by the brain for each emotional state we experience. The brain produces them and each cell in the body has neuroreceptors for receiving them. Through these chemical messages, our moods and emotions affect our organs, our immune system, and our endocrine system. When we feel powerful and invincible, our brains produce a chemical similar to interleukin 2, one of the most powerful substances known to destroy cancer cells. When we feel calm and settled, we produce a natural tranquilizer similar to Valium. When we feel depressed and hopeless, we produce higher levels of cortisol, which suppresses the immune system. This biochemical connection between emotions and immune system functioning has led to a field of study called *psychoneuroimmunology* or PNI.

Thoughts and feelings are mediated by certain neuropeptides and neurotransmitters. Diseases stimulate production of certain others, and the healing response may also involve different ones. Purely mental techniques can produce changes in the physiology. Extensive research has shown transcendental meditation (TM) to be effective in reducing blood pressure, effecting blood platelets and norepinephrine receptors, and reducing cortisol levels. Mental imagery methods have been shown to increase natural killer cell functioning to fight metastatic cancer.

The key issue, then, with PNI as applied to cancer is this:

• If certain thinking patterns and positive states of consciousness enhance immune system functioning, do these decrease the likelihood of a person getting cancer or increase the chance of a spontaneous remission if they already have the disease?
• If certain thought viruses and negative states inhibit immune system functioning, do these increase a person's likelihood of getting cancer or decrease their likelihood of recovering once they have contracted the disease?

IN SEARCH OF A CANCER THOUGHT VIRUS

Heidelberg, Germany, 1988. A group of distinguished American scientists arrives to confront Ronald Grossarth-Maticek, a relatively unknown psychologist from the former Yugoslavia.[3] Grossarth-Maticek has reported findings of the most extensive and sophisticated research on the connection of thought patterns with coronary heart disease and cancer. The results, if they hold up, could prove to be one of the most significant findings in medicine since penicillin. His studies essentially implicate faulty thinking, i.e., thought viruses, as a highly significant factor in developing cancer, as well as in how quickly the disease progresses.

Grossarth-Maticek, through long-term studies extending up to thirteen years, claims to have identified personality traits that are more reliable than anything else we know of in predicting the likelihood of someone getting cancer. He claims doing appropriate preventive counseling and therapy with at-risk personalities have produced results that are astounding—almost too good to be true.

The medical profession and many traditionalists have reacted with loud cries of protest and skepticism. They are quick to point out some inconsistencies in the numbers and the methodology. No one, however, has been able to knock down Grossarth-Maticek's numbers. Furthermore, Hans Eysenck, one of the world's best-known and most highly respected psychologists, has reviewed the work extensively and is convinced of its accuracy. He has collaborated with Grossarth-Maticek in developing and testing psychotherapy to prevent the onset of cancer or to slow down its progress once it has started.

Exercise 20
How Healthy Is Your Thinking?

These questions are based in part on a questionnaire developed by Eysenck and Grossarth-Maticek to prescreen people to see how the way they think and the way they experience emotions may impact their physical health. Answer these questions about yourself and note for each if the answer is true, rarely or frequently.

1. Do you prefer solitude as opposed to being with others?
2. Have you noticed, over the past ten years, that you have re-peatedly done things that have reaped negative emotional consequences from people who are important to you, and have you been frustrated in unsuccessfully trying to improve your interactions with these people?
3. During the last ten years, have you frequently experienced feelings of helplessness or hopelessness due to loss of a major relationship, loss of a job, or failure to achieve outcomes for yourself or to fulfill important emotional needs such as love, recognition, understanding, achievement, or success?
4. Have you consistently felt lonely or emotionally isolated dur-ing the last ten years?
5. When you consider the last ten years, have you often longed to be closer emotionally with a person or people, yet been frus-trated because the person died, there was a divorce or separa-tion, or the person just didn't understand you and created distance from you?

6. Do you regularly experience fear and anxiety—fears of being threatened, persecuted, or just unable to cope with life's problems—fears of things you potentially would have the ability to do something about or avoid if you were in a more resourceful state?
7. Do you have difficulty in expressing emotions, especially anger?
8. Over the past ten years have you been unable to maintain a consistent balance of daily life with *physical* recreation for enjoyment—such as exercise, sports, sex, or dancing?

Those who frequently experience the situations or emotions in the previous exercise may be more prone to cancer than the average person.

A CANCER VIRUS

Aside from smoking, lack of exercise, poor diet, genetic predisposition, and environmental toxins, what may ultimately *trigger* cancer is a killer virus with all three components: internal conflict (a Gemini virus), disempowering triggers, and limiting beliefs. These result in three distinct personality traits:

- inability to express negative emotions such as fear, anxiety, and especially anger
- inability to cope with stress, which results in a tendency toward feelings of helplessness, hopelessness, and depression
- a tendency toward social isolation and loneliness

Let's take a closer look at each component.

THE GEMINI VIRUS. Some NLP researchers who deal extensively with chronic degenerative disease suggest that a key emotional component of cancer is the internal conflict due to mismanagement of emotions.

Starting early in life, many of us have gotten a clear message from parents, teachers, siblings, and friends—negative emotions, especially anger, are not okay. As a result, we wind up disconnecting ourselves one way or another from our negative emotions. Negative emotions, like any other parts of us, have a positive intent, some gift for us, some way of serving us. We lose that gift by shutting off the emotions or distorting their positive intent.

As an example, when you experience fear and the fight-or-flight response, it serves a crucial evolutionary purpose, namely survival. Your veins pump with adrenaline, your heart rate speeds, blood pressure increases, alertness is heightened. Your mind and body are mobilized to engage in combat or to run away.

On the other hand, part of you realizes that neither fight nor flight may be appropriate, since what triggered your response was criticism from your boss, someone cutting in line at the movie theater, or a person giving you an obscene gesture on the interstate. There you are, steaming, with adrenaline damaging your arteries. If your thinking is cancer-prone, you will probably stuff the feelings, smile politely, and be in conflict with yourself. The body is experiencing the feelings, while the mind is denying them. You may then feel depressed because people are so mean and unfair to *you*. Elevated cortisol further damages your arteries and weakens your immune system, so you are less capable of dealing with internal menaces such as cancer cells.

A dear friend of mine, Lynn, at eighteen years old, was in the hospital with a life-threatening condition. A nurse told Lynn that if she cried, she would have to go out into the hallway. Since this meant disconnecting her life-support apparatus, Lynn thought that if she cried, she might die. Thirty years later, Lynn still can't cry, and she distorts feelings of sadness that could lead to tears and emotional release.

Recent studies on men with lung cancer and women with breast cancer have supported this point of view, and have brought to light a tendency for cancer victims to be overpatient, under-assertive, and lacking in the ability to express negative emotions.

DISEMPOWERING TRIGGERS. The trigger-virus component can automatically elicit unresourceful emotions such as helplessness, hopelessness, or depression as a response to stressful circumstances. In one British study, women who had breast cancer surgery followed by a life-changing stressful event such as a divorce, loss of a job, death of a spouse, or a forced relocation, were five times more likely to have a recurrence of breast cancer, as compared with more stress-free patients.

A trigger can also be destructive in eliciting negative emotions that are far out of proportion to the situation at hand.

LIMITING BELIEFS. Limiting beliefs about ourselves and the lack of value in reaching out to others may be a key factor. These result in social isolation and loneliness.

A Johns Hopkins study divided 1,000 men into five groups based on personality traits. People who were loners *and* were un-expressive emotionally were sixteen times more likely to contract cancer than the most risk-free group. The fact that a higher per-centage of married people at every age survive cancer, compared with singles, also supports the Hopkins findings on loneliness.

Limiting beliefs on possible "benefits" of the disease can lead to internal conflict. In the case of Roberta, the mother of my trainer Jeffrey, part of her was committed to working excessively, while an-other part of her was "dying to take a vacation." When her cancer and leukemia were discovered, part of her wanted to heal, but another, deeply unconscious part felt that to do so would be an insult to her mother, her grandmother, and other women in her family who had died from cancer.

"But what about *your* daughter, and *her* daughter? What's going to happen to them if this belief continues?" Jeffrey asked.

"Oh!" Roberta looked perplexed. Her unconscious had simply not gotten that far. Jeffrey then helped her to change these and other beliefs that stood in the way of her healing.

Limiting beliefs connected with how we visualize the disease process (V^i) can also either stand in our way *or* assist healing. Pro-ponents of PNI frequently change the way a person visualizes the internal workings of the disease as a way to heal the condition. Jef-frey asked Roberta to go inside and mentally see what was going on with her body.

"It's like hills and fields being overgrown with weeds," she said. "The weeds are taking over."

SUPPORTING RESEARCH[4]

Short-term studies designed to connect personality and cancer potentially have one major flaw. Does the personality give rise to the disease, or is the personality a result of already having the disease or early stages? Prior to Grossarth-Maticek's research in the former Yugoslavia, there were no studies of a long enough duration and a large enough scale to answer this question.

In the early 1960s Grossarth-Maticek began his research and

carried out several long term studies of ten or more years with thousands of randomly selected individuals. He divided the subjects into four groups: type 1, who he suspected would be cancer-prone; type 2, who he thought might be prone to cardiovascular disease; and types 3 and 4, who he felt were relatively more healthy emotionally. He categorized them by questionnaires and extensive interviews. The most important questions involved tendency toward helplessness/hopelessness, rational/antisocial behavior, and inability to express anger toward traumatic events in life. Exercise 20 has questions that are similar to a questionnaire published by Hans Eysenck, based on the work of Grossarth-Maticek.

Of the people in the cancer-prone group (according to Grossarth-Maticek), 50 percent in fact died from cancer during the ten years or so of the study, while only 10 percent died from other causes. Hans Eysenck points out that if these kinds of results hold up, from the viewpoint of statistics, personality would yield a six times higher probability of predicting cancer than cigarette smoking. However, don't let this sway you from quitting smoking, because nearly a third of all cancers are caused by cigarette smoke.

Hans Eysenck then collaborated with Grossarth-Maticek to answer the crucial question: Can behavior modification with cancer-prone people lower their risks of contracting cancer? They selected 100 cancer-prone people and divided them into two groups of fifty. One group received thirty hours of individual therapy involving desensitization, relaxation, expression of emotions, stress management, and generally *modeling* how more emotionally healthy people behave. In Eysenck's words, the results were astonishing. After thirteen years, 90 percent of the therapy group was still alive, while only 38 percent of the non-therapy subjects still survived.

The value of appropriate therapy certainly far outweighs the time and expense. Still, many people might think of thirty hours as being excessive, so Grossarth-Maticek and Eysenck repeated the experiment using group therapy and shorter individual counseling periods. The results still showed a marked difference between the therapy versus the nontherapy subjects. More recent research at Stanford University has found that therapy can increase survival time for people who already have cancer. The well-known Stanford study showed an average survival time of thirty-five months for women with breast cancer who received group therapy, as opposed to only nineteen months for the control group.

This research suggests that faulty thinking in the form of thought viruses may be as important as, or even more important than, the known risk factors and genetic predisposition. Given that some skeptics still question the European study, it is crucial to replicate the results. Because the research is so long-term, we may not have replication until the turn of the millennium.

THOUGHT VIRUS THERAPY

The most important therapy connected with cancer and other chronic degenerative diseases has to be prevention. The research is clear. Many if not most of us can reduce the likelihood of contracting one of these diseases or preventing it altogether.

BEGIN WITH PHYSIOLOGY. Following the usual guidelines related to smoking cessation, low-fat diet with lots of fresh fruits and vegetables, exercise, limited exposure to sunlight and environmental toxins, and regular physical checkups is just plain sanity.

Next, consider cultivating a low-risk personality.

RESOLVE TOXIC GEMINI VIRUSES. The most important one is likely mismanaging negative emotions. Part of us feels the negative emotion loud and clear, while another part tries to push the feeling away, deny expressing the feeling, or deny even having the feeling. We can resolve inner conflict by reframing the meaning of the emotion, asking power questions about the emotion, or resolving reluctance to express the emotion. Behind the feelings of the emotion there is a message, a gift. Painful feelings are the unconscious's way of getting our attention.

Exercise 21
Reframing Your Negative Emotions

1. List some of the negative emotions you experience most regularly (anger, hurt, overwhelming feelings, loneliness, etc.).
2. Suppose that for each of these emotions your unconscious was trying to communicate a meaning, some call to action through experiencing that emotion. If this was true, write

down what the meaning would be for you. Do this for each negative emotion.

In his best-selling book *Awaken the Giant Within*,[5] Tony Robbins provides some insightful and valuable ways to interpret a number of negative emotions. See how these compare with yours.

EMOTION	MEANING
Anger	You, someone else, or circumstances have violated your rules, beliefs, or standards of the way things "should be." *Remember, other people and the way things happen in the world don't always work by your standards.*
Disappointment	Some expectation or goal has been lost or is no longer achievable. *It is time for the flexibility to reset your goal or expectation.*
Fear	This is a caution signal, like a yellow light, that something is about to happen. *Beware and be prepared to take action.*
Frustration	Some goal or expectation *you still believe is possible* hasn't happened yet. *Find a new approach to make it happen or reevaluate whether the expectation is realistic.*
Guilt and shame	You have violated your own or someone else's standards. *Assess those standards to see if they are realistic and empowering, or find ways not to violate them again.*
Hurt	Someone has violated *your* rules or standards and you connect loss with that violation—loss of love, respect, or appreciation for you. *Again, the other may not have the same beliefs or rules, and there may be no loss at all.*
Overwhelming feelings	You are attempting to do too much at once. *It is time to re-prioritize things, so you can focus on what's most important to you. Chunk things down so you do one step at a time.*

Understanding the positive intent of negative emotions is a first step toward making peace with them. Beyond that, it is valuable to evaluate the appropriateness of the emotion to the circumstances at hand.

Antiviral Remedy 14
Power Questions for Negative Emotions

When a negative emotion arises, especially a habitual one, cultivate a sense of curiosity about it and ask yourself a few questions:

1. "Is what I'm feeling really _____ [anger, hurt, sadness, etc.],
   or is there some other feeling that is even more important for
   me to be aware of?" An alternative question to put you in
   touch with what you are really experiencing is, "What am I
   really afraid of here?"
2. "What is the message behind the feeling? What does my unconscious want for me through feeling this feeling?"
3. "Is the intensity of what I'm feeling really appropriate to the
   situation?" If that freeway driver I don't even know has given
   me an obscene gesture, maybe it's not appropriate to allow the
   situation to escalate into a violent confrontation. On the other
   hand, when someone is obviously being rude to me, maybe I
   should allow myself to feel and express more anger than I'm
   normally willing to.

Finally, if you regularly experience negative emotions you have
difficulty expressing, use Six-Step Reframing (pages 98–99) to resolve the inner conflict behind expressing your feelings.

DEACTIVATE DANGEROUS TRIGGERS. What can be particularly toxic to
us is the way we respond to stress. The problem may not be so
much the stressful event itself, but how we make meaning—that is,
the response *automatically triggered* in us. There are many books,
workshops, and consultants who teach life-supporting ways to handle stress. The only problem I have with their suggestions is that
you have to think about them. When confronted with stressful
triggers, you have to remember to do what they've suggested.
That's not always easy, especially when you are caught up in a
stressful confrontation or avoiding one.

One of the simplest techniques that you don't have to think
about is meditation. Extensive research with people practicing
TM shows lower blood pressure (for hypertensive individuals);
reduced levels of cortisol; reduced incidence of anxiety, hostility,
depression; and increased self-esteem and ability to relate with
others. These changes, which move you away from disease-prone
thinking, occur naturally and spontaneously.

Aside from unresourceful reaction to stress, another dangerous trigger may be involved when negative emotions are way out of proportion to the circumstance, and that particular circumstance always produces the same emotion. Here it is likely you are dealing with a common trigger virus. Use Antiviral Remedy 3 (page 58) to collapse the anchor or, even better, Antiviral Remedy 4 (pages 61–62) to reverse the trigger. What if a rude waitress *automatically* triggered a sense of compassion that she must be having a bad day? Or suppose that instead of a feeling of rejection, your friend's criticism *automatically* triggered a sense of interest and curiosity: "I wonder if I really do act that way, or what are they seeing that causes them to think like that?"

By the way, collapsing or reversing triggers is not "stuffing" feelings. You are simply choosing to have a different *conditioned response* to formerly aggravating stimuli. If a negative feeling is there, you will know it because you can feel it in your body.

A third type of dangerous trigger is one that produces feelings of helplessness and hopelessness. If you experience these feelings on a regular basis, follow the guidelines in chapter 8. Have a qualified physician eliminate possible physical causes, consider the suggestions on changing your patterns of oil consumption, and beyond that, make use of the suggestions regarding appropriate Thought Virus Therapy.

MOVE BEYOND LIMITING VIRUSES. Limiting viruses that appear to have the greatest impact on health are beliefs that promote feelings of isolation and loneliness as well as erroneous beliefs about the "value" of the disease and the beliefs related to how we visualize the disease process.

What, then, is the message behind the loneliness? For most of us it's just that we need to reach out, to connect with others. Give high priority to quality time with family and friends. Take time to help others in need of help. There's no better way to receive love than to give it. Without overindulging, let loved ones know of your fears, doubts, and frustrations. Research has demonstrated that cancer patients with social support, especially in the form of a support group, have higher levels of natural killer cells that can attack malignant cells and ward off disease. Those people live up to twice as long as cancer patients without emotional support. If you experience discomfort in reaching out to others, look for the positive intent behind the perceived need for isolation or seek counseling.

On a deeply unconscious level, part of Roberta believed that the cancer had some value, since healing herself would be an insult to her mother, her grandmother, and other family members who had died from this disease. When Jeffrey helped her change this belief, the one remaining piece was the limiting belief of how she visualized the disease within.

VISUALIZING THE HEALING RESPONSE

Proponents of mind/body healing frequently make use of visualization as a healing technique toward a possible remission of cancer. When my friend Dana participated in a support group for cancer victims in the Stanford area, she was told to visualize immune cells engaging in warfare with, and bombing, malignant cells. Dana participated in the the support group, did the visualization, and lived a year to a year and a half longer than the doctors expected. She told me, however, that that particular visualization seemed uncomfortable and odd. On some level, it just didn't fit for her.

> **WARNING: The prospect of a nonsurgical, nondrug alternative treatment for a life-threatening disease and a possible spontaneous remission presents a very attractive but potentially dangerous alternative for cancer victims. *Do not* forgo medical treatment where it may help, while waiting for a miracle, but know that miracles do happen. For many people, mind/body techniques and personality changes may enhance the effectiveness of medical treatment.**

Jeffrey approached visualization with more wisdom when he simply asked Roberta to go inside and mentally see what was going on with her body. When she reported hills and fields with weeds taking over, he asked, "Well, what do you think it would take to control the weeds?"

"I don't know. Hmm. Maybe I could bring in some sheep," she said.

"Great. Go ahead and bring in the sheep, and let them go to work," he suggested. After this Jeffrey continued to work with her to allow her thinking to become more congruent and thus coherent. Any remaining internal conflicts and limiting beliefs that Jeffrey believed helped to trigger her condition could also block Roberta's unconscious from healing her.

Some time after Jeffrey's work with Roberta, she was in her doctor's office having her blood tested. People with leukemia have a very high white–blood cell count. Her doctor looked surprised when he came out and told her that her count was normal.

"There must have been a mistake with the test," he concluded.

"Oh, that's not it," said Roberta. "It's just the sheep."

"WHAT?"

"That's right. I forgot to tell you that I brought in the sheep. But I bet if I take the sheep away, the count will go back up," Roberta said. The doctor lowered his eyebrows in disbelief that he was even hearing such nonsense.

"Yeah, let me take the sheep away, and you can retest my blood in a while," she said. After some time they retested it. The white blood cell count was now very high, as it should be with leukemia.

"See. I told you so," said the doctor. "The first test was in error."

"No, no. I'll bet if I bring the sheep back in, the count will go back down. Let me do that, and you can retest me in a while." The doctor looked annoyed, but agreed to her silly request. To his astonishment, after a short while, the count went back down to normal. Several more times in the course of her visit, she made the count go up and down with her visualizing. Finally the doctor dismissed the whole thing by saying, "It's all just in your mind!" not realizing the wisdom of his words.

Not long after that, Roberta's leukemia disappeared altogether. The doctor was both amazed and excited. With the leukemia gone they could now treat and operate on the tumor. Roberta by now was leery of Western medicine and surgical procedures, so she consulted with Jeffrey. Jeffrey assured her that traditional medicine could be useful and might be totally appropriate for her now, even though the doctors had given up on her before. Using hypnotic language patterns, he asked if he could talk with her unconscious mind. She nodded.

"Can you heal this tumor?" he asked.

"Yes," came her reply. Her tone of voice and body language reflected congruency. There was no doubt.

"How long will it take?" he continued.

"Nineteen days." Again there was no apparent doubt in her voice.

"Good. Then schedule the surgery twenty-one days from now, but be sure to have them X-ray you before the surgery," he said. She agreed and set up the surgery. The night before the surgery, the X rays revealed the tumor was gone. When I met her ten years later in the NLP workshop, she was one of the most alive and vivacious people I've encountered.

On the "rooftop" of the world, another pilgrim, a seeker, spoke with a monk, telling him of advances in mind/body healing and of occasional remissions of "incurable" diseases. "Oh, I see," said the monk. "Your people are finally discovering that."

PART THREE

THOUGHT
VIRUSES
AND
WORK

11

HOW TO END
PROCRASTINATION NOW

High achievers and great thinkers never procrastinate—true or false? It is reported that Albert Einstein once received an award in the form of a check for several thousand dollars, but he never got around to cashing it. He simply used it for a bookmark, and never quite made it to the bank. The organization that issued the check eventually contacted him to see why he hadn't cashed it, but by then it was lost.

I became interested in Einstein when I studied his physics in graduate school, because the one thing I had in common with him was that I procrastinated. I generally put off assignments to the last minute, and had a hard time getting to places on time. In contrast, Don, one of my fellow students, was one of the most focused high achievers in our Ph.D. program. I asked Don what was the secret of his success, and he said it had to do with the force of friction. I wasn't sure what he meant.

We all have *little* things, low-priority items we just never quite get around to. But the *big* things—those New Year's resolutions, that important project, those long-term goals—can be sidetracked by what Tony Robbins has branded the "silent killer." Procrastination can ultimately destroy our most important motivating force in life—dreams and visions. Procrastination creeps up on us like a thief in the night, taking away this possibility, that choice, this option.

In my workshop "Personal and Professional Empowerment," we define personal power according to the following sequence:

1. *knowing what you want,* that is, having a clear vision of your outcome
2. *having the ability to take action* to move toward your vision
3. *having the flexibility to change your action* if what you're doing is not moving you in the direction you want
4. *having a signpost*—specific, concrete evidence that lets you know when you've achieved your outcome

Once you have a clear vision of your outcome, the most crucial piece is step 2, the ability to take action. Procrastination is just the opposite—the ability to accept inaction. Without action, nothing happens. Dreams die.

WHY WE PROCRASTINATE

Very simply, procrastination is a choice, an easy way out of a Gemini virus. When it comes to any project, goal, or task, we have the choice to do it or not. Procrastination results from inner conflict; part of us wants to take action and part of us doesn't. If we perceive that something about doing the task is more painful than not doing it, unconsciously we make the choice not to do it—even though we may be convinced on a conscious level that someday we'll get around to it. We may feel that we lack knowledge of how to do it; perhaps doing the project would take away leisure time, or we just don't know how to get started. We may have *limiting beliefs* about the value of having the project completed—fear of failure or fear of success. The prospect of working on the project may *trigger* unresourceful feelings.

THE PROCRASTINATION VIRUS

The glitch in thinking that gives rise to procrastination for most of us is a combination of a complex trigger (a disempowering strategy) and the Gemini virus of internal conflicting parts. Researchers in the field of NLP have studied people who are highly motivated—high achievers—and contrasted these with people who tend to procrastinate.[1] One of the most striking differences lies in the *strategies* that members of the former group use to motivate themselves.

A person prone to procrastination is likely to experience a sequence of steps similar to what I go through when I see that my garage needs cleaning (see chapter 1). For example, you may *see* that the income tax forms need to be completed (visual external:V^e). Next you might *hear* a stern internal voice saying, "You *have to* do this" (auditory internal: A^i). This may be followed by another internal voice saying, "I don't *want* to do it!" (auditory internal: A^i). Next you might *picture* all the tedious steps and details you must go through to complete the task, and what it will look like when you don't complete it (visual internal: V^i). Finally, you feel awful and perhaps paralyzed (kinesthetic internal: K^i) at the prospect of not completing the task *and* the internal conflict of the authoritative part that says you have to do it versus the rebellious part that doesn't want to.

Try out this strategy for yourself in the following exercise:

Exercise 22
A Procrastination Trigger

1. Think of something you really need to do, but that for some reason you've been procrastinating about.
2. Now imagine a stern, authoritative, internal voice telling you, "You *have to* do this. You *have to* get it completed."
3. Next picture all of the tedious little details you have to deal with to accomplish it. Picture how things will look if you fail to complete it.
4. Now notice how you feel.

When I have seminar participants do this, the energy drops through the floor. This strategy or complex trigger leads into conflicting parts of a Gemini virus. Just thinking about the project triggers bad feelings. The unconscious solution, then, is not to think about it.

HOW TO MOTIVATE YOURSELF FOR ACTION

Now mentally erase the steps from Exercise 22, and try out a different strategy:

Antiviral Remedy 15
An Action Strategy

1. Think of that same project about which you've been procrastinating.
2. Now imagine a soft, soothing, maybe even sexy voice *inviting* you to complete the project.
3. Next picture how the completed task will appear. Imagine your feelings at that time.
4. Now again notice how you feel.

Most people notice a dramatic shift between Exercise 22 and Antiviral Remedy 15. What's the difference? The difference is in both the content of steps in the strategy and different submodalities.

High achievers may not hear an internal voice at all. If they do, it is likely soft , soothing, supportive, and possibly playful or sexy. What they visualize is not so much the sequence of steps to get from here to there, as how the task will appear once it's completed and the resulting feelings are motivation to do it.

Occasionally, if you have a part that strongly objects to completing the project, you might need to do the Six-Step Reframing (Antiviral Remedy 8, pages 98–99) to maintain the positive intent of the objecting part.

MODELING HIGH ACHIEVERS

One of the more powerful tools from NLP as applied to Thought Virus Therapy is the process of *modeling*—making use of the beliefs and strategies of high achievers. Aside from the action strategy we covered in the previous section, high achievers make use of three more tools:

PROCRASTINATION LIST. Make a list of projects, tasks, and goals about which you've been procrastinating for a month or two or longer. I find that if I start the day doing one of those items from my list, my energy goes up as the list shrinks. It's a direct relationship.

DAILY GOALS AND ACTIVITIES LIST. Almost all experts on time management agree that *writing down* and *prioritizing* a list of daily goals and activities you want to accomplish is a major step toward achieving your goals and making the best use of the day. The rule of thumb is to start with the most important items first, so that if there are things on your list you don't get to, you have the most important items out of the way.

If you tend to procrastinate, first read the list and ask yourself, "What's the one thing here that I least want to do?" Do that that item first. It might not be particularly important—maybe apologizing to someone or signing some papers—but for some reason you have resistance to doing it.

When I ask seminar participants who do this about their experience, they report feeling that a load has been lifted from them. They know anything else on the list will be easier. Be careful, however, that it's not too big an unpleasant item. If it's too big, break it into small chunks, and start the day with one chunk.

CHUNKING DOWN AND MICRO-CHUNKING. When I ask, "How do you climb the tallest mountain?" people instinctively respond, "One step at a time"—the principle from NLP of *chunking down*. Formidable projects that appear huge and intimidating become manageable one step at a time. If you have a difficult project about which you've been procrastinating, try getting the project started by initially spending just forty or forty-five minutes a day on it. Knowing that you are going to stop after just forty or forty-five minutes makes it easier to get started. That's how I began this book—just doing forty-five minutes a day. Once I got the project moving, I found it easier to spend more time working on it. Even now, this far along, on my busiest teaching days at my college I spend just one forty-five-minute chunk in the morning and one in the afternoon. If you keep doing those chunks each day, they add up quickly.

For the *most* difficult-to-start projects, try micro-chunking. For me, such a project might be preparing my income taxes. On the first day I decide not to actually work on the taxes, but I'm willing to spend just ten minutes planning the information I need and familiarizing myself with the computer program I need to do the taxes. Now even if I am getting into the project or starting to enjoy it, after ten minutes I have to stop. The next day I again won't actually work on the taxes, but I might start bringing together some of the forms and receipts I need for them. Again, even if I'm starting to get into the project, I have to stop after ten minutes. After a few days of this, as the project starts to move, I might reward myself by allowing an extra ten minutes each day. Finally, as I pick up steam, I can work in forty-minute chunks or more.

Have you noticed that once you get up a head of steam with something you've been procrastinating with, once you get it moving, it's much easier than you expected? In fact, I might even find myself enjoying understanding how the tax laws work.

It wasn't until years after graduate school that I finally understood what Don meant about the force of friction. There is a principle in physics that states, "Static friction is greater than kinetic friction." That means it's harder to start something moving than to maintain motion once it *is* moving. Don's success as a self-starter was due to his knack for gently easing himself into whatever he was working on, just to start things moving. For tasks and projects that are truly important, about which you have felt a sense of resistance or friction, the strategies in this chapter should make a difference.

If they're not that important, then you might do as Einstein did, and put your attention on other things. When the awarding organization contacted him to find out why he hadn't cashed the check, he realized it was lost, and asked if they would be willing to issue another one. Shortly afterward, when he received the new check, he called them back and asked, "What's this for?"

12

OVERCOMING FEAR OF FAILURE
AND FEAR OF SUCCESS

YOU MAY BE DISAPPOINTED
IF YOU FAIL,
BUT YOU ARE DOOMED
IF YOU DON'T TRY.

—BEVERLY SILLS

The Boundary Waters Wilderness Area, Northern Minnesota. I had always wondered why Minnesota is called "The Land of Ten Thousand Lakes." When I arrived in this wilderness area I found out. This region is covered with hundreds of lakes that stretch many miles from northern Minnesota well into Canada. The topography is flat, with rolling hills, and has a unique blend of hardwoods and evergreens characteristic of the northern divide. Most people know that rivers to the west of the Continental Divide generally flow toward the Pacific, and that most rivers to the east, as far as the Appalachians, flow toward the Mississippi. My guides here told me that this *northern* divide creates a similar transition. Rivers south of here generally flow south toward subtropical hardwood foliage, while rivers to the north flow toward the pines and eventual desolation of the polar regions.

It was August, and I was attending a wilderness seminar that was part of an academic summer program. Most of my camping experiences were backpacking excursions in the High Sierra of California. This seminar promised a whole new adventure called portaging—hiking and camping with canoes. We were also to study wilderness writers, visit a true pioneer who lived in the wilderness, and learn the ultimate secret for overcoming writer's block.

One of the first things I learned here was how costly mistakes and failure can be. When you portage your canoe from one lake to the next, it is crucial to pay attention to exactly where you come out of one lake and where you enter the next. After a while one lake looks like the next. If you make the mistake of not paying attention, and fail to notice subtle detail of the terrain, you can get hopelessly lost. Unlike the High Sierra, you can't climb to the top of the mountain, scan the terrain, and see where you are. Success here means survival. Failure might mean the opposite. Nature can be unforgiving that way.

One night while we were sitting around the campfire, Bob, a fellow student, pulled out a guitar and began strumming. The instrument was badly out of tune, and Bob was just a beginner. His efforts to tune the guitar only made it sound worse, and nearby timber wolves began howling. I was concerned for our safety, so I grabbed the guitar and managed to tune it in a couple of minutes. Bob asked me how I could hear the pitch so easily. I remembered back to when my first music instructor explained tuning. He said that it is based on making mistakes and on physics. Unless you start by *failing* to match the tones you are tuning, they can be difficult to hear. He said that failure can sometimes be valuable. Some of the most successful and famous people are paid because they fail most of the time.

I wondered then how our thinking becomes distorted, so that for most of us fear of failure shuts us down from trying out new things, taking new directions in life, taking risks. When we do attempt to better ourselves through self-improvement programs, why are they almost always doomed to failure? How can we learn to fail successfully, to use failure as a springboard to success? And how can we learn to recognize our own success and adjust our internal rules, so it is easy to succeed and hard to fail?

WHY MOST SELF-IMPROVEMENT PROGRAMS FAIL

Remember the components of personal power from the last chapter:

1. *knowing what you want,* that is having a clear vision of your outcome

2. *having the ability to take action* to move toward your vision
3. *having the flexibility to change your action* if what you're doing is not moving you in the direction you want
4. *having a signpost*—specific, concrete evidence that lets you know when you've achieved your outcome

Part of step 2, the ability to take action, is being able to move through procrastination using suggestions from the preceding chapter. Aside from procrastination, what else holds us back from taking the *action* necessary to achieve our goals and visions in life? In my Personal and Professional Empowerment Seminars, I've identified four reasons why most efforts toward self-improvement are doomed to failure.

EXTERNAL OBSTACLES. These include *prioritizing* the necessary time, having the money that might be required, getting the education or training needed, and having social support. Although external obstacles can be formidable, they are probably the easiest of all to deal with. Most can be handled by chunking the obstacle down into smaller manageable pieces. My former wife wants to earn a Ph.D., but lacks the time and money to be a full-time student, so she takes only one or two courses of graduate study each semester. It may take her ten or fifteen years to complete, but she will eventually have her Ph.D.

INTERNAL OBSTACLES. These include fear of failure, fear of success, fear of rejection, and other parts of us—Gemini viruses— that create internal conflict and resistance. Part of us wants to be successful, while another part, or parts, objects. Books and self-development seminars don't provide the means to deal with such objecting parts. And if we have conflict with what we want to do consciously versus unconscious resistance, we know from a lifetime of experience that the unconscious resistance wins out.

From the viewpoint of Thought Virus Therapy, the solution is simply a matter of integrating the positive intent of the resistance through Six-Step Reframing or The Visual Squash—Antiviral Remedys 8 or 9 in chapter 5. This works for most internal resistance, *other than the fear of failure.* Such fear may trigger a fight-or-flight survival response, and requires a special approach we will consider shortly.

PERCEIVED FAILURES AND SETBACKS ALONG THE WAY. In learning to play a new musical instrument, to change a self-defeating habit, or to set a new course for your career, you are bound to make some mistakes and have a few setbacks or failures along the way. Generally, self-improvement programs don't provide a way of handling such bumps on the path. We will consider some suggestions shortly that allow all of us to turn failure into useful feedback.

EXPECTATION VERSUS PERFORMANCE. The most overlooked and perhaps the most interesting obstacle to self-improvement involves learning curves. When learning a new skill or installing a new behavior, the performance with time does not improve along a straight line. More likely, mastery proceeds along a learning curve, as illustrated here:

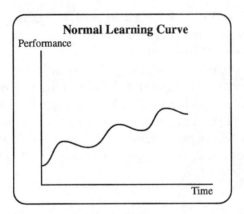

As you can see, performance proceeds upward, then levels off or even goes down a little as new skills are integrated. This is followed by the next cycle. The next figure (see facing page) shows the so-called Bandura Curve,[1] comparing expectation with actual performance for one learning cycle:

The top curve is expectation, the bottom is actual performance. At point 1 both the performance and expectation are increasing with initial enthusiasm. At point 2 performance is leveling off, while expectation continues to rise. At point 3 the expectation has now leveled off and the performance has dropped a little. Point 3 is crucial because this is where the biggest gap between expectation and performance occurs. Here is where most people get discouraged and are most likely to quit. If the person gets coaching or some support, or simply finds a way to continue

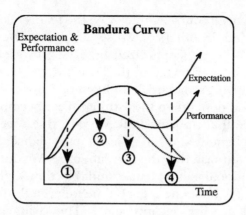

on, then at point 4 both curves continue upward into the next cy-cle, or the person quits and the curves fall off.

This is why I encourage seminar participants to continue meet-ing as a group or even with just one other seminar participant. The skills of applying the antiviral remedies presented in this book and performing the exercises are just that—skills. The way to master them is not just to read them and understand how they work, but rather to practice using them again and again. That is usually easier with another person. Besides that, whenever some-one attempting to integrate a major change into her life reaches point 3 on the Bandura Curve, she will have the ongoing support of a caring partner or a continuing group.

THE FEAR-OF-FAILURE VIRUS

Several well-respected psychologists contend that there are only two emotions: love and fear. They say fear is simply the absence of love, and in itself is a "useless" emotion. There may be a grain of truth in this, but other emotions do exist, and each has unique neurotransmitters that "fingerprint" that state. Furthermore, fear, like any other negative emotion, does have a positive intent and a message. The positive intent is survival, and the message is *"Be prepared,* both mentally and physically, to take drastic action if nec-essary."

A trigger virus occurs when fear is inappropriately anchored to something we have no business being afraid of, such as taking dance lessons, approaching that attractive single, or signing up for a foreign-language course. Quite often the fear is related to fear of rejection—either by others or, worse yet, by ourselves.

Our survival is *not* jeopardized by having two left feet at the dance lesson, being rejected by the attractive single, or being confused by German grammar. The physiology, however, reacts as if our survival did depend on these things. Fear becomes F.E.A.R.—*F*alse *E*vidence that *A*ppears *R*eal. We miss out twice, because we don't get the benefit and fun of learning to dance, having a new relationship, or mastering the new language. We do, however, get all of the emotional pain of failure and rejection, as if what we fear most has already happened. Each time we even think about it, we get to experience the negative states. The saying that a coward dies a thousand deaths and a courageous man only one illustrates the point.

The trigger virus linking fear with not having things turn out the way we'd like them to (i.e., possible mistakes and failures along the way) keeps many of us from trying out new things, taking new exciting directions in life, experiencing new adventures. Instead, many of us are sentenced to the same old routine, doing only those things we feel comfortable with, and living life in a rut. A saying that has recently become popular is

> "Ask yourself what you would do,
>   if you knew,
>   you could not fail."

Think about that. What would *you* do? What new things might you try out? What new directions would you take in life, if failure were no longer a possibility for you? The good news comes from a presupposition in NLP:

> "There is no such thing as failure,
>   there is only feedback."

This is something Thomas Edison believed. It is reported that before making his first successful lightbulb, he tried several thousand that did not work. How many of us could do something a few thousand times, fail a few thousand times, and keep going—*not knowing that what we're attempting will eventually work?* Even Edison didn't know for sure that someday he would produce a successful lightbulb. After he succeeded, someone asked him about it. He said that he never really thought of the first few thousand attempts as failures. Each one actually taught him something: it taught him how *not* to build a lightbulb, and he learned something useful.

Somewhere between early childhood and our school years, most of us pick up some very unpleasant associations with making mistakes and with receiving criticism. Teachers, parents, siblings, and friends send us a clear message—it is not okay to make mistakes. They inadvertently help anchor us to feeling embarrassed, humiliated, or guilty when what we are attempting to do doesn't work out the first time we try.

In my Powerlearning seminars, an important principle is to create an atmosphere that is childlike. I ask participants why we would want a childlike state. They are quick to remember that as young children, *before we had negative associations with failure,* we were wide open to learning, especially to language acquisition. Dr. Lin Doherty, formerly at the University of Massachusetts, taught the German language using principles I teach in my seminar, one of which is to create a playful, childlike environment in which *it is okay to fail.* By using these methods, his students were able to master two years' worth of university-level German in one quarter. In fact, at the end of the quarter, students staged a dramatic production in German—something the average German major could probably not do after four years of study.

Now, understand there actually are times when it is crucial that the learner knows clearly when mistakes are *not* okay—in performing brain surgery, for instance, or in military combat. But to have powerful negative triggers associated with not remembering the fifth president of the United States, or how to spell *dyslexia,* or some lack of physical coordination on the playground—these triggers can cripple us as learners for the rest of our lives.

LEARNING TO FAIL SUCCESSFULLY

When things don't go the way we'd like them to, the advice from most spiritual traditions is to look at the bright side of things, to see the good in whatever is happening, to find something positive. People like my friend Dana, who naturally had this ability, are an inspiration. They are like magnets; people are naturally drawn to

them. Unfortunately, no one tells us *how* to find the good in whatever has happened; when we are upset enough, we don't even
want to look at things that way.

There is a story of a sage in ancient India who supposedly had
mastered this skill. A seeker sought out the sage to test him. The
seeker and the sage walked from village to village, observing victims of crime, homeless beggars, unfair taxes on the poor, yet the
sage could always find something uplifting in the situation. Finally
they came across a dead tiger that had been decaying for several
days. The sight and smell were so disgusting, the sage was ren-
dered speechless, and the seeker concluded that he had met his
match. Perhaps, then, not everything has redeeming qualities.
However, mistakes, failures, and criticism are certainly events we
can learn to handle resourcefully. We can learn how to fail successfully—how to use failure as a springboard to success.

Have you had even one experience in life when something dis-
appointing happened—a major mistake, a setback, a failure—yet
you were totally resourceful in how you handled it? When you
look back on what happened, you know you did just the right
things. If you can think of even one experience like that, then
your unconscious already knows how to fail successfully. The trick
is to discover how you pulled it off—that is, what was your unconscious *strategy?*

Antiviral Remedy 16
Discovering How You Fail Successfully

Think back to a specific time when you experienced what appeared to be a major failure or setback, yet you were totally resourceful in how you handled the situation. As usual, begin with
physiology. Being back in that situation as if it were happening
now, how does your body feel? What sensations do you notice with
your facial muscles? How is your posture and your breathing?

To unlock the strategy, be in touch with all of the feelings,
sights, and sounds from that particular experience. It is crucial to
be in touch with that experience as if it were happening *now*.

1. Once you feel yourself back in that experience of being totally
   resourceful, notice the very first thing that must happen to begin triggering a resourceful response to the apparent setback.

Is it something you see (visual external—V^e), something you hear (auditory external—A^e), or something you touch (kinesthetic external—K^e)? Write down this very first step that triggers your resourcefulness.

2. Next notice what happens on the *inside* once you have seen, heard, or touched what started your resourceful response. Do you now visualize something inside, hear some words or self-talk inside, or have some internal feelings (V^i, A^i, or K^i)? Once you are aware of this step, write it down.

3. Once you have seen, heard, or felt something inside, does something else internally or externally need to happen for you to be completely resourceful? Write down that step. Continue the process until it feels complete. A typical strategy may involve two to five steps.

4. After you have listed each step, you might conjure up another time when you were totally resourceful in the face of apparent failure. Put yourself back in that situation as if it were happening now, and see if the experience involves the same sequence of steps. This may lead to some refinement in your strategy.

5. Often the first step in your strategy is your dominant modality (V, A, or K), although this step is also the one most likely to change from one situation to another. The last step in your strategy is a kinesthetic internal state of feeling totally resourceful. Notice how you feel the feelings in your body.

6. Once you are convinced you have the correct sequence of steps, write it down. This is your recipe for failing successfully.

7. To refine your strategy, check for submodalities of the internal steps.

Once you have your strategy, carry it with you or post it someplace where you will see it daily. This is your recipe for bouncing back when things don't go your way, your way of seeing the bright side of things.

Beyond having your strategy in place, asking yourself certain power questions about the situation can help transform the way you make meaning about it, and reframe your point of view. Here are a few possibilities:

• What could be great about what has happened, if I were willing to look at it that way?

- What have I learned from this, or what could I learn if I wanted to?
- How might this mistake or setback be moving me toward what's most important for me in life, if I were willing to take that viewpoint?
- What am I willing to do to move through this and keep going?

Tony Robbins uses a football metaphor: When things don't work out, at least we've run a play. As long as we keep running plays, we're still in the game. Deepak Chopra says that when things don't appear to be going as he would like, he *trusts* that things are happening as they should, that the events are part of a bigger picture he can't see just yet. Notice his shift in submodalities. He is looking at the picture too closely. Later he will be able to back off and see a bigger picture.

The skill of failing successfully is a powerful tool in the second quality of personal power: having the ability to take action. You can keep running plays even if they don't work. This should, however, be tempered by the third quality: *having the flexibility to change your action, if what you're doing is not moving you in the direction you want.* This refines the fine art of failing successfully. Edison didn't keep attempting to make a successful lightbulb by doing exactly the same thing over and over, thousands of times. With each attempt, he carefully observed what worked and what didn't. He then changed his approach accordingly.

After the seeker and the sage encountered the rotting dead tiger with the horrible stench and had retreated to a safe distance, the sage turned to the seeker with a smile and said, "Did you notice how white and shiny its teeth were?"

THE FAST PHOBIA CURE FOR PAST FAILURES

The emotional link between past failures and disempowering feelings can be so powerful it is almost like a phobia. Whenever we even *think* about approaching that attractive single, or trying that new sport, or taking an accounting course, the triggered feelings of rejection, humiliation, or low self-esteem may literally paralyze us into inaction. Here is a quick process you can do in about ten to fifteen minutes. It allows you to dissipate emotions from past failures, and gives you a clean slate to move on with life.

Antiviral Remedy 17
The Fast Phobia Cure for Past Failures

Pick a *context* in which you've had a number of failures or set-backs—applying for jobs, getting through calculus, flirting with attractive singles—one area in which you would like to clear the slate.

1. Think back to a specific time when you experienced a major failure in this context, maybe a time you would rather not remember or talk about. Before proceeding, ask your unconscious to preserve whatever you've learned from these setbacks, so you don't have to make the same mistakes in the future.
2. Picture a protective wall of Plexiglas sliding down in front of you to protect you from whatever you see on the other side.
3. Next, picture yourself out in front of the Plexiglas, watching or remembering a black-and-white movie of the events around that failure. Make sure to keep yourself and the movie on the other side of the Plexiglas.
4. Now remove the Plexiglas and imagine seeing what happened in color, as you saw it, only speed the movie up and run it *backward*. Start at the end and quickly move back to the beginning. When you're done, replace the Plexiglas.
5. Repeat steps 2 and 3, only this time run the movie a little faster, both forward and reverse. Do this two or three times, each time increasing the speed.
6. Test your response to the memory by thinking about it. If the feelings are cleared, you should feel neutral, or you might even feel some humor, with scrambled images going backward and forward. If you still have some residual feelings about what happened, repeat the process.
7. Pick two or three other memories in the same context you are working with, and do steps 1 through 5 for each of these.
8. Finally, ask your unconscious to take *all* emotionally charged memories in the context you're working with, put those memories in black and white, and move them farther away from you. With the Plexiglas in place, start at the beginning and see yourself watching a sped-up movie of all of these.
9. Finally, remove the Plexiglas, and quickly run the composite movie backward.

An alternate approach to this process is to do Antiviral Remedy 13, the Eye Movement Scrambler (pages 152–153) while thinking about each of the highly charged memories in the area you have chosen, then all of them collectively. Some people respond more easily to one process than to the other. People who think of themselves as being nonvisual may find the Eye Movement Scrambler an easier process.

FEAR OF SUCCESS: THE THERMOSTAT VIRUS

How can some of the things we want most in life—especially a rewarding career, financial independence, and a great intimate love relationship—be the things we are most afraid of actually having? For many of us, fear of success infects our motivation as powerfully as, or more powerfully than, fear of failure.

Fear of success is like a thermostat. Many of us have adapted to a certain low level of success, a certain comfort zone. If we move beyond that level, a glitch in thinking, a *thermostat virus,* shuts us down, just as an electrical thermostat keeps our homes from overheating. The model presented on pages 45–47 in chapter 3 illustrates how the thermostat virus works. If we are not making progress toward a certain vision or outcome, it is because of the following factors:

- We sense something positive or comfortable about *not having* the outcome.
- We perceive something negative about the *process of achieving* the outcome.
- We sense something negative about *having the outcome,* i.e., fear of success.

The unconscious fear of having success may be a trigger. Maybe one time you had a great job that felt especially rewarding and fulfilling, when suddenly you were laid off and felt devastated with the loss. Inadvertently, feelings of job satisfaction got anchored with fear of loss. In the future, if a job starts to feel too rewarding or fulfilling, suddenly you become fearful, or begin feeling a deep sense of loss. This may lead to sabotaging advancement of your career.

Fear of success might also involve limiting beliefs. This is especially true with having abundant money. Think of the beliefs many of us grew up with:

- Money is the root of all evil.
- It is harder for a wealthy person to get to heaven than for a camel to pass through the eye of a needle.
- You can't buy happiness.
- Money won't solve your problems.

Whatever the reason for fear of success, it results in conflicting parts of a Gemini virus. Part of us longs for the man or woman of our dreams, and part of us is scared to death of that prospect, owing to a trigger or ambivalence caused by limiting beliefs. We will focus on such *intimate thermostat viruses* in the next chapter.

Thought Virus Therapy for fear of success involving triggers makes use of Antiviral Remedy 1 (pages 53–55), 3 (page 58), or 4 (pages 61–62). On the other hand, you can handle fear of success based on limiting beliefs with Antiviral Remedy 6 (page 81) or 7 (page 87). Beyond that, Six-Step Reframing (pages 98–99) is a way to resolve the internal conflict of wanting success and not wanting it.

Beyond fear of success, there are other important issues that keep success elusive for many of us.

EXPERIENCING SUCCESS

The fourth characteristic of personal power is having a *signpost*—specific, concrete evidence that lets you know when you've achieved your outcome. Many people—movie stars, corporate executives, political leaders, sports heroes, even religious leaders—whom everyone else might think of as extraordinarily successful don't think of themselves that way. Most likely they never set up a signpost. They get so caught up in achieving, and having the vision always out of reach, that their mindset does not support recognizing when they have achieved it and acknowledging themselves for being successful.

On my first job after graduate school, as an engineer with a microwave company, my boss, a senior engineer, had a strange management style. Whenever I made a mistake, or did something

differently from the way he would have done it, he was right on my
case. Whenever I did something well or put in extra hours, I never
heard anything about it. Without acknowledgment and positive
feedback, success was almost impossible. Trying to be successful
was like trying to fill a bottomless pit. How many of us have bosses
like this inside our heads?

Exercise 23
Your Internal Rules For Success

1. Ask yourself, "What area of life [career, personal growth, family, relationship, recreation, finances, spiritual, social, etc.] is
   less than magnificent? In which area do I feel least successful?
   Write this down.
2. Now ask yourself, "What would it take for me to feel successful
   in my _____ [the area that needs work]?" or "Success in _____
   [the area] means _____." Pick four or five specific and *measurable* criteria. Such statements as "having a better love relationship" or "being in a more fulfilling career" are too nonspecific.
   How would you know you had a better love relationship or a
   more fulfilling job? What specifically would it take? Elicit the
   rules or beliefs and write them down.
3. As you consider the four or five rules or beliefs of what it
   would take to be successful in your chosen area, ask yourself:
   - "Do these conditions for success give me a reasonable
     chance of achieving it, or do they just keep success out of my
     reach?"
   - "Whose rules are these? Did I ever sit down and consciously
     design them as part of a master plan for success, or did I just
     randomly adopt them?
4. Finally, pick an area of life in which you feel most successful,
   and repeat steps 2 and 3 to find four or five specific and measurable things you are doing that let you know you are successful, and how these rules serve you.

Rules or beliefs for what it takes to be successful are rarely conscious decisions, but evolve in a chaotic manner from a lifetime of
attempting to make meaning. If they keep success at a distance,
because we are unclear what it takes to be successful, or if the conditions are not realistically achievable, they constitute a limiting
virus that holds us back. If this is the case in that area of life in

which you are lacking success, consider changing your beliefs to ones that make it easy to succeed.

Antiviral Remedy 18
Changing Your Rules for Success

1. Identify the positive intent, or the value each rule is connected to, by asking yourself, "What's important to me about doing _____ [the rule]?" Maybe one rule for me to feel successful at being physically fit is that I think I need to exercise every day for an hour and a half. What's important to me is that I want to be *consistent,* so that exercise will become a *habit,* and to have a long enough session to do stretching, weight-bearing exercise, and aerobics.
2. For each rule, ask, "What's important about *not* doing this?" This is an interesting and crucial question. If there is something you feel you need to do to be successful, and you're not doing it, guess what? There's a good reason why you're not doing it. If I'm really honest with myself, the reason I don't exercise this long and this often is that I find long exercise sessions too hard, too much work, and I have too many other things to get done.
3. For each rule, ask yourself, "Is there a new rule I could adopt that would satisfy what's important about doing _____ [the old rule] *and* what's important about *not* doing _____?" Maybe you could exercise regularly on alternate days three or four times a week, and break the exercise into three or four shorter sessions during the day for a change of pace.
4. For each new rule, ask your unconscious if it would be okay to try it out as a way of feeling successful. Use them for a week or two and see if they are working and if you are allowing yourself to feel success.
5. If the new rules work, that's great. If not, repeat steps 4 and 5 to generate some different new rules to try out. Once you have achievable rules, and you are experiencing success regularly, you may want to use Antiviral Remedy 6 (chapter 4, page 81), for locking in the new beliefs by changing their submodalities.

Sometimes people are concerned that if their beliefs make it easy to be successful, they will become complacent or demotivated. That's not the case. Success along the way inspires the desire for more success, just as a competent manager motivates a subordinate by acknowledging achievements and progress rather than just focusing on mistakes and setbacks.

One of the guides, a leader for my wilderness seminar, had promised to share the secret of getting beyond writer's block. He said, "Get it written and *then* get it right." I thought that was a wonderful illustration of failure and success. When it comes to writing, many of us get caught up in creating ideas and *simultaneously* editing. This arises from a faulty belief that even when we just begin to create, it is necessary to get it right the first time—no mistakes in grammar, style, or logical expression. Physiologically this is almost impossible to do, because creative writing involves a balanced functioning of the left and right sides of the brain, while editing is primarily a left-brain process. The secret is first to fail successfully. Just write down the ideas, allowing them to flow, no matter how poorly you think you are expressing them. Once the words are all down, then you can turn the job over to your left-brain editor. The writing now becomes like a sculpture. With the rough form present, the sculptor can now refine and polish the final artwork.

If, as in the Boundary Waters, your very survival *does* depend on careful observation and *not* making mistakes, then have a healthy respect for that need, and allow some fear to be your ally. On the other hand, if you are simply working to complete a project or wanting to flirt with that grocery cashier, have your strategy in place for failing successfully, and ask yourself empowering questions if things don't work out.

My first music teacher reminded me that Ted Williams was the last great big-league baseball player to finish a season hitting over .400. That means he failed 60 percent of the time! Team owners paid him a high salary, fans cheered him, and he made baseball's Hall of Fame for failing one and a half times more often than he succeeded.

I also realized, when I tuned Bob's guitar, that failure was the key to success. Most musicians know that when sounding two tones together, you *deliberately* make the one you are tuning slightly different from the one that's already tuned. Failing to be exactly tuned results in a wavering sound called *beats*. Once you hear the beats, the slower the wavering, the closer you are to being tuned. To complete your success, you simply adjust the instrument until the beats, your failure, goes away.

PART FOUR

THOUGHT
VIRUSES
AND
LOVE

13

INTIMATE VIRUSES

THE CHEMIST WHO CAN EXTRACT FROM HIS HEART'S
ELEMENTS COMPASSION, RESPECT, LONGING, PATIENCE,
REGRET, SURPRISE, AND FORGIVENESS AND COMPOUND
THEM INTO ONE CAN CREATE THAT ATOM WHICH IS
CALLED LOVE.

—KAHLIL GIBRAN

One of the most romantic days in my first marriage occurred when Helen and I backpacked to a wilderness lake in the High Sierra. The lake was surrounded by rocky granite mountains on one side and forested hills on the other. After we set up camp next to the lake, we hiked up the hillside to get a better view of this magnificent setting. Just as we reached a vista, as if by magic, the air became still, the last ripple left the lake, and it cast a perfect reflection of mountains on the other side. The lake remained ripple-free all night, reflecting evening shadows, wilderness starlight, and the love and attraction we felt for each other.

I think we've all had that initial thrill of feeling in love and incredibly attracted to another person. We felt witty, charming, and happy for no apparent reason. As we broke through the walls of isolation and alienation, sensory awareness heightened. We began to see and hear things we had rarely noticed before. We felt strong, yet at the same time completely vulnerable. Being in love is one of the few times we can truly open up to tell our life story, and know the other is really listening.

Romantic love is described as being anything from the "single greatest energy system in the Western psyche"[1]—replacing religion as a path toward wholeness, ecstasy, meaning, and psychological healing—to illusion and pure narcissism. Men and women devote enormous amounts of energy to finding that perfect partner. They struggle to create and preserve a relationship that is satisfying to both partners, in spite of almost no cultural under-standing about how to make love work. One researcher, Catherine Johnson, carried out a study of 100 happily married couples who had been together from seven to fifty-five years.[2] In spite of a wide-spread belief that more meaningful, mature love grows slowly with time, she found that almost all of the couples felt at home with each other right from the start—a quality more characteristic of romantic love. Being "in love," as a standard for intimate relation-ships and marriage, is a concept that is peculiar to the West. This standard is not considered important elsewhere, although the warmth, stability, and devotion shared by couples in many other cultures would put us to shame.

When I pondered the connection between romantic love and thought viruses, I wondered why some of the things we want most in life can be the same things that we are most frightened of. What is this "romantic chemistry" that both draws and eludes so many of us, and does being in love serve any useful purpose? What are the major land mines that destroy most intimate relationships? And can the magic of falling in love be rekindled after it has faded?

INTIMATE VIRUSES

No other area of human experience provides a better breeding ground for thought viruses than love relationships. Glitches in thinking—*intimate viruses*—that infect love relationships cause more suffering than any other except killer viruses. In fact, inti-mate viruses in both love and parent-child relationships are the basis of many killer viruses. Because of intimate viruses, more than 50 percent of marriages end in divorce. As a result, many disgrun-tled people are convinced that romantic love doesn't work. Carl Jung once described our failure to make intimate love relation-ships work as a "great wound in the Western psyche," and the "pri-mary problem of Western culture."[3]

The problem is that, in spite of the feelings of ecstasy, being in love can bring with it loneliness, alienation, frustration, and a host of unspoken, unagreed-to expectations owing to limiting viruses. One's *partner* should always continue to provide intense, pleasur-able, in-love feelings. He or she is *expected* to be a passionate lover, a friend, a family psychologist, someone who is there for us when we need them and willing to give us space when we need that.

These days the partner should also be a co-breadwinner who still has the energy to comfort us at the end of the day.

We are high in expectations and low in energy and resources. Many of us can maintain these expectations for a while during the initial courting stage, but sooner or later one partner returns to a more realistic, routine way of living. The other partner may then feel abandoned. Worse yet, heaven forbid, one partner might find something in the other to criticize, and the recipient of the criticism feels betrayed. When the early unspoken promises of romantic love appear to be crumbling around us, we are more likely to feel angry with our partners or ourselves than with the expectations we brought to our relationships.

In addition to the unrealistic expectations of limiting viruses, intimate viruses include *disempowering triggers* and *unfulfilled strategies* that trigger deep feelings of love and attraction. Internal parts can also distort our perception of who the partner is as another person. This is like looking into a mirror and forgetting we are looking at ourselves.

Carl Jung said further that if you discover the psychic wound of an individual or a society, you have also discovered its quickest path to healing and growth of consciousness. For us in the West, intimate love relationships provide a potentially powerful tool—a path that can either destroy us or move us onward toward our highest dreams and ideals.

RELATIONSHIP PHASES

For the past twenty years I have read accounts of three natural phases in the evolution of an intimate love relationship. Phase One is the experience of initial ignition. We are strongly attracted, euphoric, and often feel a deep sense of expansion and completeness—as if missing parts of us had suddenly come together. The partner has an uncanny feeling of familiarity, and such statements as "I feel like I've always known you" are common. From this vantage point we tend to see all the great qualities in our partner (and in ourselves), and to overlook the not-so-pleasant ones.

Phase Two is characterized by withdrawal—feelings of disappointment, disillusionment, anger, and betrayal. This phase is sometimes referred to as the power struggle. Fights, moodiness, and withholding love are attempts to hold on to, or to force one's partner to bring back, the idyllic times of Phase One. We now see all of the flaws in the other and overlook the great qualities that brought us together. Most relationships die in Phase Two.

Phase Three, for couples who get this far, is characterized by compromise, resolution, and balance. We are well aware of and accept the partner's flaws. This actually creates a space that improves the likelihood that the partner will choose to change. We also haven't forgotten the good qualities that brought us together. More recent studies show that even within the general structure of the phases, couples run through mini-cycles of each phase.[4] The way to judge where you are in your relationship, and the quality of it, is to notice what states you experience when you are with your partner. Notice, in particular, how you feel about yourself as a result of being together.

I've wondered, over the years, why these phases occur and what happens to the initial excitement and passion. Can we prevent the disillusionment of Phase Two, or rekindle that initial spark once it has slipped away? Do the discomforts of Phase Two have some value?

THE FIVE "LAND MINES"

There are five potential "land mines" that destroy the initial joy and excitement that brought us together, ending most intimate relationships.

WORN-OUT TRIGGERS AND ROUTINE STRATEGIES. If we are around anyone long enough, it is just human nature to get used to that person and to start taking him or her for granted. The initial triggers that sparked feelings of newness and excitement begin to fade. Still, everything seems fine with our partner, so we get *caught up*— in work, in paying the bills, in taking care of the kids, in doing the laundry. We forget about the spontaneity and playfulness that brought us together.

Routines are strategies that serve the purpose of allowing us to accomplish daily tasks expediently. If we had to spend our time constantly thinking up new and creative ways of getting out of bed, brushing our teeth, taking a shower, drinking our morning coffee, and commuting to work, we would get little else done in life. We just do those things and don't think much about them. In a relationship, however, acting the same way, day after day, and being totally predictable, is one of the surest ways *out* of the relationship.

The first step toward avoiding this land mine is through mindfulness. Know that the tendency toward routine exists. Look for those areas in your relationship where things are becoming routine, and maybe a bit too predictable. Be on the lookout for ways in which you can become more spontaneous and surprise your partner.

NEGATIVE TRIGGERS. If you are around your partner long enough, there are bound to be times when you are angry, fearful, hurt, or depressed, and they may not have anything to do with your partner. Perhaps you had a bad day at work, or a financial investment went sour. You are experiencing the state, while simultaneously seeing your partner's face, hearing her voice, feeling her touch, and your partner can get inadvertently linked up with the negative state. If, over time, that happens again and again, all you have to do is to see her face, hear her voice, or feel her touch, and you become angry, fearful, hurt, or depressed.

Fifteen years ago, when I began doing nationwide seminars on innovative learning methods, I would sometimes schedule three seminars per weekend. By the time I finished the last seminar, on Sunday evening, I was tired. Just before leaving to return the rental car to the airport and start back home, I would call my wife—at that time—just to let her know how things had gone, and that I was on my way home.

As time went on, I began to notice something. When I called her from the college in the middle of the afternoon, I might be feeling great, but as soon as I heard her voice, I felt tired. Once I became aware of this pattern, I wondered, "What's going on here? Is the romance gone? Are we slipping into Phase Two? Why am I so tired?" Fortunately, at about the same time, I was reading about triggers, and finally recognized what had happened. I followed the procedure outlined in Antiviral Remedy 3 (page 58) to collapse this disempowering anchor, and was fine with her voice after that.

Trigger viruses that sabotage relationships may date back to a time well before the relationship started. Maybe one of your parents or a sibling had a mannerism, a gesture, or a tone of voice that made your hair stand on end. If your partner just happens to have that same mannerism or use that tone of voice, you get upset for no apparent reason.

One of the most powerful negative triggers is perceived criticism, because of childhood experiences with criticism and failure. The test of whether you are experiencing a trigger virus is to observe whether your response to something your partner does always elicits the *same* emotion, and if you feel that the response is automatic—that is, you have no control over it.

Over time, once you have enough negative triggers with your partner, it's just not much fun being around that person. You experience more pain than pleasure in his or her company. The best way to avoid this land mine is to be aware of the power of negative states and be careful not to focus on your partner when you are intensely experiencing one. Martha Washington was probably one of the first Thought Virus Therapy specialists. Whenever she was in a foul mood, she would sit in a certain chair. If George or the servants saw Martha sitting in that chair, they knew to leave her alone until she was ready to get up.

If negative triggers are already in place with you and your partner, use Antiviral Remedy 3 or 4 (pages 58 and 61–62) to collapse or reverse the triggers; or get a therapist to help you with one of these processes. A partner's response to criticism can be almost phobic, as it often is with past failures. Procedures from the preceding chapter can be helpful in such cases.

UNFULFILLED ATTRACTION AND LOVE STRATEGIES. Each of us has a unique sequence of external and internal experiences—a strategy—to feel strong attraction to a potential partner, and another strategy to feel a deep sense of love. Some people are more *visual;* you need to *show* them that you love them by taking them places, buying them flowers or gifts, gazing at them with that certain look in your eyes. For others, the *words* are more important. They need to *hear* "I love you" in that special tone of voice. For others, what makes them feel most loved is that special touch, or how someone holds them.

When we are courting and in Phase One, we tend to be multisensory—gifts, candlelight dinners, starry-eyed looks, "I love you" said in so many ways, and touch all over the place. After a while, though, we may groove back into the modality (V, A, or K) with which we are most comfortable. If the partner's preferred modality is different from ours, after a while he or she will feel unloved. Maybe the husband is more auditory and the wife is more visual. After a while, each may feel unloved.

"What do you mean, you feel unloved? I *show* you all the time," he responds.

"Yes, but I need to *hear* the words. You never talk to me the way you used to when we were dating," she says.

"Well, I take you places, I buy you clothes, and what about that diamond ring? Doesn't that show you how much I care?" he counters. Of course they aren't communicating, because they are speaking different languages based on preferred modalities.

It is such a simple thing to discover what makes your partner feel attracted to you, and what triggers feelings of deep love. These strategies are normally unconscious. Once we bring to conscious awareness the steps we go through, we have the keys to maintaining or even rekindling the magic that brought us together in the first place.

Exercise 24
Eliciting Your Attraction Strategy

Think back to a particular time when you were totally attracted to a potential love partner. To discover how this happened, begin as usual with your physiology. When you are totally attracted, how does your body feel? What is the expression on your face? What gestures or movements do you make? How are you breathing? How would you be sitting or standing right now, if you were experiencing that same attraction?

To discover the steps in your strategy, imagine that time as if it were happening *now*. Be in touch with all of the feelings, sights, and sounds when you were totally attracted.

1. Once you feel yourself back in that experience, notice the very *first* thing that must happen to trigger your feeling of attraction. Is it something about what you see in the other (visual external—V^e), or something about the way they speak (auditory external—A^e), or something about the way they touched you (kinesthetic external—K^e)? Write down this first step.

2. Next, notice what happens on the *inside*, once you have seen, heard, or felt what started your attraction. Do you now visualize something inside, hear some words or self-talk, or have some internal feelings (V^i, A^i, or K^i)? Once you are aware of this step, write it down.

3. Once you have seen, heard, or felt something inside, does something else internally or externally need to happen for you to be totally attracted? Write down that step. Continue the process until it feels complete. A typical attraction strategy involves two to four steps.

4. After you have listed each step, you might conjure up another time when you were totally attracted to another potential love partner. Put yourself back in that situation as if it were happening now, and see if that experience involves the same sequence of steps. This may lead to some refinement in your strategy.

The attraction strategy is what gets a relationship started. What *sustains* it is what your partner does that triggers a deep sense of love.

Exercise 25
Eliciting Your Deep Love Strategy

Think back to a particular time when you felt deep and total love with a partner. To discover how you did this, begin again with your physiology. When you are feeling the deepest level of love, how does your body feel? What is the expression on your face? What gestures or movements do you make? How are you breathing? How would you be sitting or standing right now, if you were experiencing that same love?

To uncover your strategy, again imagine that time as if it were happening *now*. Be in touch with all of the feelings, sights, and sounds from that experience that you remember. Unlike other strategies, the deep love strategy normally involves just two steps. You experience a visual, auditory, or kinesthetic stimulus, and this triggers the kinesthetic state of feeling deep love.

1. Once you feel yourself back in that experience of feeling deep and total love, what is the *most important thing* that has to happen to *trigger* that love?
   - Is it most important that he or she looks at you in a certain way, or brings you flowers or presents or takes you places (visual external—V^e)? *Or:*
   - Is it even more important that he or she tells you something in that certain tone of voice (auditory external—A^e)? *Or:*

- Is it even more important that he or she touches you in a certain way? (kinesthetic external—K^e)?
2. All of these things may be nice, but usually one is most important. This may or may not be the same as your strongest modality—VAK.

CONFLICTING BELIEFS AND VALUES. Any disagreement, argument, or upset in a relationship is based on conflicting beliefs and values. One partner *expects* that the other will act in a certain way, and it doesn't happen like that. Sometimes two people can even have the same value, but different beliefs or rules of what it takes to realize that value.

A dear friend and I both value feeling close and connected during the rare moments we have together as I've been completing this book. I have noticed that whenever I am getting close to finishing a section or a chapter right before a date, it is important for me to complete it if possible, even if it means I'll be *a little late.* That way I won't be thinking about what I haven't completed. I can then put my full attention of being present with my friend, and we feel close and connected. It turns out, however, that she feels it is important that I be *right on time.* That way she knows that I value her, so we can feel close and connected. We both *value* feeling close and connected, and we each had different ways of achieving this until we discovered the conflict, and compromised on our expectations.

The heart of virus-free communication presented in the next chapter is to re-create rapport between the opposing lovers and to fish out the differences in beliefs and values that underlie the conflict.

THE ELUSIVE MIRROR. To be discussed later in this chapter.

CHILDHOOD THOUGHT VIRUSES

Remember, the basis of internal conflict is unconscious parts. A part (or a thought virus) is a portion of the nervous system (the unconscious mind) that is more or less functionally detached. It is incongruent because the behavior it produces is at odds with its positive intent. Given the theory that most of us are born into wholeness—that wholeness is shattered at least partially by the formation of three major parts.[5]

THE MASK. What traits did you have to develop as a child to get people to like you? What do you have to do, or how do you need to act now, to be socially acceptable? The collection of such beliefs is commonly called the *mask*. This part no doubt originates with childhood beliefs of what it takes to get love and acceptance from parents or caretakers. The mask is a group of limiting thought viruses that are incongruent because of the presupposition that you are unlovable to begin with. You are attempting to become something you aren't, by taking on behaviors that aren't you. Parental suggestions that promote formation of this glitch in thinking include the following:

- "Big boys don't cry."
- "Don't touch yourself there."
- "We don't act like that in this family."
- "You don't really hate your little brother."

THE SHADOW. I wonder, when you were growing up, if you ever heard statements like, "You'll never be able to _____," or "You're just not cut out for _____," or "Your sister was the one who got all the good looks." Maybe as an adult you even say things like, "I could never learn computers," or "My memory is like a sieve," or "I just can't have orgasms." These statements identify self-imposed limitations—more limiting viruses—based on past failures and suggestions of parents, siblings, and teachers. In a sense we put these natural abilities *behind us,* in our *shadow.* The fabric of our shadow is limiting viruses—all of the qualities and capabilities we think we could never have. The good news is that these natural abilities are still potentially there, if we are will-ing to recover them. The bad news is that some of the qualities and capabilities we most admired in our parents may now reside in our shadow. On some level we may feel incomplete, because we lack these desirable attributes. According to Dr. Harville Hendrix, these are the attributes we are most likely to seek and recognize unconsciously in a potential mate.[6] We then per-ceive that person as a way to make us feel whole. This phenome-non is called *transference.* The shadow as a part is incongruent because of presuppositions that we cannot have certain natural abilities and qualities, and that another person is necessary to complete us.

BLIND SPOTS. By adopting a mask that includes beliefs and values from our parents or caretakers, we also take on some of their negative traits without being aware of it. If others criticize us for being stingy, unfeeling, overemotional, selfish, or distant, we may deny being that way, because we are unaware of, or blind to, having adopted these qualities. These are either limiting beliefs or trigger viruses that are invisible to us. It is especially ironic when a person says something like, "I'll never be like my mother," yet she is exactly like her mother. This part is totally incongruent, because the intent is that you are free of those undesirable attributes, while your behavior displays the same qualities.

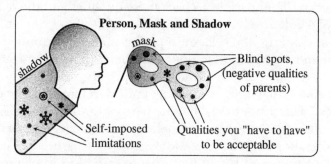

Many psychologists believe that on some level we still have memories of the feelings of wholeness and completeness with which we began life. A fundamental human drive is somehow to recover that wholeness. For many of us, this need fuels our spiritual quest and our desire for personal growth. One of the quickest and most striking ways to at least glimpse what that recovered wholeness would be like is through an intimate relationship.

THE ELUSIVE MIRROR

The fifth land mine, called *the elusive mirror,* occurs because our unconscious is quite adept at recognizing positive qualities in another that we feel are lacking in ourselves—qualities we have banished to our shadow. We also recognize a similar mask and blind spots, which provide some level of comfort, because they are familiar. Thus the statement, "It feels so comfortable being with you. I feel like I've always known you." A partner with closely matched unconscious parts is like a good mirror for viewing our potential wholeness. The more similar his or her unconscious parts to our own, the better the mirror, and the more difficult to recognize as such. Falling in love is like turning on the light to view ourselves. The better the lighting, the more distinct the shadow.

When we first gaze into the mirror, we see an expanded self that includes our shadow—all the great qualities of our parents we never thought we had. Self-imposed limitations are momentarily lifted. The early promise of romantic love is to recover the primordial wholeness through our partner. The limiting thought virus is called *transference*—ascribing desirable parental qualities and "missing" pieces of oneself to one's partner. We act as if that person can somehow give us back these qualities and the resulting sense of wholeness.

As we continue the relationship, that is, as we continue to gaze into the mirror, we begin to notice our blind spots. We attach these qualities to our partner through the process called *projection:* "I can't believe how stingy, unfeeling, and overemotional *you* can be at times." This is not to say that the partner doesn't have his or her own faults and blemishes, but looking into the elusive mirror, it is hard to know whether you are looking at your partner's shortcomings or your own. It is said that what we are most intolerant of in others is what we are most intolerant of in ourselves.

As Carl Jung suggested, intimate love can be a powerful tool in our quest for integrating parts, wholeness, and coherent thinking. We are, however, confronted with a dilemma. Our greatest emotional needs to become more whole are probably the same as our partner's, and what we most need from that person is probably what he or she is least able to give. The good news is that if we give to our partner what *we* most need, we experience the *state* we desire. Putting ourselves in the states we want, and simultaneously helping to heal our partner, allows for self-healing and integration.

- If what you most need is nurturing, nurture your partner.
- If what you need is intellectual stimulation, provide intellectual stimulation.
- If you need admiration, admire your partner.
- If you need love, provide love.

In summary, love is one of the quickest paths toward wholeness, self-actualization, and spiritual progress. Unfortunately, this path requires great patience and courage, because it is fraught with danger. When the path becomes dominated by the desert landscape of Phase Two, most of us feel we have had it, and slip over the *threshold*.

- *Land mine 5*. We look into the elusive mirror and don't like what we see, so naturally we blame the mirror. We may feel the partner has betrayed unspoken initial promises to provide wholeness and completeness.
- *Land mine 4*. We begin to notice conflicting beliefs and values.
- *Land mine 3*. Love and attraction strategies are not being fulfilled.
- *Land mine 2*. We experience negative triggers in which just being with the partner elicits negative emotions.
- *Land mine 1*. The relating has lost playfulness and spontaneity. We take the partner for granted. . . .

B   O   O   M!

On to the next relationship. There is only one problem with this scenario: When you go on to the next relationship, you have to take *you* with you. If the next partner is an equally good mirror, you will probably get to look at the same things.

WHAT IS ROMANTIC CHEMISTRY?

If you have ever experienced it, you clearly know what *romantic chemistry* is, even though it's hard to describe in words. Let's consider it from the perspective of how we make meaning.

First of all, if we experience strong initial attraction, our attraction strategy has been activated. Similarly, if at times we feel a deep sense of love, our partner has unconsciously activated our deep love strategy. It is really useful to know what your strategies are, so that if someone comes along and inadvertently but powerfully activates them, you have a choice; you aren't just swept off your feet with the wrong partner.

Once two partners feel initial attraction, they normally enhance chemistry by establishing feelings of rapport. They will *mirror and match* each other—that is, they use similar body language, similar gestures, and similar speech patterns, and spend much time searching out common beliefs, values, and interests, while overlooking ones that don't match. Then each is amazed at how comfortable and familiar the other seems.

In addition, the unconscious recognizes similar positive and negative qualities of our parents or caretakers, reflected in our partner's mask, shadow, and blind spots. A crucial consideration in dating is to know whether chemistry is present to the point that commitment is appropriate—if that is what you are seeking. Although most people say they just know chemistry intuitively, there are some questions worth asking yourself.

Exercise 26
Chemistry Questions

1. *Are you clearly attracted to this person?* Ask yourself this question, listen to your body, and *be honest.* If you aren't honest, the resulting incongruence will eat you alive. Misgivings about basic attraction usually show up as discomfort somewhere in your body, when you ask yourself the question. Do yourself a big favor and make sure your attraction strategy is lively *before* committing yourself to a relationship. This will make it much easier to get through conflicts, disillusionment, and the hard work connected with Phase Two.

2. *Is the type of person you are attracted to relationship material?* Some people, for whatever reason, are habitually attracted to unavailable partners, addictive personalities, or physically or emotionally abusive types.

   Find a good thought virus therapist (see Appendix 2) or an NLP practitioner to assist you in changing your clearly self-defeating attraction strategy. The process of changing unconscious strategies is relatively straightforward.

3. *How do you feel about yourself, being with this person?* Do you feel
   - more energy?   - heightened spiritual awareness?
   - a healthier outlook on life? - more loving and accepting of others?
   - more playful?   - better about yourself in general?

   These questions provide a good measure of chemistry being present. The last question also provides a good gauge for the health of an ongoing relationship. If these questions clearly indicate chemistry, yet you still feel some ambivalence about being with this person, you might ask yourself:

4. *Is there something important to me about* not *being in a relationship?* In other words, are *you* really available, and if not, how do you benefit by not being in a relationship?

CURING THE INTIMATE THERMOSTAT VIRUS

Question 4 in the previous exercise is especially interesting. I'm sure we've all had the experience of feeling deep love for another. Our heart is wide open, we feel especially close, when suddenly— whammo!—our beloved ends the relationship and leaves. There we are with the pain of having our heart ripped to shreds, and the unconscious anchors being close and in love with the excruciating pain of grieving. In the future, anytime we start to feel closeness and deep love, those very feelings we most desire *trigger* fear and apprehension of grieving, and we are in the grips of an *intimate thermostat virus*. Most of us at this point shut down emotionally, and unconsciously find some way to sabotage the relationship. This is one example of *fear of success* as a trigger virus. It is one of the most common major obstacles for getting the love we want.

A good therapeutic approach for such a fear of success is to begin with Antiviral Remedy 17—The Fast Phobia Cure for Past Failures (page 201), as a means to dissipate the nearly phobic reaction many of us have to the vulnerability of being in love. Beyond that, the intimate thermostat virus involves a Gemini component— the internal conflict between the part of us that wants closeness and intimacy and the other part that is scared to death of that closeness.

In the morning the lake was still perfectly calm. I realized in that calmness why so many of us crave an intimate love relationship that truly works, yet it is what we are most afraid of. I then walked down to the water's edge and meditated to bring within me the peaceful silence all around. Suddenly I realized the illusion of love. I had been ascribing the delicious feelings of wholeness, and strengths I never thought I had, to my partner. When I opened my eyes, I saw on the water's surface a perfect reflection of myself, and knew: That is what an ideal partner is. I also noticed how a reflection reverses right and left, just as we reverse or confuse what we see "out there" with who we are within.

14

VIRUS-FREE COMMUNICATION

GOOD COMMUNICATION
IS AS STIMULATING AS BLACK COFFEE,
AND JUST AS HARD TO SLEEP AFTER.

—ANNE MORROW LINDBERGH

Duryea, Pennsylvania. "Tell me, Aunt Teresa, what is the secret of successful marriage?" I had just returned to this small former coal-mining town, where my mother, her parents, and many of their relatives grew up. I hadn't been back since I was seven years old, and was curious to see whether any of my relatives here were still alive. To my surprise, the people who lived in the house where my grandmother once lived led me to my great-aunt Teresa. She had been married for more than fifty years, which is certainly an accomplishment these days, especially since her husband, who had died recently, occasionally had an unpleasant disposition and a bad temper. Since so many people have problems with commitment and staying married, I had to know her secret for a long, happy, lasting marriage, "What *is* your secret?"

She looked me straight in the eyes and said without flinching, "Ear plugs!" She had a great sense of humor, but I knew she was serious, so I decided not to pursue the subject. I couldn't help wondering, though, what my friend Dr. John Gray, who is an expert on men's and women's communication styles, would think of her approach.

I thought back to a weekend workshop I had attended with John. He knew that I was a physicist, so he had asked me how I, as a scientist, thought of love relationships. I said I thought they were like cosmic rays.

"WHAT?" he responded. He must have thought that I had gone off the deep end with my left-brain science, and was out of touch with my feeling side—that part which is so important for relation-

224

ships. I explained that cosmic rays are very *high-energy* subatomic *charged* particles that bombard Earth from *outer space*.

"Oh, I get it. You think that relationships can have high energy, but also a lot of emotional charge, so you need some space," he concluded.

"Well . . . I guess, but not exactly. These particles have so much energy, they move close to the speed of light, and strange things happen," I said. I was thinking about one particle in particular, called a *muon*. This is a secondary cosmic ray that is produced in subatomic collisions about 32,000 feet above the ground.[1] These particles only last about two-millionths of a second before changing into an electron, so a big mystery is how muons can make it all the way to the ground in their "lifetime." Even at the speeds they go, they should only be able to travel about 2,000 feet—one-sixteenth the 32,000 feet they manage to cover.

Albert Einstein provided an explanation through his Theory of Special Relativity. From our point of view, time slows down for the high-speed muons, and they "live" sixteen times longer than they are supposed to. Therefore they can travel sixteen times farther than they should, and make it to the ground. On the other hand, if you take it from the muon's viewpoint (if they had one), they still only live two-millionths of a second, and can still travel only about 2,000 feet. What's fascinating is that, according to Einstein, each viewpoint—ours and the muon's—is equally correct. So the question still remains: How are the muons able to make it to the ground, some 32,000 feet away? I thought this was like relationships, because each partner has a viewpoint that is equally valid, yet different viewpoints can lead to conflicts and even paradoxes—like the paradox of love reception viruses.

Dr. Harville Hendrix, a researcher and couples counselor, made a rather remarkable observation some years ago. When things are not going well in love relationships, most people will complain that they feel unloved—the partner is not loving as he or she did in the beginning. Dr. Hendrix developed a number of powerful exercises for couples to rekindle ways of expressing love for each other. After some time, people doing these exercises agreed, the partner really was loving them more, and many of the relationships dramatically improved. However, a number of relationships actually got worse.[2] For some of us, the very thing we most crave in a relationship, the thing we complain about not having—feeling deeply loved—can make things worse if we actually get it. I have labeled this phenomenon the *love reception virus*. One researcher has gone so far as to say that expressing love to our partner can be detrimental to our love life. I didn't understand his statement at the time, but, knowing how devious thought viruses can be, I figured anything was possible.

When I began my research on thought viruses as they apply to intimate love relationships, I believed that the most crucial skill to make love last is effective communication. I soon recognized that that skill itself was subject to infection by thought viruses. I wondered what caused the conflicts and arguments so characteristic of Phase Two. How does communication break down? If thought viruses have a positive intent, what *is* the intent behind arguments? We also know that overindulging such negative emotions as hostility may be a significant factor in coronary heart disease, and ignoring feelings as Aunt Teresa did may lead to cancer. How, then, do we strike a balance of appropriately communicating love and the negative emotions—hurt, anger, feelings of betrayal—in a way that works for both partners?

WHY CONFLICTS AND ARGUMENTS ARISE

The focus of Phase One is discovering likeness and fostering rapport with our partner. Recognizing those great qualities in our partner that had been banished to our shadow, allows us to feel a greater sense of wholeness as we view ourselves in the mirror of an intimate partner. The sense that the partner is really listening to us may provide the feeling of being understood and valued.

When the focus in Phase Two shifts to differences, this breaks down rapport and promotes polarization. Conflicts and arguments are simply ill-fated attempts to reestablish rapport by defending our viewpoint and trying to *persuade* the partner to think as we do. We are hurt, upset, or angry because the partner has violated some belief or value of ours. Many of us feel that *our* values are universal, that anyone in his right mind knows this is the way things should be. If our partner doesn't agree, we feel the need to point out the flaws in his or her thinking. Unfortunately, when our partner challenges our blind spots or mask, that's essentially challenging our acceptability and lovability as a person. To challenge our beliefs and values is to challenge our very identity.

The death rattle for most relationships may not be so much the frustrations, hurts, and anger that are bound to surface, as much as how we communicate the feelings—or don't communicate them, as in the case of my Aunt Teresa.

The core of any disagreement boils down to one simple truth: No matter how much our partner is like us, in many ways he or she still makes meaning differently. If I work long hours, I might think it means that I want to go the extra mile to provide my family with material comfort, because I care about them. To my family it might mean that I'm a workaholic who cares more about his job than time with his family. The heart of virus-free communication is for each partner to discover the meaning behind the other's point of view and, like Einstein, regard the other viewpoint as equally valid.

There are many ways for categorizing how people think: visual versus auditory versus kinesthetic; right-brain versus left-brain; introverted versus extraverted; moving toward versus moving away from people; Martians versus Venusians; and so on. These and other systems all contain some truth as models. Some provide clever and interesting insights. The problem I have with these various ways of categorizing people is how to remember it all—the myriad characteristics described by each model. I think a much simpler and more realistic approach is to recognize that whenever a conflict arises, our partner is making meaning differently than we are.

As we pointed out earlier, the unconscious is skilled at recognizing similar unconscious parts in a potential mate. Even if that person displays negative qualities of our parents or caregivers, and those qualities are uncomfortable, they are familiar. For many of us, even if being familiar means pain, it is still more comfortable than that which is unfamiliar. Dr. John Gray points out the fundamental human drive for understanding. Our unconscious is driven to re-create situations from childhood that we did not understand, in order to resolve them now.

COMMUNICATING LOVE VIRUS-FREE

Many people I talk with who are having trouble in their intimate love relationships acknowledge that thought viruses may be the culprit. Yet they are still convinced they are great communicators. The problem lies in their *partner's* distorted thinking.

There is a presupposition in NLP that you can measure the effectiveness of your communication by the results you get.

This is a challenging point of view, because it puts the responsibility for results squarely on the communicator. If you have experienced less-than-magnificent relationships during your adult life, there is a good chance that not only is the relationship suffering from faulty thinking, but your only tool for repairing the relationship—communication—is itself contaminated with thought viruses.

Most partners are convinced that they know how to express love to their partner, that they communicate that love, yet often feel frustrated because the partner doesn't appreciate the love they're expressing. As we pointed out in the last chapter, we generally feel unloved because our deep love strategy and possibly the attraction strategy are not being activated. What's crucial here is not just to communicate your love, but to communicate it in a way that your partner really gets it—that is, through *their* love strategy. I think this is what that one researcher had in mind when he claimed that communicating love with your partner can be detrimental. Unappreciated gestures of love can breed resentment.

The first step to communicating love effectively is to discover the deep love and attraction strategies for you and your partner through Exercises 24 and 25 (pages 215–16 and 216–17). If, after doing these exercises, you are still not clear about what works for you and your partner, invest a little time and money. Have a thought virus therapist or an NLP practitioner* help you with the process. It is one of the most valuable investments you can make if you value a relationship that really works.

Beyond that, you can enhance expressions of love and attraction by creating a "Gifts of Love" list.

Exercise 27
"Gifts of Love" List[3]

1. Write down all the things that make you feel loved, and title it "My Gifts of Love List." If you are not in a relationship, think back to your last significant one and what that person did that made you feel deeply loved.

---

* See Appendix 2.

2. Next, think back to the beginning of your current relationship or the last significant relationship you had. What were some things your partner did in the beginning of the relationship that made you feel especially loved, which after a while he or she stopped doing? Add these to your list.

3. Now think of things that no one has ever done for you that you *imagine* would make you feel deeply loved. Add these to your list.

4. Next read back over your list and rate items from four stars (having the biggest impact), down to one star (having the least impact).

5. If you are in a relationship, exchange lists with your partner. Put a check mark next to items that would be easiest for you to do, and a question mark next to ones that would be difficult.

6. Keep written copies of your partner's attraction strategy, his or her love strategy, and this "Gifts of Love" list someplace where you will see them regularly. Remember to employ his or her attraction and love strategies, as you probably did when you were first dating. In addition, once or twice a week, do one of the items from your partner's "Gifts of Love" list as exactly that, a gift—not an expectation. Do this regardless of how you are feeling about your partner. By giving love freely, you are putting yourself into a loving state.

ARGUMENTS

Do you remember the well-known fable of the three blind men examining an elephant for the first time? One feels the tusk and concludes that the animal is hard and lancelike. The one feeling the trunk concludes the elephant is flexible and snakelike. The third, feeling the body, concludes the elephant is like a massive wall. These men have quite an argument about their perceptions. Each is convinced of the accuracy of his careful observations: Any reasonable man, being as careful as he was, would have come to the same conclusion; the other two blind men must simply be out of touch with reality. Each tries to convince the others that he is right and they are wrong.

Arguments are counterproductive because we are out of rapport with our partner, and the underlying presuppositions are likely to make the lack of rapport worse. Most of us assume, like the blind men, that any reasonable person would think as we do, that *our* viewpoint is universal, with the one strange exception of our partner. We assume further that if one person is right, that means the other is wrong. If my partner is right, that means I must be out of touch with reality.

Arguments are dangerous, because in the heat of the moment we might inadvertently say something that we wind up regretting for a long time. Once those words are out, there's no way to erase them.

One useful approach to arguments is to set up an agreement with your partner ahead of time. If you are ever in an argument that is getting out of control, one of you must momentarily get sane enough to do something outrageous to *interrupt the pattern* of the argument and bring it to a stop.

> Practically anything you say
> will seem amusing,
> if you're on all fours.
> —P. J. O'Rourke

This is an example of a great pattern interruption, if you are both willing to do it. Anyway, decide ahead of time on something either of you can do or say that is outrageous enough to shock the other and stop the argument. Agree to process the feelings with the advanced communication model, *later,* when you have both calmed down.

COMMUNICATING SMALL-TO-MODERATE ANNOYANCES

"I can't believe what a slob you are. Every time I come over to visit, you have dirty dishes and old spoiled food scattered around your house," snapped Dan.

"Oh yeah? Look who's talking. When I come over to *your* place, I can smell your uncleaned cat box a block away," retorted Linda. These are not major resentments—yet—but they may very well become major with this style of communicating. Some couples actually do better in handling major, deep-seated feelings and crises than in dealing with the small-to-moderate annoyances that can accumulate and ultimately do in the relationship.

A much less confrontative and more effective way of communicating and clearing up such annoyances is to create a request list. The key to the process is to fish out the value important to you *and* to the well-being of the relationship that is being violated, and how specifically your partner's behavior violates that value, *before* communicating with your partner. For example, if I were working with Dan and Linda in couples counseling, I might ask Dan, "What's important to you about Linda having the dishes cleaned and picked up?"

"It makes my skin crawl to see that mess, and I feel like I don't want to be there," Dan says.

"What's important to you *and* Linda about not having your skin crawl and wanting to be there?" I continue.

"Well, I want to be close with her, and I think it would bring us closer if I could be comfortable with her in *her* home as well as mine," Dan responds. We now have the value. Dan values being close with Linda, and being comfortable in her home might help toward that end.

"Specifically how do you know that you're not comfortable in Linda's home and not getting close to her?" I ask.

"When I see the dirty dishes with uneaten old food, it feels unsanitary to me. I feel repelled, and don't want to be there. I guess my ex-wife was like that, and it made me sick," Dan responds. Dan's reaction may be a trigger—discomfort anchored to dirty dishes and clutter in the past—or it may be that he simply values clean, sanitary surroundings. If Dan's reaction is a trigger, there are two approaches to remedy the conflict. I could assist Dan in collapsing the anchor, or Linda could change her habits. Since I personally value sanitation, I would probably show Dan how to clearly request that Linda change her pattern. On the other hand, if what annoyed Dan was Linda's occasionally using a certain tone of voice, a certain look, a certain gesture—something over which she has little *conscious* control, it would be more appropriate to assist Dan in collapsing or reversing his trigger.

A key component in any request is the word *because*. This is a very powerful and persuasive word. We habitually like to ask "Why?" The natural answer, just as when we were children and asked our parents why we had to eat our peas, or why we couldn't go to the circus, is "Because!" The University of Pennsylvania did an office study in which people were lined up to use a copy machine. A fellow worker came in and said she was in a hurry, she had only ten copies, and could she cut in line? Sixty-two percent of the time, the people in line would let her. When she changed the request to, "I'd like to cut in, *because* I'm in a hurry, and I have only ten copies?" people accommodated her 92 percent of the time.

In the session with Dan and Linda, I'd suggest this format for Dan's request, "I'd like you to _____ [specific behavior to satisfy your rule], *because* _____ [your emotional reaction now], and I want to feel _____ [the value] with you when _____ [the context of the annoyance]."

In the present example it comes out like this: "I'd like you to keep your dishes picked up and clean, *because* old dirty dishes make my skin crawl, and I want to feel comfortable and close with you when I visit you in your home." Notice how clear this request is. There's no blaming, no having one person be right and the other wrong, no aggressive demands, no defensiveness. Here is how to clean up the backlog of annoyances you might have with your partner.

Antiviral Remedy 19
The Request List
(for Small-to-Moderate Annoyances)

1. Each partner separately takes three blank pieces of paper. Label the first "Annoyances." Make a list that answers the following statement: "I am annoyed when my partner _____."
   - Avoid for now behaviors that will likely be a *major* source of conflict.
   - Any annoyance that is likely a trigger—a certain look, a certain tone of voice, a certain gesture or touch—that your partner has little conscious control over, but automatically triggers a strong response in you, is better handled with collapsing or reversing the trigger.
   - Do not share this list with your partner.
2. Divide the second sheet into two columns. Title the first "Values," and the second "Rules and Beliefs."
   - *Chunk up* on each annoyance until you have a value by asking yourself, "What's important to me about my partner doing _____ [opposite of the annoying behavior], and what's important for us about this?" Repeat the question until you find your value that's being violated. Write this down.

- *Chunk down* with the value by asking yourself, "How *specifically* do I know that I'm not getting the _____ [value] that I want?" This gives your rule that is being violated. Write this down next to the value, but in the next column. (For example, I might value feeling safe with my partner while he or she is driving the car, and my rule is that I feel unsafe when my partner barrels around hairpin turns at twice the speed limit.)

3. Label the third sheet "Requests for My Partner." Create a request for each annoyance, based on the following structure:
   - "I'd like you to _____ [specific behavior to satisfy your rule], *because* _____ [your emotional reaction now], and I want to feel _____ [the value] with you when _____ [the context of the annoyance]."
   - "I'd like you to drive at or under the speed limit when we're together, because I get carsick and frightened at high speeds, and I want to feel well and safe with you when we drive."

4. Prioritize your requests by labeling the most important ones with four stars, and descending to one star for the least important.

5. Exchange the request list (not the first two pages) with your partner. Put a check mark next to items that would be easiest for you to do, and a question mark next to ones that would be most difficult. You may need to deal with the most difficult items by using the advanced communication model.

6. Each week, give as a gift one or two of your partner's requests, along with one or two items from the "Gifts of Love" list.

COMMUNICATING DEEPER-SEATED EMOTIONS

The heart of virus-free communication is, even in the midst of intense emotional upset, to establish and maintain rapport, to communicate feelings without insults, and to fish out and resolve differences in rules and values that caused the upset in the first place. The model I have adopted has six distinct steps:

SET THE STAGE. This involves getting your partner's permission to share your upset, as opposed to just springing or dumping the feelings. "I'm feeling angry [upset, hurt, etc.] with you. Are you willing to listen to me now?" This gives your partner mental and emotional space to prepare, and reduces the likelihood of nonlistening defensiveness. Your partner may want a few minutes to finish up what he or she is doing at that moment. Agree to talk, ideally within ten minutes, or at least within twenty-four hours if possible.

Remind each other that the *purpose* of talking is to resolve *just the feelings at hand,* and not just vent, dump on the other, or bring up issues from the past. Having a clear outcome in mind helps you maintain focus in this process.

ESTABLISH RAPPORT. NLP researchers have noticed that when people are in a strong state of rapport, they tend to unconsciously mimic or *mirror* each other; they assume a similar posture, use similar gestures and speech patterns, and make more prolonged eye contact. One of the most powerful expressions of rapport, however, is synchronized breathing. If you want to establish strong rapport with someone, simply notice his or her breathing, and mirror it without being obvious about it. After a while you can test for unconscious rapport by speeding up or slowing your breathing, and checking to see if he or she keeps pace. If so, you have established unconscious rapport. This greatly increases your chances of gaining conscious rapport.

Exercise 28
Rapport and Auditory Mirroring

1. Sit opposite your partner. One of you breathe normally, and have the other observe and synchronize breathing for about a minute. Switch roles and continue for another minute.
2. Next, one of you takes on the role of the *sender* and the other the *receiver*. The sender talks about something going on in his or her life that is *not* emotionally charged.
3. The sender speaks about two or three sentences, then the receiver practices auditory mirroring by paraphrasing the sentences and asking, "Did I get that right?" If not, ask for clarification and re-paraphrase. Continue the mirroring for a few minutes, then switch roles for a few more minutes.
4. Talk with each other about how each part of this process felt, and if you felt really listened to during the auditory mirroring.

Exercise 28 is a useful way to experience rapport-building through mirroring, and to begin to lay the foundation for listening skills necessary for effective virus-free communication.

AUDITORY MIRRORING. This is the heart of diffusing the emotional charge behind the upset. It is the essence of what Deepak Chopra calls being defenseless—letting go of having to defend your point of view. One of the things we want most, when we are upset with our partner, is to be heard. We want to know that our partner understands and cares about what has upset us.

The person who is upset, the *sender*, writes a love letter describing what happened and the resulting feelings; *or* simply talks to the partner, the *receiver*, about the issues. Just as in the previous exercise, the receiver reads or listens to two or three sentences at a time, and paraphrases the information back to the sender.

The sender needs to follow two guidelines:

1. No name-calling, insults, or character assassination.
2. Express only that which others could not debate or take issue with.

For example, such statements as "When you looked at her that way, *everyone* knew you wanted to undress her on the spot," *or* "You're a lazy, irresponsible son of a bitch!" could be debated by others. On the other hand, a statement like "When you forgot my birthday, I felt angry, hurt, and was afraid I'm not important to you," can't be debated. This is your truth.

The receiver also has two guidelines:

1. No commentaries, disagreement, or any reactions. Hold your tongue just for now.
2. Paraphrase back a few sentences at a time, then ask, "Do I have it right?" If not, ask for clarification and re-paraphrase.

The first guideline here is the most difficult part of the whole process. Most of us are so conditioned to the idea that it is unacceptable to make mistakes or to be wrong that we immediately jump in to defend ourselves, without even hearing what the other person has to say. Unless you already have the magnificent relationship you'd like, your pattern of responding to your partner probably hasn't worked. This auditory mirroring provides a great

236 THOUGHT VIRUSES AND LOVE

way to interrupt our usual patterns of arguing and being defensive. In order to paraphrase back what your partner is saying, you actually have to listen to him or her. Trying to devise a counterattack is too confusing.

When the message appears complete, the receiver asks, "Is that it?" The sender will now likely feel truly heard. However, you still may not have uncovered the deeper meaning each of you has around the issue.

UNCOVER RULES AND VALUES FOR THE SENDER. This involves chunking up to get the *value* by asking, "What's important to you and us about having _____ [opposite to the behavior the sender objected to]?" Maybe what's important to me about, for example, your remembering my birthday is that I want to know that you value me and our being together. That is my value.

You next chunk down to get the rule(s) being violated: "Specifically how do you know that you're not getting the _____ [values] you want in this situation?" For example, how I know that you're not valuing me and our being together is that you forget the little things, like birthdays, anniversaries, and taking out the garbage on Tuesday nights.

Another question you can use to unearth the emotional impact of what is going on is "What are you afraid of in this situation?" The most basic emotion underlying anger, frustration, disappointment, and sadness is usually fear. If I'm honest, what I'm afraid of is that if you don't value me and our being together, our love might die, and we might end up separating.

UNCOVER RULES AND VALUES FOR THE RECEIVER. Swap roles. The receiver may or may not have any values connected with the behavior. My partner might say that she thought it would be more spontaneous and surprising to give me gifts on days other than birthdays, anniversaries, and so on, because I wouldn't be expecting them. Her value may be to be spontaneous and unpredictable. On the other hand, she may say she has been putting in too many hours at work, simply got caught up, and forgot my birthday. Or maybe in her family, birthdays weren't celebrated. Whatever the receiver offers, the sender mirrors back, with no comments or contradictions.

THE CREATIVE LEAP. The receiver asks the sender, "How can we change our behaviors or our rules so that you can have the _____ [sender's values] you want, and I can have the _____ [receiver's values] that I want." Seek some creative alternatives. These may result in additions to the "Requests" list for each of you.

Antiviral Remedy 20
The Advanced Communication Model
(for Clearing Deeper-Seated Negative Emotions)

1. Set the stage by
   - *getting permission* to share feelings versus just springing them on your partner ("I'm having feelings, and can we process them now or sometime in the next ten minutes to twenty-four hours?")
   - *reminding each other* that the purpose of your processing is to resolve the feelings and issue at hand and not just to vent, dump on the other, or bring up other things from the past
2. *Establish rapport* by mirroring breathing for one to two minutes.
   - The sender (the one who is upset) breathes slowly and deeply.
   - The receiver mirrors the sender's breathing and visualizes the sender as a hurt child.
3. *Auditory mirroring.* The sender expresses feelings and issues two to three sentences at a time verbally, or the receiver reads two to three sentences at a time from a love letter (see from experience which works best for you and your partner).
   - The sender follows two guidelines:
       a. no name-calling, putting down, or character assassination
       b. express only that which *others* could not debate or take issue with
   - The receiver follows the two guidelines:
       a. No commentaries, disagreement, or any reactions. Hold your tongue just for now.
       b. Paraphrase back a few sentences at a time, then ask, "Do I have it right?" If not, ask for clarification and re-paraphrase.

When the message appears complete, the receiver asks, "Is that it?" The sender will now likely feel truly heard.

4. Uncover *rules and values for the sender.*
   - Receiver asks, "Is it okay now to look for your rules and values behind this issue?" If okay, proceed.
   - Receiver chunks up: "What's important to you and to us about having _____ [opposite to the behavior the sender objected to]. Continue chunking up until you have one or several values.
   - Paraphrase the values. Ask "Do I have it right?" then write them down.
   - Receiver chunks down: "Specifically how do you know that you're not getting the _____ [values] you want in this situation?"
       a. Get an expression of the rule or rules being violated.
       b. Paraphrase the rule(s) and ask "Do I have it right?" and write them down.
   - Receiver asks, "What are you afraid of in this situation?" Paraphrase and write these down.
5. Uncover *values and fear for the receiver.* Swap roles.
   - Receiver asks "Is it okay if we find my rules and values behind this issue?" If okay, proceed.
   - Sender chunks up: "What's important about doing things the way you did them?" There actually may not be anything important to the receiver. It may be an oversight or a bad habit. If there are values, continue chunking up until you have one or two values. Sender paraphrases, and asks, "Do I have it right?" Write them down.

   Note: If you chunk up far enough, you may find that the receiver and the sender have the same value.

   - Sender asks receiver, "What are you afraid of in this situation?"
6. *Creative leap.* The receiver asks the sender, "How can we change our behaviors or our rules so that you can have the _____ [sender's values] you want and I can have the _____ [receiver's values] I want?" Seek some creative alternatives. These may result in additions to the "Requests" list for each of you.

Note: If the sender is extremely upset, he or she may not be able to swap roles and listen to the receiver (step 5). If this is the case, stop after step 4. Steps 1–4 are enough for now, and should greatly dissipate the emotional charge. Agree to continue the process at another time.

If one of you loses it emotionally during these steps, and the process falls apart, use a prearranged pattern interrupt to stop. Agree to a later time when you can come back and make the process work.

Sometimes when couples first start using this process, one member will object, saying it feels too mechanical, too step-by-step, too left-brain. When revealing deep-seated negative emotions, it is, without a doubt, *not* the time to be spontaneous and wing it. Most of us have spent a lifetime using self-defeating communication patterns. The fact that this process can at first be a bit awkward and step-by-step is valuable if you stay with it. It forces you to deviate from your old way of communicating. It's also like learning to play music and starting with mechanical scales and arpeggios. It's mechanical at first, yet it's the quickest way to gain skill to master the instrument.

THE LOVE RECEPTION VIRUS

In spite of our partner's best efforts to elicit our love strategies, provide gifts of love, comply with items from our request list for small to moderate annoyances, and communicate deeper-seated emotions clearly, sometimes it doesn't work. Harville Hendrix and others have observed that some relationships get worse with increased expression of love. Some of us are plagued by the paradox I call *love reception viruses.* The more love our partner shares, the more uncomfortable we become. This can certainly be frustrating and baffling to our partner.

The notion is actually similar to the love thermostat virus—what we *say* we want is what creates the most discomfort when we get it. It is also different, because the cause of the love thermostat is usually a trigger—past feelings of hurt and grieving, anchored with being close. On the other hand, the love reception virus results from limiting beliefs. If a child in a dysfunctional family didn't have the experience of being deeply loved, then receiving love can be threatening to him as an adult, because it is unfamiliar. Even though being unloved has its own discomfort, we are used to it. If part of us desires to be loved, and another part is un-comfortable when the love actually comes, the solution is first to find the positive intent of each part. These may very well be the same. Then it is simply a matter of reintegrating the parts using Six-Step Reframing or The Visual Squash (pages 98–99 and 103).

As I reflected on the problems couples have in communicating, I realized that the one tool we have to resolve glitches in thinking that sabotage relationships is *communication*. When communica-tion itself is infected with explosive triggers and limiting beliefs—trying to defend our point of view, or to get the partner to think as we do—we lose the whole perspective of seeing an equally valid universe from a sometimes strange and sometimes fascinating point of view.

Aunt Teresa had the wisdom to avoid arguments, but may have excluded a whole new way of looking at things—as we would, by not taking the viewpoint of the cosmic ray muons. The only way they can reach the ground *from their perspective* is that the distance to the ground *is* only about 2,000 feet instead of 32,000. In other words, the whole universe from their perspective, parallel to their velocity, appears to be flattened to only one-sixteenth of the size we see it to be. Just as in relationships, one point of view (ours), that time slows down for the muons, and the other point of view (the muon's), that the universe has shrunk to one-sixteenth the size that we see, are equally valid.

PART FIVE

MOVING TOWARD WHOLENESS

15

GETTING THE RESULTS
YOU WANT IN LIFE

July 1976, Fairfield, Iowa. "Hey, Don. Come on outside and see what I just saw. It's the northern lights!" Steve knew I was a physicist, so he thought I'd be impressed. It was a sweltering summer night in central Iowa, as we were finishing our evening meeting—part of a monthlong teachers' conference on consciousness and education. I thought to myself, "Northern lights? In central Iowa? In the middle of the summer?" I told Steve that I thought that it was possible, but not too likely. Maybe it was town lights reflecting off clouds.

"No, no, I saw it clearly. The lights are due north, they are pretty bright, and flickering!" he insisted.

"Okay, let's take a look." We stepped outside, and when my eyes got used to the dark, I saw what he was talking about. In spite of the oppressive humidity, the sky was reasonably clear, and due north, near the horizon, there were steady flickering lights. I had never seen the northern lights before, so I was excited. As I watched carefully, though, I began to notice outlines of darkness within the light, and suddenly realized what it was—a distant thunderstorm, far enough away that we couldn't hear the thunder. The storm was so intense, though, that it displayed one lightning flash after another, almost continuously.

Steve asked me what caused the northern lights, and I explained it was subatomic particles from outer space electrifying the air in the upper atmosphere and causing it to glow.

"Oh! Well, how come they have cosmic rays at the North Pole, but not here?" he asked. I said I thought we had just as many cosmic rays here.

"Then why doesn't the air glow here? Why don't we have the Midwestern lights?" he continued.

"That's a good question," I responded. "When I was in college, I once asked Professor Hibbs something like that. He said it's sort of like life. If you move in the direction set out for you, progress is effortless. But if you move counter to your direction, progress is almost impossible, and you go in circles." I told Steve I hadn't understood that at the time, but that the present workshop was giving deeper meaning to his words.

Steve was a political science professor from a university in Mississippi, and was interested in consciousness and government. He reminded me that the three founding values for our country were life, liberty, and the pursuit of happiness. Unfortunately, our political forefathers didn't tell us *how* to pursue happiness.

Even today psychologists are divided about this. What is happiness? How do inner standards contribute to such states as happiness, fulfillment in life, and getting the results we want? How do we determine what it takes to be successful in life? And how can we free ourselves of the thought viruses that cause inner conflict, so we can move toward a destiny we will be proud of?

THE PURSUIT OF HAPPINESS

In working with clients, I've noticed that once a person is able to reintegrate conflicting parts of a thought virus, coherence of thinking and action noticeably improve. People appear more focused, more decisive, more in tune with their direction in life, and generally more happy. This was one of the striking qualities I sensed in Dana's way of thinking that led me to another revelation.

CLUE NUMBER 8: TO FIND TRUE HAPPINESS, BRIDGE THE GAP BETWEEN YOUR HIGHEST VALUES AND THE WAY YOU LIVE DAY-TO-DAY LIFE.

In a study reported in the *British Journal of Social Psychology*,[1] psychologists at Bar-Ilan University in Israel reported some definitive findings that may make happiness and fulfillment in life less elusive. Their work tested and expanded on the findings of an earlier researcher, E. T. Higgins. In Higgins's model, the *ideal self* reflects our core values, the *ought self* reflects how we think others expect us to be, and the *actual self* is how we think we actually are.

Exercise 29
Feelings of Congruence

1. Ask yourself, "What area of life [career, personal growth, family, relationship, recreation, financial, spiritual, social, etc.] do I feel *best* about? Which area seems to be working best for me right now?" Write down your answers.
2. Now ask yourself, "In this area that seems to be working the best for me, what in particular am I *doing* that makes me feel proud?" Write down at least one thing you are doing. Maybe you feel good about your family life because you spend an hour of quality time each evening with your children, and take them on occasional outings.
3. Next, find the value associated with what you wrote down in step 2, by asking yourself, "What's important to me about doing _____ [what you are doing]?" Chunk up further by asking, "What's important to me about _____ [the answer to the previous question]?" Keep asking until you have a value. Maybe you value showing your children that you love them in a way that they really get it.
4. Finally, ask yourself, "When I do _____ [the answer from step 2], that supports _____ [the value from step 3], how do I feel?"

When the Israeli psychologists asked university psychology students questions along the lines of the questions in Exercise 29, the answer to question 4 was generally "a state of short-term happiness." In other words, short-term happiness results when activities from our *actual self* are in line with the values of our *ideal self*. On the other hand, when what we do is in line with values from the *ought self*, we feel more tranquillity and peace of mind. Some values from the ought self may be the same as those from the ideal self, and some may be quite different.

Exercise 30
Feelings of Incongruence

1. Ask yourself, "What area of my life [career, personal growth, family, relationship, recreation, financial, spiritual, social, etc.] is *less than magnificent?* Which area needs the most work right now?" Write this down.
2. Now ask yourself, "In this area that needs the most work, what in particular am I doing, or *not* doing, that I don't feel good about?" Maybe you're not exercising, or you're still smoking, or you haven't taken the first step toward that New Year's resolution that's been on your list for the past ten years. Whatever it is, write it down.
3. Next find the value associated with what you wrote down in step 2, by asking yourself, "What's important to me about doing _____ [what you're *not* doing in step 2]?" or "What's important to me about not doing _____ [what you're doing in step 2]?" Chunk up further by asking, "What's important to me about _____ [the answer to the previous question]?" until you have a value. Maybe it's important to you to follow through on that New Year's resolution, because that would make you feel that you are in control of life, that you can set your own direction.
4. Finally, ask yourself, "When I do (or don't do) _____ [the answer from step 2] that goes *against* _____ [the value from step 3], how do I feel?"

Again, in surveying students roughly along the lines of the questions in Exercise 30, the researchers found that the answers to step 4 were depression, sadness, and dissatisfaction. In other words, a large discrepancy between the perceived actual self and the ideal self produced the opposite of happiness. In contrast, a large gap between the actual self and the ought self was more likely to produce feelings of guilt and anxiety, the opposite of peace of mind.

It appears, then, that one major component of short-term happiness and fulfillment is congruence, i.e., freedom from the internal conflict of thought viruses that prevent us from living the values we most cherish. The key issues to getting the results we want in life are

- to *know* clearly our most cherished values, dreams, and visions (i.e., our *mission* in life)
- to find a way to bridge the *gap* between our highest values and the way we live day-to-day life

If your value is to train for a new career, find a way to make that work. If your value is to live on a tugboat, as it was for Dana, live on a tugboat.

YOUR MISSION, SHOULD YOU CHOOSE TO ACCEPT IT . . .

To bridge this gap, and to attune our thinking with our life's purpose, we need to know clearly what our values and life purpose are. The ten exercises presented in Appendix 1 of this book constitute a *vision quest* to clarify these issues for you. The vision quest consists of four parts:

- discovering your present life values, personal uniqueness, and visions in life
- discovering why you have "chosen" this particular life—with all of its joys, sorrows, triumphs, and tragedies—and what it would take for you to be able to look back at the end and say, "Now *that* was a successful life!"
- formulating your mission statement based on what you have discovered
- realigning your present values, goals, and visions to support you and automatically move you toward completing your mission and a destiny you will be proud of.

The exercises will probably take a few hours, and the time spent could very well be the most important time investment you've ever made toward a fulfilling life. Stop reading here until you have completed your vision quest. . . .

Based on the mission statement you completed in Section Three of Appendix 1, and all that you've written in your vision quest so far, go back to your Life's Values (Exercise 31, page 259) and answer the questions in the following antiviral remedy:

Antiviral Remedy 21
Realigning Your Values

1. Which values most support moving you toward your mission? Put a star next to these, and write just these values down on another sheet of paper titled "Values Supporting My Mission." Prioritize them in terms of relative importance.

2. Are there any values *missing* from your new list, which, if they were here, would be especially important in moving you toward your mission? Write these down in the proper order of priority.

3. Look at your old list and see if you would like to add a few more of these to your new list, just to make the path toward your destiny more fun, interesting, and exciting. Add these according to proper priority.

4. Notice those items on your new list that are moving-away-from values, such as, "I never want to be in another abusive relationship," or "I don't want to feel rejected," or "I'm not willing to lose money again, as I did on that last investment." For each of these values, ask yourself if there is still some unhealed issue behind that value, some emotional charge. If you sense there *is* a strong unhealed emotional component, you can do several things to change the meaning of what has happened in the past.

   - Use the Fast Phobia Cure (Antiviral Remedy 17, page 201) or the Eye Movement Scrambler (Antiviral Remedy 13, pages 152–53) to reduce or eliminate feelings from all the times in the past that you experienced the negativity—being in an abusive relationship, being rejected, or losing money on bad investments.

   - Reframe the meaning by asking yourself questions like, "What was important to me about being in that abusive relationship, or what could be important, if I chose to look at it that way? How could I have benefited from having that experience? How could having that experience be moving me toward my mission in life, if I chose to think of it that way?" You might also check your moving-toward values to see if any of them are based on moving-away-from experiences. Follow the last two steps above for any of these.

5. To reprioritize your new values list on your unconscious level, so that you automatically think this new way, do an ecology

check first. Ask yourself, "Is there any part of me that would object to reprioritizing my values this way?" If so, find the positive intent of the objecting part. If not, continue.

- Elicit submodalities of how you *picture* your former number-one value. This process can work with auditory or kinesthetic submodalities, but visual is generally easier. Elicit the corresponding submodalities for a less important value, and find the one or two submodalities that are most different, for example, the *driver(s)*.

- If your former number-one value is life-supporting and has some usefulness in moving you toward your mission, you might consider keeping it as your number-one value.

- Follow steps 4, 5, and 6 in Antiviral Remedy 6 (page 81) to use the driver submodalities to shift (unconsciously) the importance of your other values, according to your new list.

This completes your vision quest. One optional additional step is to go back and reprioritize your goals—life goals, five-year goals, and six-month goals—in light of your mission statement and your new set of values.

Now that you have your mission statement, your new values list, and possibly your new set of goals, keep copies of these somewhere where you can review them every two to four weeks. Whenever you face a difficult major decision, simply consult with your mission statement to see which choice is most in line with your chosen direction. Having your values aligned is one of the most powerful steps you can take toward congruent, virus-free thinking. Progress for you should now become increasingly automatic, on some levels even effortless.

The Israeli researchers pointed out that we don't know for sure how short-term happiness connects with long-term happiness and fulfillment. More than likely, though, happy moments make for a happy time. Happy times make for happy days, and happy days make for a happy and fulfilling life.

Israel and the Middle East are a long way from the northern lights—which are connected with Earth's magnetic field. Our planet is a giant magnet, and the farther we are from polar regions, the more the Earth's magnetic field is parallel to the ground.

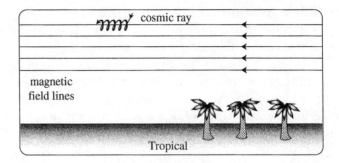

A major cause of sadness, depression, anxiety, and guilt is moving against our chosen direction in life—our highest values, our mission. This is like cosmic rays attempting to *cross* Earth's magnetic field lines. The magnetic field throws them off course by pushing them sideways, just as thought viruses can derail life's course from the track of our cherished values. The cosmic rays wind up spiraling in circles and getting stuck well above the atmosphere. No doubt, most of us feel as though *we* are moving in circles, when we get stuck with internal conflict.

Congruent thinking allows us to act in accord with the values of our ideal self. This is like moving with the flow of life, as Professor Hibbs pointed out. It is like cosmic rays moving toward the Earth in polar regions. Here, the Earth's magnetic field lines point straight into the ground.

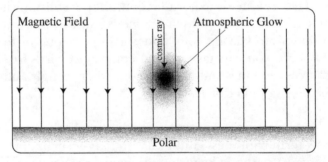

As long as the cosmic rays move *with* the direction of the magnetic field, as when we move *with* our mission, they experience no opposing force. They enter the atmosphere, electrify the air, and cause it to glow—like a person free from internal conflict.

16

BEYOND THOUGHT VIRUSES

CHARMING PEOPLE
LIVE UP TO THE VERY EDGE
OF THEIR CHARM,
AND BEHAVE JUST AS OUTRAGEOUSLY
AS THE WORLD WILL LET THEM.

—LOGAN PEARSALL SMITH

Washington, D.C., June 1993. Like most other major cities, Washington, D.C. has experienced steadily increasing crime, drug use, and other noncoherent, antisocial behavior for the last twenty years. The noncoherence here is just a reflection of the noncoherence across the country, caused by an epidemic of thought viruses. In this year alone, well over one million people will die from smoking, drugs, preventable chronic degenerative disease, violence, child abuse, and drunk driving. Millions will endure allergies, many will endure perceived failure, and millions more will bog down in the slow quicksand death of depression. Countless others will experience the death of dreams, careers, love relationships, and passion for living. Worst of all, most people aren't even aware of the cause as an epidemic in how we think and make meaning.

A group of 4,000 specialists in coherent thinking has just arrived in Washington to conduct a psychosocial experiment that could have monumental repercussions. The individuals perform an advanced mental practice that produces the highest level of brain-wave coherence yet observed. Statistics over the years have suggested that when a certain number of people do this mental practice together, coherence seems to radiate into the environment, and the crime level and other noncoherent thinking in surrounding areas decreases. This group proposes to demonstrate this definitively.

The President, every member of Congress, the chief of police, the media, and social scientists at various universities have been notified that the group anticipates a 15 to 20 percent drop in the crime rate by the end of the eight-week experiment. The officials react politely, and sympathetically, to the proposal. People in the street, when told of the experiment and interviewed on TV, express frustration that nothing else has worked to reduce crime, so why not try something new like this? Still, there is pessimism. The chief of police, when asked what must happen for the crime rate in Washington, D.C., to drop by 15 to 20 percent in June and July responds, "It would take a blizzard and the Washington Redskins football team playing every day."

The phenomenon the group is attempting to demonstrate, whereby only 4,000 people might influence the coherent thinking of millions of people in the city, is not unnatural. Consider this: The human voice carries remarkably little energy. A group of 10,000,000 people talking at the same time would produce barely enough sound energy to light a common flashlight.[1] Yet a *single person* singing just the right note can shatter a glass. Marching soldiers, when crossing a bridge, will break step to create deliberate noncoherence so that their marching cadence won't set up a resonance in the bridge's structure that might cause it to collapse.

Can individuals merely practicing coherent thinking really cause people and the environment around them to resonate with coherence? As individuals become increasingly free of thought viruses, what common characteristics do they display? What is the potential power of coherent thought?

QUALITIES OF VIRUS-FREE THINKING

In the course of my research, teaching seminars, and consulting, I have observed that people who are recovering from thought viruses, or whose thinking is becoming more virus-free, increasingly display six distinct qualities:

SELF-REFERRAL. This is a term I borrow from Deepak Chopra. It means that these people judge themselves more by their internal standards than by what other people expect and think. They enjoy others, but success does not depend on other people's opinions, or even on external circumstances. Their inner values are aligned. This allows them to automatically and unconsciously move toward what is important in life.

ABILITY TO MANAGE THEIR STATES. They do this as Dana did, by

- putting attention on the here and now
- collapsing or reversing triggers, that for most people would automatically produce unresourceful states
- changing the way they feel about undesirable things that have happened, by changing the meaning. This is most effectively accomplished through taking care of one's physiology (exercise, massage, breathing techniques, and power moves), and through Power Questions, as in Antiviral Remedy 12 (page 135).

ABILITY TO FAIL SUCCESSFULLY. These people naturally possess or have cultivated the skills from chapter 12, and no longer fear failure. They use setbacks as feedback, as Thomas Edison did. They have the ability to make meaning in such a way that they naturally see something positive, useful, or at least humorous, in whatever takes place for them.

BALANCE between solitude and spending time with others. They enjoy other people without judging themselves by others' standards. Solitude allows them to center and reconnect with their inner essence, to further bridge the gap between their highest values and the way they live daily life. They are also focused and productive with structured time, yet have the balance to equally enjoy unstructured time for being spontaneous and playful.

THINKING IS CONGRUENT AND ECOLOGICAL. Again, *congruent* means all their unconscious parts are aligned toward their vision. *Ecological* means that their success allows other people to be successful. Success, for these people, is not achieved at someone else's expense.

SOCIAL INTUITIVENESS AND CREATIVITY. These people become visionaries, with the uncanny knack of seeing some social need—to advance knowledge, to effect social change, to invent a new product or a new business, or to serve others in some innovative manner. They have a way of being in the right place at the right time.

Living your inner uniqueness brings out a childlike innocence and charm that can magnetize the people around you. I think part of the reason people were so drawn to Dana was that they recognized the charm in her that they wanted to experience for themselves. It is like wanting to recapture magical qualities of childhood.

When Dana was sick and being treated for ovarian cancer for more than a year and a half, she, like most people in similar circumstances, was devastated financially. She lost her savings, her forest cabin, and the Porcshe that she had much pride in owning. One day when she was in the hospital, her brother showed up with a brand-new Cadillac for her. He had taken on a second job, after hours, working in a garage for a year, so he could save enough money to buy her the new car. I observed this and other selfless acts of love for Dana from the people around her.

I said, "Dana, it's no accident this quality of love comes to you. Because of the way you think, the universe responds with love like this." My observation led me to the ninth clue for her way of thinking.

CLUE NUMBER 9: WHEN YOUR THINKING IS CONGRUENT, IT ATTUNES WITH YOUR LIFE'S PURPOSE, AND THE WORLD AROUND YOU WILL RESONATE.

RESONANCE

One of the great mysteries in the field of mathematics is the discovery of that branch called *the calculus*. At the time of Sir Isaac Newton and Gottfried Wilhelm Leibniz, who independently conceived of the calculus, geometry had been known for over 2,000 years, and algebra for over 500 years. Calculus represents an enormous quantum leap in our understanding of mathematics and physical motion. It is truly remarkable that, *simultaneously*, two powerful minds would independently conceive of the idea. Some people suggest, from a metaphysical perspective, that when a new way of thinking—a new paradigm—is ready to present itself, it is somehow present in the air. Those people whose thinking is clear enough will pick up on it.

You might think, "That's easy enough for people like Einstein and Newton, because they were geniuses. But how can an ordinary person have any significant impact on the world, even if that person is free of thought viruses?" Part of the answer is that we can each serve as a model, a vision of possibilities for those around us, an inspiration for what can happen.

When an electric guitar that's not plugged in is played, you can barely hear it. Guitar strings by themselves make very little sound. Those same strings, on an acoustic hollow-body guitar, sound much louder. How come? The guitar string stimulates the air inside the body to vibrate sympathetically; that is, the air inside resonates to the string and greatly amplifies its sound. This is also like the singer who sings a high pitch. If the singer matches her pitch to one of the natural frequencies of vibration of glass, the glass vibrates or resonates sympathetically. The energy in the glass keeps building until it shatters.

When I think of people who have changed the course of history, I think of Mahatma Gandhi, Ralph Nader, Mother Teresa, and Rachel Carson (author of the book *Silent Spring*, which sparked the environmental movement in the United States). On some level, each of these people picked up on some important need for humanity, something that was in the air, and they simply started thinking and acting, using congruent, coherent thought. Because the need was there, it *resonated* with many other people, and the ideals of that one person grew into a movement. I think the same is true of three of the most influential thinkers in the last ten years, Dr. Deepak Chopra, Tony Robbins, and Dr. John Gray. Each worked to refine the clarity of his own thinking, and each picked up on some crucial social need, that in a sense was already in the air. The overwhelming response to their books and talks shows how their ideas have resonated with and benefited large numbers of people around the world.

Increasing numbers of people are becoming aware of various antiviral remedies that produce powerful thinking and quick change. Virus-free individuals are causing people around them to resonate harmoniously. People whose thinking causes the world around them to resonate are said to have charisma.

When the 4,000 coherent-thinking specialists arrived in Washington, D.C., during June 1993, they approached coherent thinking from a different angle. They were trained in an advanced mental practice that produces the highest level of brain-wave synchrony and coherence yet observed. The idea was that a large enough group of people experiencing ultra-synchronized and co-herent brain waves might somehow cause the environment to res-onate harmoniously. Based on past data, the organizers predicted to the media, political leaders, and social scientists a 15 to 20 per-cent decrease in crime within two months. The D.C. police de-partment agreed to monitor crime figures.

Halfway through the experiment, the crime rate had dropped by 4 percent. By the end of eight weeks it had dropped by 18 per-cent, well within the predicted range.[2] After the group left Wash-ington, the rates returned to their previous high levels. These 4,000 people did not patrol the streets or perform any police ac-tivity; they simply sat quietly in dormitory facilities of three major universities and practiced an advanced meditative technique called the TM Sidhis.

I remember during this time looking up at a full moon, think-ing of the fullness of life, and what an exercise in coherent think-ing it took to land astronauts on the moon. I thought of the strange new light source they could actually see from the moon, even at levels as low as fifteen watts. When they observed this new coherent light, it echoed from the corner reflectors they had put in place. What they witnessed was the first laser beam successfully reflected back from the moon. The laser experiment allowed Mis-sion Control the ability to measure the distance from the Earth to the moon with an accuracy of less than several inches.

Ordinary light is noncoherent, like a person caught up in the distorted thinking of a thought virus. The particles of light pro-duced from various atoms vibrate randomly, do not reinforce each other, and scatter in all different directions.

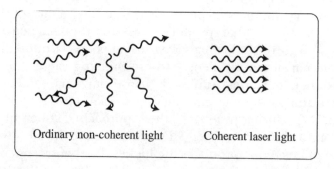

Ordinary non-coherent light   Coherent laser light

In contrast, *coherent laser light* consists of vibrations that are all synchronized, that all add together constructively, and are focused in one direction, like a person experiencing the congruence of having internal parts all aligned toward their dreams, their vision, their mission in life. Then I remembered that the millions of watts of noncoherent light from New York City were not enough for the astronauts to even see. Fifteen watts of coherent light from a laser beam is not only visible, but it has the power to burn a hole through steel. I wondered how much more powerful coherent virus-free thinking might be.

APPENDIX 1:
YOUR VISION QUEST

In this series of ten exercises constituting your vision quest, you will discover your uniqueness, how you live, what values most motivate you, and what ultimately is your mission in life. You will find which present values move you toward your desired purpose and which interfere, and ultimately realign your values to achieve congruence—all of your inner parts being aligned toward your mission in life.

Find a quiet place to complete these exercises where you will be undisturbed for a couple of hours.

SECTION ONE: YOUR PRESENT VALUES, UNIQUENESS, AND VISIONS

Exercise 31
Present Life Values

1. As you think back over your life as a whole, look for one time you were especially motivated. What was the emotion or state you felt just as you began to feel this motivation? Put a label on it.

   Keep in mind it could be positive, like feeling connection, a sense of adventure, feeling creative, or it could be a moving-away-from value, such as fear of being fired, or of losing your love relationship. Whatever it is, write it down. Don't judge right or wrong.

Next, think of another time when you were particularly motivated in living life. Again, what was the emotion or state just as you began to feel motivated? Write this down. Repeat this process until you run out of examples.

2. Ask yourself, "What would it take for me to become discouraged with, or give up on, wanting to go on with life?" Write down whatever comes up. This will provide you with further motivating values. If failed health or severe depression would derail your desire to keep living, then having vibrant health or avoiding depression may be an important value. Add to your list of values based on the question here.

3. For each situation that would cause you to become discouraged with life, or want to give up on being alive, ask yourself, "If this were to happen, is there anything else that could happen that would rekindle my enthusiasm for life, even though *this* thing has happened?" If your health failed, but you could still maintain resourceful states, think clearly, and learn new things, maybe that would turn things around for you. State management, clarity of thinking, and learning new things might be some additional values for you. Write down whatever comes up. If nothing could rekindle your enthusiasm, you have discovered one of your top values in life.

4. Prioritize the values you came up with in steps 1 through 3. Which is the most important value, which is the second most important, and so on?

5. Expand your list of life values as follows:
   - Elicit moving-toward values by asking, "What else is most important to me about life?" Go for ends values—states—such as feeling vibrant, feeling enthusiastic, feeling healthy, feeling loved, feeling excitement, feeling creative, feeling secure, or feeling outrageous. For means values that come up, such as having more money, traveling, or being in a love relationship, simply ask, "What is important about doing or having that?" This should lead to the ends values. Blend these new values into your prioritized list according to their importance.
   - Elicit moving-away-from values by asking, "What states would I do almost anything to avoid having to experience?" These may include depression, grieving, humiliation, shame, fail-

ure, rejection, or physical pain. Which are most important to avoid? Again, blend these into the list by priority.

6. Are the five most important values on your list being met in your present circumstances? If not, what changes would be necessary to fulfill them?

These values are what *most motivate you*—the things you are most drawn to, in anticipation of pleasure, and what you most fear as potentially painful. The next exercise provides more clues on your uniqueness.

Exercise 32
Personal Uniqueness

Write down answers from the following clues:

1. What do you do in life that is as natural as breathing? This could be anything from serious to silly—smiling, understanding how things work, cooking, arguing, socializing with others, criticizing, explaining things, playing the devil's advocate. What comes most naturally to you?

2. What especially attracted and fascinated you as a child? What did you love to do—no matter how silly (daydream, fantasize, explore new places, collect coins or stamps, play house)?

3. Does it feel as if there is a part of you that still loves some of those childhood things? Are you doing any of them now? What would life be like if you did?

4. What *values* were most important to you as a child?

- Elicit moving-toward values by asking, "What was most important to me about life back then?" Again, go for ends values—states—such as having fun or adventure, feeling loved, learning something new, feeling excitement, security, freedom, and so on. For means values that come up, such as having a new bicycle or getting to go to a basketball game, simply ask, "What was important to me about doing or having that?" This should lead to ends values. List and prioritize them.
- Elicit moving-away-from values by asking, "What states did I do almost anything to avoid?" Blend these into the list from the preceding question in order of importance.

5. Ask, "What changes would I make in life if I knew I could not fail?" Write these down.

Do any of your childhood values belong on your list of present-day values? Are some already the same? Modify your present-day values list accordingly.

A third step toward understanding what motivates you is to trace your direction through time via your dreams and goals. Here are three processes I first encountered in Alan Laikin's pioneering work, *How to Get Control of the Time in Your Life*. If you haven't done something like this in the last two or three months, it would be very useful to do these exercises *now*.

Exercise 33
Life Goals

On a blank sheet of paper, list the things you would like to accomplish during the rest of your life. Write as fast as you can, and go for quantity. Be sure to include all of the playful as well as practical and even outrageous possibilities, like skydiving or going on that African safari—whatever you have dreamed of doing, even if it doesn't seem practical or sensible. *Do not spend more than two minutes making the list.* Check your clock or watch and start now.

Once you have finished, take one more minute to go back over the list for additions or modifications.

Exercise 34
Five-Year Goals

On a second blank sheet of paper, not taking more than two minutes, list all that you would like to do in the next five years. Some items may be the same as items on your first list, and some may be different. Again, go for quantity and avoid censoring the possibilities. When you are ready, *start*.

When the two minutes are up, take one more minute to go back over the list to make additions or changes.

Exercise 35
Six-Month Goals

On a third blank sheet of paper, spend another two minutes on the following. Suppose you knew you would be dead in six months. All of the funeral arrangements and legal matters have been taken care of, and money is not an obstacle. What would you *do* during this last six months? Again, go for quantity.

Once you have completed the list, spend one more minute to go back over it, checking for possible additions or corrections.

Exercise 36
Priorities in Life

Take one minute each to go back over your three lists and pick the five items from each you would most like to do—the ones that are most dear to you. Start with the six-month list, then the five-year one, and finally the life list. Again, spend no more than one minute on each.

Once you have completed this, take a maximum of thirty seconds each to go back over your choices and verify that these are what you most want.

After doing the exercises, do you notice any patterns in your goals? How do the three lists compare? As you might imagine, the six-month list contains the things in life that are most important to you. Did any new values emerge? If your life goals are fairly consistent with your six-month list, your direction in time is congruent. On the other hand, if your life goals are very different from your six-month goals, you may want to take another look at your course in life.

Before going through the next part of your vision quest, you might enjoy reading something I have posted in my office, called "Guidelines for Life." I'm not sure where these came from, but I always find them to be an inspiration.

Guidelines for Life

1. You will learn lessons. You are enrolled in a full-time school called "Life on Planet Earth." Every person or incident is your teacher.

2. There are no mistakes—only lessons. "Failures are only stepping-stones to success."

3. A lesson is repeated until learned. It is presented in various forms until you learn it. If you are here, there are still lessons to learn.

4. If you don't learn the easy lessons, they get harder. Pain is one way in which the universe gets your attention.

5. You'll know you've learned a lesson when your actions change. Only action can transform knowledge into wisdom.

6. "There" is no better a place than "here." When "there" becomes "here," you'll notice another "there" that again looks better than "here."

7. There is no right or wrong—but there are consequences. The universe never judges us; it only gives us opportunities to balance and learn.

8. Your life is up to you. Life provides the canvas; you do the painting.

9. Your answers lie inside you. All you need to do is look, listen, and trust.

10. You'll tend to forget all this.

SECTION TWO: WHY YOU HAVE "CHOSEN" YOUR LIFE CIRCUMSTANCES AND YOUR RULES FOR SUCCESS

For the next several exercises you'll need to know how your brain organizes time. When we think of various events, some in the near past, some in the remote past, some in the future, and maybe others happening right now, the brain must have some way to sort or categorize each event by where it is located in time.

Exercise 37
Discovering Your Time Line

1. When you think of events that have occurred in the past, and if you were to point which way the past is for you, which way would you point? Go ahead and point in that direction. Is it

- behind you?
- to one side?

- underneath you?
- above you?

Which way, physically, is the past for you? If you are not sure, trust whatever comes up for you from your unconscious.

2. When you think of events in the future, and if you were to point toward the future, which way would you point? Go ahead and point in that direction. Is it
- in front of you?
- to one side?
- above you?

Which way, physically, is the future for you? Again, trust whatever your unconscious presents.

3. Now if you imagine the connection of events in the past with the present and events in the future, can you imagine a line or curve connecting all these events? This line or curve is called your time line. For many people the line goes from behind them (the past), through them (the present), to in front of them (the future). For many others it stretches from the left (the past), to directly in front of them (the present), toward the right (the future). For others the pattern is different. There is no right or wrong configuration for time lines. It is just the brain's way of sorting past, present, and future events.

Time lines are unique and individual. Many people have a time line with the past behind them and the future in front. These people often live in the moment and are good at putting the past behind them. Many other people have the past toward their left and the future toward their right. These people may have a broader perspective of being able to learn from the past and seeing the relationship of past, present, and future. We will use a metaphor of floating way up above your time line to gain a clearer perspective on your direction in life.

Exercise 38
In the Beginning . . .

1. Think about your mother (or other caregiver who was a mother for you). If she lived to learn certain lessons or to resolve certain issues, what would those issues be? Maybe she needed to develop more self-esteem, or the ability to take care of herself as well as she took care of others, or to accept her feminine side as

opposed to being focused and competitive in the workplace. What do you think her lessons and issues were? Write them down.

2. Now think about your father or alternate caregiver father figure. What were some of his issues to learn in life? Maybe he needed to be more in touch with his feeling side, maybe he neglected the family because he worked long hours, or maybe he needed to learn gentleness as opposed to being verbally or physically abusive. Whatever you think his issues were, write them down.

3. Next, get yourself into a comfortable relaxed position and imagine floating way up in the air above your time line. Float all the way back to the point of your conception. Float to a point where you are well up above your conception, a little *before* it occurred.

4. From this vantage point, imagine the following. Suppose we lived in a universe where, as a spirit, we *chose* to come into life with certain parents, and we *chose* all the positive and negative occurrences that were destined to happen in this life. I'm not suggesting this is the way it is, but just imagine for a second that it were this way. From this vantage point, answer the following questions:

- Why would you have chosen the mother you did? With all of her issues, what she needed to learn, her great qualities, her shortcomings, why would you choose her? What could you learn from being with her, and how would *you* benefit, with her as a mother?
- Why would you have chosen the father you did? Again, with all of his good qualities and shortcomings, how would being with him promote your being a better or stronger person?
- Look along your time line from this beginning point all the way to the present, and see all of the joyous events, the frustrating events, the times of personal triumph, the times of tragedy. Ask yourself why you would choose to come into a life with *these particular issues* to face. If there *were* reasons—ways that these occurrences would somehow make you stronger and wiser—what would those reasons be? Once you have a sense of these, write them down.

5. Now slowly float forward, well above your time line, and settle back down into the present.

Exercise 39
In the End . . .

1. Review all that you have written from Exercises 31 through 38.

2. Again, get yourself into a comfortable relaxed position and imagine floating way up in the air above your time line. Float all the way forward to the end of it. Float to a point where you are well up above the end and *looking back* over all that has occurred during your life.

3. From this vantage point, answer the following. Make sure to stay well above your time line to maintain your perspective and objectivity.

   - What would you like your life to have been about? What issues would you like to see resolved? What would you like to have done and experienced in life? What would you like to have learned? Write these down.
   - What needed to happen along your time line, so you can look back from this perspective at the end, and think to yourself, "Now, *that* was a successful life!" Write these down. Are your standards realistic and achievable? If not, would you be willing to change them?

4. Now slowly float back well above your time line, and settle down into the present.

Note: The most crucial piece here is what you have answered to the second part of the last question. Do your rules or beliefs for a successful life empower you by being easily achievable? If they keep success out of your reach by making it impossible to succeed, use Six-Step Reframing (pages 98–99) to find the positive intent behind unrealistically high standards. Reintegrate this part with the other part of you that wants to succeed in life. Some people are concerned that if they make it too easy to succeed, they will be unmotivated. That turns out *not* to be the case. The more we experience success, the more driven we are to experience even more.

SECTION THREE: YOUR MISSION

At this point, review all that you've written from Exercises 31 through 39, then continue.

Exercise 40
Discovering Your Mission

Based on all the data you have so far—all these different view-points on your life—write down a paragraph or two, or a list, or a poem stating what you feel your mission in life is. By now it should be pretty clear, but if not, write down your best guess. Your mission might change with time as you gather more data about life.

The last step in your vision quest is to return to pages 248–49 in chapter 15 and use Antiviral Remedy 21 to realign your values to automatically support your mission statement.

APPENDIX 2:
RESOURCES

Powerlearning Systems offers seminars, consultations, books, and tapes on issues of personal empowerment and innovative learning methods. For information on available services, training in the methods of Thought Virus Therapy, speaking engagements, products, or referrals for therapists in your area, write to

Dr. Don Lofland
P.O. Box 496
Santa Cruz, CA 95061

- Corporate Seminars
- Certification Training
- Individual Consultations
- Accelerated Learning Books, Tapes, Seminars, and Resources

If you are a counseling professional who is certified in NLP and would like to be listed as a referral for your area or to receive additional training in these methods, please contact Powerlearning Systems at the address listed above.

Visit us on the World Wide Web:
http//:www.power-learning.com/

Pat Wyman, M.A., with The Center for New Discoveries in Learning, offers *Super Teaching Strategies* and dyslexia-correction videotape training courses (with college credit available) for parents and teachers working with children and students who want to circumvent thought viruses connected with learning blocks. She also offers a *Spelling Strategies* video based on NLP methods.

Pat Wyman
P.O. Box 1019
Windsor, CA 95492
707-837-8180

APPENDIX 3:
THOUGHT VIRUS TYPES

BASIC VIRUSES

Trigger Viruses

• *Simple Triggers*

Components: V/K, A/K, or K/K synesthesia—a visual, auditory, or kinesthetic stimulus triggers an unresourceful kinesthetic state.

Positive Intent: Memory retrieval, safety in being able to act without having to think about what is happening.

Antiviral Remedy: #3—Collapsing Anchors (page 58) or #4—Setting Reverse Triggers (pages 61–62).

• *Complex Triggers*

Components: A sequence of external and internal experiences, i.e., a strategy, triggers an unresourceful state.

Positive Intent after: The same as simple triggers.

Antiviral Remedy: #1—Overcoming a

Phobia by Changing Submodalities (pages 53–55).

Limiting Viruses

• *Limiting Beliefs*

Components: An erroneous way of interpreting events to make meaning.

Positive Intent: Protection, making meaning, and providing a measure of whether or not our values are being met to experience pleasurable states and avoid painful ones.

Antiviral Remedy: #7—Eliminating a Disempowering Belief (page 87).

• *Unhealed Moving-Away-from-Values*

Components: Putting attention on values we don't want helps to bring about these values and leads to sequential incongruence.

Positive Intent: Avoiding painful states that occurred in the past.

Antiviral Remedy: #13—The Eye Movement Scrambler (pages 152–53),#12—Power Questions (page 135) to reframe the meaning, or #17—The Fast Phobia Cure for Past Failures (page 201).

• *Misplaced Values*

Components: Important values have too low unconscious priority or unimportant ones have too high priority.

Positive Intent: Experience pleasure or avoid pain.

Antiviral Remedy: #6—Reprioritizing Values (or Beliefs) (page 81).

Gemini Viruses

Components: Two internal parts are in conflict, which leads to procrastination, inaction, or self-sabotage.

Positive Intent: Seeking balance through harmonizing different viewpoints, yet the highest intention of each conflicting part is usually the same.

Antiviral Remedy: #8—Six-Step Reframing (pages 98–99) to reintegrate a weaker problematic part or #9—The Visual Squash (page 103) when the parts carry nearly equal weight.

SPECIALIZED VIRUSES

The Addiction Virus

Components: A trigger in the form of an erroneous association, limiting beliefs to rationalize the addiction and internal conflict of a Gemini component when one recognizes the destructive consequences of the addiction.

Positive Intent: Usually a devious way of changing one's state.

Antiviral Remedy: #10—Eliciting Your Motivation Strategy (pages 116–17), #11—Tips to Free Yourself from Substance Addictions (page 117–18), and help from a counseling professional.

The Allergy Virus

Components: A trigger—the allergen and a limiting belief in which the immune system mistakes the allergens for invading viruses.

Positive Intent: Possibly a backup defense or warning system against toxins or an evolutionary system to ward off parasites.

Antiviral Remedy: A trained thought virus therapist together with a medical professional if the allergy has any potential to be life threatening. See Chapter 9.

The Cancer Virus

Components: Internal conflict (a Gemini Virus), limiting beliefs, and disempowering triggers, personality traits including the inability to express negative emotions, inability to cope with stress, which results in a tendency toward feelings of helplessness, hopelessness, depression, and a tendency toward social isolation and loneliness.

Positive Intent: It is doubtful the cancer itself has any positive intent, but the triggers, limiting beliefs, and internal conflict that might help trigger the cancer all have positive intents.

Antiviral Remedy: Eliminate known risk factors and use prevention measures suggested in Chapter 10 for physiology and cultivating a low-risk personality. #14—Power Questions for Negative Emotions (page 177). Medical attention if cancer is already present.

The Depression Virus

Components: Trigger viruses linking circumstances and memories with painful, depressed states, and limiting viruses with circumstances violating our rules of the way things are supposed to be.

Positive Intent: To maintain a system of making meaning and order based on rules that have now been violated—"How could this have taken place? It never *should* have happened!"

Antiviral Remedy: #12—Power Questions (page 135), #13—The Eye Movement Scrambler (pages 152–53), exercise and dietary considerations from Chapter 8, and professional help for severe or chronic depression.

The Fear of Failure Virus

Components: An erroneous trigger linking embarrassment, humiliation, or guilt with things not turning out the way we'd like.

Positive Intent: Safety and protection from disempowering feelings.

Antiviral Remedy: #16—Discovering How You Fail Successfully (pages 198–99), #17—The Fast Phobia Cure for Past Failures (page 201).

The Fear of Success Virus

Components: There are no rules or beliefs to measure if success has occurred, or beliefs keep success out of reach, or success is uncomfortable because it is unfamiliar.

Positive Intent: Safety and protection from disempowering feelings, and maintaining comfort with what is familiar.

Antiviral Remedy: #18—Changing Your Rules for Success (page 205).

The Intimate Thermostat Virus

See the Thermostat Virus.

Killer Viruses

• *Alcohol and Drug Viruses*	*See* Addiction Viruses.
• *The Gambling Virus*	*See* Addiction Viruses.
• *The Sex Addiction Virus*	*See* Addiction Viruses.
• *The Suicide Virus*	*Components: See* the Depression Virus.

Positive Intent: An attempt to escape the way one feels by escaping life.

Antiviral Remedy: Immediate professional help. Aside from this, see the Depression Virus.

• *The Tobacco Virus*   *See* Addiction Viruses.

The Love Reception Virus

Components: Limiting beliefs from childhood during which it was familiar not to receive love. Receiving love in a love relationship feels uncomfortable because it is unfamiliar. A Gemini Virus also occurs when part of oneself desires love and closeness while another part is afraid of it.

Positive Intent: Familiarity and comfort.

Antiviral Remedy: #8—Six-Step Reframing (pages 98–99), or #9—The Visual Squash (page 103).

The Math Anxiety Virus

Components: A trigger virus and limiting beliefs.

Positive Intent: Same as the Fear of Failure Virus.

Antiviral Remedy: #3—Collapsing Anchors (page 58), #4—Setting Reverse Triggers (pages 61–62), #7—Eliminating a Disempowering Belief (page 87), and #17—The Fast Phobia Cure for Past Failures (page 201).

The Phobia Viruses

Components: A simple or complex trigger.

Positive Intent: Safety and protection.

Antiviral Remedy: #1—Overcoming a Phobia by Changing Submodalities (pages 53–55), #13—The Eye Movement Scrambler (pages 152–53), or #17—The Fast Phobia Cure for Past Failures (page 201).

The Procrastination Virus

Components: Inner conflict of a Gemini Virus.

Positive Intent: On some level not doing *appears* less painful than doing.

Antiviral Remedy: #15—An Action Strategy (page 188) and suggestions in Chapter 11.

The Thermostat Virus

Components: Similar to the Fear of Success Virus. There is a negative association with having the outcome, the process of achieving the outcome; or a positive association with not having the outcome.

Positive Intent: Safety and protection from disempowering feelings, and maintaining comfort with what is familiar.

Antiviral Remedy: #3—Collapsing Anchors (page 58), #4—Setting Reverse Triggers (pages 61–62), or #6—Reprioritizing Values (or Beliefs) (page 81).

APPENDIX 4:
EXERCISES

APPENDIX 5:
ANTIVIRAL REMEDIES

CHAPTER REFERENCES

Chapter 2: Viruses

1. "Viruses," *National Geographic,* July 1994, 64–86.
2. "The Outbreak of Fear," *Newsweek,* 22 May 1995, 48–55.
3. John R. Wilke, "How Scientists Stalk Crafty Computer Viruses," *The Wall Street Journal* 29 August 1994.
4. "Is There a Case for Viruses?" *Newsweek,* 27 February 1995.
5. Dr. Tad James, *The Basic NLP Training Collection* (Honolulu: Advanced Neurodynamics, 1990).

Chapter 3: Trigger Viruses

1. Deepak Chopra, M.D., *Quantum Healing* (New York: Bantam Books, 1989), 86–87.

Chapter 4: Limiting Viruses

1. Dr. Tad James, *The Advanced Neuro-Linguistic Programming Training Collection: Master Practitioner Training Tapes* (Honolulu: Advanced Neurodynamics, 1989).

Chapter 5: Gemini Viruses

1. Dr. Tad James, *The Basic NLP Training Collection* (Honolulu: Advanced Neurodynamics, 1990).

Chapter 6: Killer Viruses

1. R. J. Samuelson, "Great Expectations," *Newsweek,* 8 January 1996.
2. "Kicking Butts," *Psychology Today,* September/October 1994.

Chapter 7: Thought Virus Therapy

1. Dr. M. Colgan, *The New Nutrition* (San Diego: C.I. Publishers, 1994); L. Larson, *Acta Physiol Scand* 36(S) (1978), 457.
2. Anthony Robbins, *A 30-Day Program for Personal Power,* audiotape series (Irwindale, Calif.: Guthy-Renker, 1989).
3. Ibid.
4. Ibid. These questions are based on the morning questions Tony Robbins suggests using.
5. Donald Lofland, *Powerlearning®* (Stamford, Conn.: Longmeadow Press, 1992), chapter 12.
6. J. P. Banquet, "Spectral Analysis of EEG in Meditation," *Electroencephalography and Clinical Neurophysiology* (1975) 35.
7. P. C. Ferguson and J. C. Gowan, "TM: Some Preliminary Findings," *Journal of Humanistic Psychology* 16 (1976), 51–60.
8. W. P. van den Berg and B. Mulder, "Psychological Research on the Effects of the Transcendental Meditation Technique on a Number of Personality Variables," *Gedrag: Tijdstrift voorPsychologie* 4 (1976), 206–18.
9. Allan I. Abrams, "Paired Associate Learning and Recall: A Pilot Study of the Transcendental Meditation Technique" in *Scientific Research on the Transcendental Meditation Program: Collected Papers* (New York: MIU Press, 1975).
10. R. K. Wallace, M. Dillbeck, E. Jacobe, and B. Harrington, "The Effects of Transcendental Meditation and the TM Sidhis Program on the Aging Process," *International Journal of Neuroscience* 16 (1982), 53–58.

Chapter 8: Depression

1. B. Bower, "Brain Images Show Structure of Depression," *Science News,* 12 September 1992, 165.
2. "10 Physical Reasons You May Be Depressed," *Prevention,* June 1992, 69.
3. *Science News,* 11 March 1995, 157.
4. "10 Physical Reasons You May Be Depressed"
5. Donald Lofland, *Powerlearning®,* (Stamford, Conn.: Longmeadow Press, 1992), chapter 7.
6. I first encountered this method in Los Gatos, California, in therapy sessions with Francine Shapiro who I believe developed the method. It was later presented by Connirae Andraes.

Chapter 9: Allergies

1. Dave Cutler, "The Season's Best Allergy Busters," *Prevention* (September 1993), 117–24.
2. E. Pennisi, "Food Allergies Linked to Ear Infections" (Otitis Media; research by Talal M. Nsouli), *Science News*, 8 October 1994.
3. "Learned Histamine Response," *Science*, 17 August 1984.
4. B. L. Benderly, "Emotions and Allergies: The Pavlov Connection," *Psychology Today*, June 1989.
5. Robert Dilts and Todd Epstein, NLP Practitioner Certification Training, NLP University at the University of California, June–July 1991.

Chapter 10: Cancer

1. Marc Barasch, "The Mind/Body Connection," *Psychology Today*, July/August 1993.
2. Devra Lee Davis and Harold P. Freeman, "An Ounce of Prevention," *Psychology Today*, September 1994.
3. Joshua Fischman, senior editor, *Psychology Today*, December 1988.
4. Hans J. Eysenck, "Health's Character," *Psychology Today*, December 1988. This test is based in part on a questionnaire written by Hans Eysenck, and published in this *Psychology Today* article. The test also incorporates results of concurrent and more-recent research.
5. Anthony Robbins, *Awaken the Giant Within* (New York: Simon & Schuster, 1991), 267–275. An excellent discussion of the value of negative emotions.

Chapter 11: How to End Procrastination Now

1. Steve and Connirae Andraes, *The Heart of the Mind* (Moab, Utah: Real People Press, 1989).

Chapter 12: Overcoming Fear of Failure and Fear of Success

1. Robert Dilts and Todd Epstein, *NLP Practitioner Certification Training*, June–July 1991.

Chapter 13: Intimate Viruses

1. Robert A. Johson, *We* (New York: Harper & Row, 1983), xi–xiv.
2. Catherine Johnson, *Lucky in Love* (New York: Viking, 1993).
3. Carl Jung, quoted in Johnson.
4. "A Forecast for Couples," *Psychology Today.*
5. Harville Hendrix, *Getting the Love You Want* (New York: HarperCollins, 1990). This section parallels Hendrix's Imago model of the unconscious.
6. Ibid.

Chapter 14: Virus-Free Communication

1. Arthur Beiser, *Physics,* third edition (Menlo Park, Calif.: Benjamin Cummings, 1982), 648.
2. Harville Hendrix, *Getting the Love You Want* (New York: HarperCollins, 1990).
3. Hendrix, *Getting the Love You Want.* This is part of a process that Hendrix calls "re-romanticizing your partner."

Chapter 15: Getting the Results You Want in Life

1. *British Journal of Social Psychology* 30: 21–35.

Chapter 16: Beyond Thought Viruses

1. Paul Hewitt, *Conceptual Physics,* sixth edition (Boston: Scott Foresman, 1989), 344.
2. The Institute of Science, Technology, and Public Policy, Fairfield, Iowa.

INDEX

Magnetic field, of Earth, 249–50
Mahabarata (Indian sage), 168
Mask, as childhood thought virus, 218, 219
Massage, 128
Math anxiety, 55–59
Meaning, 59
  changing, 60–61, 124–25
  in life, 4, 8
Means values, 70
Meditation, 139–40
  See also Transcendental meditation
  and aging, 138
Memory, 18
  and triggers, 41–42
Michelangelo virus, 26
Micro-chunking, 189–90
Mind, empowering, 139
Mind/body healing, and cancer, 168–69
Minerals, 145
Minor personalities, 95
Mirror (elusive), and intimate viruses, 219–21
Misplaced values, 77–78, 81
Mission, 247–49
Mistakes, reframing past, 134–35
Modeling, 37, 138
  high achievers, 188–90
Montana, Joe, 123–24
Mother Teresa, 113, 255
Motivation, 12–13
  to change careers, 96–99
  eliciting, 116–17
  and goals, 13
  and procrastination, 188
  strategy, 114–19
Moving-away-from values, 70–71, 76–77, 81, 88, 91
Moving-toward values, 70, 77
Multiple personalities, 33, 34
Multiple personality syndrome (MPS), 33, 157–58
Muon particle, 225
Murder, incidence of, 107, 109

Nader, Ralph, 255
Negative emotions
  power questions for, 177
  reframing, 175–76
Neuro-Linguistic Programming (NLP), 8, 10–12, 14, 16, 37, 75, 196, 228

Neurological model, perception of, 16
Neuropeptides, 109, 143, 168, 169
Neurotransmitters, 109–10, 143, 168, 169
Newsweek, 6
Newton, Sir Isaac, 254, 255
  First Law of, 118, 119
NLP. See Neuro-Linguistic Programming
Nominalization, 66
Noncoherent thinking, vs. coherent thinking, 19–20

Object referral, 44
Obstacles
  external, 193
  internal, 193
Oils, unsaturated, 144–45
O'Keeffe, Georgia, 142
Omega 3 oil, 144
Omega 6 oil, 144
O'Rourke, P. J., 230
Ought self, 245
Outbreak (film), 25
Outcome, well-formed, 130–31
  feasibility, 131
  signpost, 131
  vision, 130–31
Ovarian cancer, 165
Overwhelming feelings, meaning of, 176

Particles, location and frequency of, 89–90
Parts of creation (twin), 89–90
  See also Separate parts; Twin parts
  conflicting, 90–92
Performance, vs. expectation, 194–95
Perls, Fritz, 10, 20, 93, 138
Personalities, minor, 95
Personal power, according to sequence, 186
"Personal and Professional Empowerment" workshop, 186
Phase transition, and orderliness, 123, 124
Phobia cure for past failures, 200–202
Phobias, and submodalities, 53–55
Physiology, 14–15, 57, 127–30, 145, 175
  body, listening to, 130
  diet, 114, 128–29,145
  exercise, 127–28
  power moves, 129–30
  of states, 129–30